Public Religions in
the Future World

Public Religions in the Future World

POSTSECULARISM AND UTOPIA

David Morris

The University of Georgia Press

ATHENS

Chapter 2 previously appeared, in slightly different form, as "Intellect and Activism: The Secular Authority of *Left Behind*," *Cultural Critique*, vol. 90, 2015, pp. 64–87, published by the University of Minnesota Press. Chapter 3 previously appeared, in slightly different form, as "Octavia Butler's Revolutionary Movement for the Twenty-First Century," *Utopian Studies*, vol. 26, no. 2, 2015, pp. 270–88. © 2015 The Pennsylvania State University. This article is used by permission of the Pennsylvania State University Press.

Most University of Georgia Press titles are
available from popular e-book vendors.

Printed digitally

Library of Congress Cataloging-in-Publication Data

Names: Morris, David, 1980– author.
Title: Public religions in the future world : postsecularism and utopia /
    David Morris.
Description: Athens : The University of Georgia Press, 2021. | Series:
    Since 1970: histories of contemporary America | Includes
    bibliographical references and index.
Identifiers: LCCN 2021022951 | ISBN 9780820360621 (hardback) |
    ISBN 9780820360645 (paperback) | ISBN 9780820360638 (ebook)
Subjects: LCSH: American fiction—21st century—History and criticism.
    | Utopias in literature. | Religion in literature. | Neoliberalism in
    literature. | Religion and literature—United States. | Christianity
    and culture—United States. | Postmodernism (Literature)
Classification: LCC PS374.U8 M67 | DDC 813/.5409372—dc23
LC record available at https://lccn.loc.gov/2021022951

CONTENTS

ACKNOWLEDGMENTS

The project that would eventually become this book began years ago. Backed by the resurgent power of American fundamentalists, George W. Bush promised to rid the world of evil in 2001. Religious visions of the future were everywhere, and I felt they warranted more attention. Many things changed since then, but the power of these visions is not one of them.

With insight and patience, Susan Koshy guided me through my earliest efforts to produce something out of a disparate set of texts and a disorganized group of ideas. Trish Loughran gave my work its closest reading and sharpest criticism; further, she was instrumental in the project's greatest leaps toward its current form. I can't thank either of them enough.

Several friends, colleagues, and former teachers of mine provided help at various stages of this project. Special acknowledgment goes to John Claborn and Lisa Oliverio, who read countless drafts and provided helpful comments and encouragement. Further reading and support were offered by Jonathan Ebel, James Engelhardt, Patrick Fadely, Waïl Hassan, Jamie Jones, Bob Markley, Justine Murison, Kimberly O'Neill, Bob Parker, Christopher Simeone, Michael Simeone, Derrick Spires, James Treat, Jeff Tucker, and Ted Underwood. Kay Emmert, Dana Kinzy, Kristi McDuffie, and Andrew Moss all helped create a work environment wherein I had time and energy to research and write. Additionally, this project would not have been possible without the librarians of the University of Illinois library.

Lynn Itagaki approached me at a conference and introduced me to Mick Gusinde-Duffy. I want to thank them and everyone at the University of Georgia Press for their capable support as I completed this book. Thanks to Kaelin Broaddus, Jon Davies, Michelle Martinez, Thierry Ramais, Merryl Sloane, and Beth Snead for helping me prepare for publication.

I started thinking seriously about utopia after attending the Midwest Conference on Utopian Studies in 2012. I want to thank Carter Hanson and Mardy Philippian for organizing that conference and welcoming me into its intellectual community. The scholars in the Society for Utopian Studies were equally stimulating and welcoming. Similarly, interacting with members of the American Religion and Literature Society of the American Literature Association was immensely helpful in making final revisions to this manuscript; special thanks to Kathryn Ludwig for welcoming me into that community.

Academic research in the humanities and the career paths that support it are undergoing a dramatic change. It's in this context that I want to recognize the Non-Tenure Faculty Coalition (Local 6546) for securing for my colleagues and me health insurance, a living wage, and a small research fund. Much of the foundation for their work was laid on our campus by the Graduate Employees' Organization (Local 6300) over the past four decades. In a rapidly changing profession, organizations like these crucially protect research and teaching by securing and supporting academic workers.

I have the privilege of working in a large, intellectually diverse department of professors, adjunct faculty, grad students, academic professionals, English majors and minors, and indispensable staff. Utopian thinking energizes my department's greatest publishing achievements, its best teaching, and its most rancorous conflicts. Our tiny island of the academy positively crackles with utopian energy. For better and worse, this environment made me the scholar and teacher I am now. With respect and love, fear and frustration, and hope and dreams, I dedicate this book to my colleagues and students. May we with vision and humility work toward a better world while we live in this one.

Finally, to my brilliant partner, Gwen Rudy. Thank you for your encouragement, your engagement, and your belief that the world can be better. It's my great joy to live with you in the world as it is—even if that includes a long quarantine.

Public Religions in
the Future World

INTRODUCTION

Religion in the Social
Dreams of the Present

Early in Tom Perotta's 2011 novel, *The Leftovers*, the city of
Mapleton gathers for the "first annual Departed Heroes' Day of Remembrance
and Reflection" (12), the anniversary of the Sudden Departure, a worldwide
Rapture-like event wherein 2 percent of the world's population disappeared in
an instant. As one of the main characters, Nora Durst, delivers a speech mourning her husband and two children, several members of one of the many new
post-Departure cults, the Guilty Remnant, appear behind the other spectators
and unfurl a banner: "STOP WASTING YOUR BREATH," it declares (Perotta 27).
The Guilty Remnant members dress all in white, live communally in houses,
observe a vow of silence, and disrupt public events and private lives with their
constant presence. They even keep surveillance records of all the town's citizens so that they can intrude at maximally disruptive times (115–19). The Guilty
Remnant organization has no clear or consistent theology or religious mission:
"it had no priests or ministers, no scripture, and no formal system of instruc-
tion" (208). Instead, the Guilty Remnant disrupts all settled human relations:
"the post-Rapture world demanded a new way of living, free from the old, discredited forms—no more marriage, no more families, no more consumerism,
no more politics, no more conventional religion, no more mindless entertainment. Those days were done. All that remained for humanity was to hunker
down and await the inevitable" (208). By showing us the lives of many of the
characters, *The Leftovers* makes clear that the Guilty Remnant's mission to dis-
mantle relationships is helping along a process already well under way.

The confrontation between the secular, civil religious Heroes' Day ceremony and the nihilistic religious devotion of the Guilty Remnant embodies
a central problem for literature of the late twentieth and twenty-first centuries: the dissolution of meaning and the frustration of social connections under the fragmentary logics and material practices of neoliberalism. The novel's
two central protagonists, Nora Durst and Kevin Garvey, try to find meaning
through public and personal rituals. They also try to connect to each other

1

but have difficulty doing so; Nora's grief and Kevin's bafflement in the face of it stand in the way. While official community events in Mapleton—Heroes' Day parades, city council meetings that remind Kevin of church with their set liturgies (Perotta 231), and city recreational events—try to bring people into community, they routinely fail. At the same time, new post-Departure religious movements like the Guilty Remnant only mark the absence of meaning and community rather than restoring it. Indeed, the Guilty Remnant even enacts a sadistic ritual wherein it allows friendships to form between adherents before forcing them to murder each other. Meanwhile, Matt Jamison, Mapleton's mainline Protestant pastor, spends his time in pointless theological disputation, trying to prove that the Departure was not the biblical Rapture (an argument almost no one is making).

The novel offers a small glimmer of hope for the characters at the end, one that suggests the possibility for new models of kinship within the nuclear-family-oriented symbolic order of the suburb. Kevin's son, Tom, brings home a baby (the abandoned daughter of the disgraced charismatic faith healer Holy Wayne and one of his "spiritual brides," an underage woman). He leaves the baby on the doorstep of his father's house and drives away. Nora, on her way out of town, finds this child (abandoned, mixed race, without a name) and waits for Kevin, ending the novel with a simple exclamation: "Look what I found" (355). Nora, Kevin, and the child suggest a new model of kinship: a pair of people who have lost their families adopting the child of a fraudulent spiritual movement. A visitor from outside the insular suburban community (a child without history and without clear origin) potentially shatters the very notion of the normal. Nonetheless, the appearance of the child and Nora's inclination to immediately care for it with Kevin suggest a happy Hollywood ending—a restoration of the nuclear family and of the same symbolic order they had lost in the Sudden Departure.

In *The Leftovers*, the Sudden Departure exacerbates the absence of meaning that cements functioning publics and private relations. Community rituals and aggressive fundamentalist cults equally serve as simulacra that mark the absence of secure publics rather than reviving them. To see *The Leftovers* as engaging with religion is easy enough, with its cults, its civil religion, and its Rapture-like event. It's harder to see it as a dystopian text with a backward look: loss of meaning, the novel seems to say, dissolves human connection. The novel expresses doubt that such meaning can be restored. This hasn't stopped other authors of utopian literature, however, from looking for that meaning in one of the chief sources rejected by *The Leftovers*: religion, at least in some form. A significant portion of contemporary utopian literature, I argue, finds in some version of religion keys to reviving and reimagining publics in the face of their neoliberal dissolution.

Lyman Tower Sargent defines utopia as "social dreaming": "the dreams and nightmares that concern the ways in which groups of people arrange their lives and which usually envision a radically different society than the one in which the dreamers live" ("Three Faces" 3). Sargent's broad definition allows him to address utopia as both a literary genre (with its cogenre, dystopia) *and* as a real-world political ideal.[1] While the term comes from Thomas More's 1516 satire, *Utopia*, utopian fiction, proposals, thought experiments, and communities can be traced at least as far back as Hesiod in the West and perhaps further elsewhere. Many of these real and imagined utopias from the early modern period on (especially in the New World) were religious.[2] But in the case of contemporary utopian writings, the religious elements have only sometimes been included in scholarly examinations of utopian literature. Conversely, while religion has received intensified scrutiny since the mid-2000s by scholars of American literature, utopianism has made only brief appearances.[3] Remedying this gap, in this book I argue that contemporary literary utopianism is deeply inflected with diverse religious ideas, with the visions, values, and ambitions of Christianity, mysticism, Buddhism, Islam, and other traditions. This religiosity in turn resonates with and underwrites a range of competing political projects, including imperialism, globalization, neoliberal capitalism, ecological action, and the pro-migration movement. While these texts are religiously and politically diverse, their engagement with the broad logics and organizations of neoliberalism unites them. They all use religion to reimagine publics within and against the multivalent tendency toward privatization under the dominance of late twentieth-century neoliberalism.

Public Religions in the Late Twentieth-Century United States

Contemporary utopian thinking engages with the desire to rethink and re-create publics in a neoliberal environment that defines publics primarily in economic terms. Surprisingly, utopian literature since the 1980s has turned to religion as material to build imaginative alternatives to neoliberal public degradation. Scholarship on postsecularism in literature, however, has largely left the utopian underpinnings of religion in literature unexamined. Instead, scholars in postsecular studies tend to work within a binary opposition: on the one hand, postsecular, "weak" religions inflect progressive secular ideas with religious affect. Two particularly influential works in postsecular literary studies, John A. McClure's *Partial Faiths* and Amy Hungerford's *Postmodern Belief*, both take on religion as private and weakened—that is, as individual, non-organized, even detheologized manifestations in postmodern novels. Both Hungerford and McClure emphasize how individuals think and feel through partially religious affects and ideas.[4] On the other hand, "strong" religions that reject doubt and invest in concrete structures remain just as present in American life and literature. Taking up strong religion in new and old forms, Melani McAlister, Erin A. Smith, Amy Johnson Frykholm, and a variety of others have engaged the organized networks of literary production and consumption in American fundamentalist churches. Further, in a particularly insightful 2014 article in *American Literature*, Danielle Haque shows how the tendency to ignore recognizable, organized, strong religion in literature totally erases a good deal of American Muslim literature, which often does not fall easily within the weak and strong categories conceived mostly with Christianity in mind.[5] If nothing else, the striking political power of religious fundamentalism in the 1990s and 2000s has established the urgency for a continued examination of strong religion, yet John A. McClure, Amy Hungerford, and others show that partial and secularized religious forms occupy a powerful place in American culture. Moreover, much like separating religion from the secular, drawing an absolute distinction between strong and weak religions would require artificial and limiting separations too. Therefore, I want to cut across the strong-weak distinction, because I think it has in some way prevented scholars from excavating the complex interaction of religious and secular forms in contemporary culture. Like Tracy Fessenden in *Culture and Redemption*, I worry that the distinction has, perhaps accidentally, enabled a tendency to categorize religions somewhat simplistically as good or bad, liberatory or oppressive (*Culture* 2).

Instead, I want to use the category "public religion," a term I mean to cover the myriad, networked ways people use religion to influence cultural and political economies. I've borrowed the term "public religion" from one of the founding works of the postsecular turn, José Casanova's *Public Religions in the Modern World* (1994). Casanova argues that seemingly dramatic appearances of religion across the world in the late twentieth century—from the Islamic revolution in Iran to the anticolonial movements of South America to the rise of the New Christian Right (NCR) in the United States—represent not an *increase* in religion but a "deprivatization" of religion. For Casanova, a public religion is a deprivatized religion—that is, religious practice and expression that leave the private spaces of conscience, home, and house of worship and enter the public arenas of politics, economics, and culture (5–6). Further, according to Casanova, these religious movements enter public arenas both to influence public policy and in response to secular invasions into their religious "lifeworlds" (145–46). Casanova's deprivatization thesis alerts us to two important things: first, he counterintuitively suggests that much religious organized public action aims to influence the regulation of the private sphere (home, family, and related matters, such as education). For example, members of the NCR in the United States organized in part for the right to teach their own curricula in private and home schooling (145–57). Second and relatedly, Casano-

va's work calls for careful attention to the power dynamics of the relations between public and private.

Deprivatized religions carry ambitions that might cause discomfort among
more secular-minded readers. In *The Leftovers*, for example, religions occupy
no positions between the cultish Guilty Remnant and the inadequate, frustrated mainline Protestantism of Matt Jamison. However, in utopian literature
that imagines future social alternatives, public religion often provides bases to
imagine new modes of social organization. Further, utopian and dystopian fiction imagines futures with new models of publics, plural, just as literary texts
hail and circulate within publics, plural. Throughout this book, I use "public"
in two senses: first, as opposed to private; and second, in Michael Warner's
terms, wherein publics are multiple, overlapping, and held together by circulating texts.[6] That is, making utopian, democratic publics requires extending
influence beyond a given public and into something more like Jürgen Habermas's "public sphere." However, as the ongoing civil rights, feminist, and gay
rights movements (among others) have clearly shown, this has never worked
as well as Habermas and others have hoped.

This volume begins in the late 1970s, a key moment in the co-arising dominance of neoliberalism and postsecularism. The shape of inequality that privileges some people and publics over others changed dramatically in the latter
half of the twentieth century with the dominance of neoliberalism as a system of political-economic philosophy and practice. While neoliberalism has
many faces,[7] for my purposes, three important developments in the 1970s are
paramount: the shrinking of the public sphere under privatization; the shift
in values structures from political citizenship to economic participation; and
the atomization of social activism and responsibility. In his first inaugural address, Ronald Reagan famously declared, "government is not the solution to
our problem; government is the problem," a succinct mission statement for
privatization. Reagan's electoral victory represented the coalescing of a variety of economic shocks, cultural shifts, conservative organizing, and the creation of a new Republican coalition.[8] While the Reagan administration is well
known for its efforts at shrinking the public sphere, it was a small part of nationwide attempts at the state and local levels to roll back New Deal and Great
Society reforms (Schaller 50–51). These moves toward privatization matched
with a growing shift away from political participation and toward economic
thinking. Bruce J. Schulman notes, for example, the rise of the "yuppie" as a figure in the 1980s representing an economic philosophy that entrepreneurship
and the profit motive produced better social results than public policy and
programs did (243–44). Not unique to the yuppies by any means, this change
both economized social benefit (measuring programs first by their profitabil-
ity and second by their social benefit) and atomized responsibility by directing
it toward small groups and individuals rather than the common good.

These developments in the late 1970s fit neatly within neoliberalism. In *Undoing the Demos*, Wendy Brown defines neoliberalism not just as a set of policies, but as a "normative order of reason" that "transmogrifies every human domain and endeavor, along with humans themselves, according to a specific image of the economic" (9–10). Brown argues that under the cultural economy of neoliberalism, the "public" in a Habermasian sense privatizes into fragmented, narrowly defined economic interests. In classical liberalism, albeit selectively, state and ideological apparatuses privilege *Homo politicus*, the human person as political actor and entity with rights, interests, conflicts, and so on. Neoliberalism, she says, centers *Homo economicus*, the human as economic actor whose worth and status are determined by their economic activity. Further, Brown argues, neoliberalism in the present privileges two interrelated things: investment, where *Homo economicus* does all things to invest in themselves entrepreneurially, and economic growth, where it is the duty of citizens and communities to sacrifice themselves for the sake of economic, rather than political, health (32–35). Under neoliberal logics, a restructured political economy produces harsh economic effects for the least protected people but through responsibilization makes their struggles a matter of personal morality: "Responsibilization tasks the worker, student, consumer, or indigent person with discerning and undertaking the correct strategies of self-investment and entrepreneurship for thriving and surviving" (132–33).

The utopian visions I examine in this book offer different responses within and against neoliberalism. While I'm interested particularly in religion, broadly, the novels in this study offer a range of reactions that in some way mimic the range of available political responses to neoliberalism. In *Undoing the Demos*, Brown offers a thorough description of how this ruthless neoliberal logic infects and changes the culture and institutions of a democratic society. She argues that liberal arts education (something increasingly sacrificed under neoliberal dominance) offers the kind of citizenship preparation needed by people to oppose this economization of society (178–79). Other responses include Bonnie Honig's argument for investment in material objects and spaces that anchor people together into a broad public even as symbolic and social orders change; Jodi Dean's argument for a revival of the Communist Party and revolution; and Michael Hardt and Antonio Negri's redefinition of "public" toward the common, the non-ownership of resources and spaces.[9] All of these possible democratic structures (publics, commons, liberal education, revolution) provide material for Sargent's "social dreaming." All of these models consider the relations among people, texts, and objects. The texts that I examine in this study similarly build their imagined futures not just on human words and actions but also on nonhuman factors: lands, resources, objects, technologies, environments, and even supernatural realms and new planets.

Postsecular Responses to Neoliberalism

My purpose here is not to select one of the theories in this debate and side with it or use it extensively. Given the range of competing political projects represented in the texts with which I engage, all of the theories are useful, for some utopias imagine fluid publics, others rigorously differentiated publics, others commons, and still others revolution for good and ill. Taken together, however, they raise three important items for attention when reading religion and utopian fiction. First, beginning in the late 1970s, politically conscious texts unavoidably engaged the ubiquitous logics of neoliberalism (whether indirectly or in an intentional effort to resist those logics). Second, just as there are various models of *the* public, *a* public, or *multiple* publics, texts imagine publics in a wide variety of models and combinations. Third, people, texts, and nonhuman objects network in complex and overlapping ways to constitute publics, commons, and demoses. Given this, understanding how utopian fiction uses religion to respond to neoliberalism requires that we rigorously contextualize each piece. In other words, religious or otherwise, utopian responses to neoliberalism vary widely in orientation and scope. There is no one identifiable set of qualities or outcomes that religion produces. Rather, religions represent one source of contribution to the building of utopian visions.

Religion energizes, underwrites, and inflects utopian reactions to neoliberalism in a wide variety of ways, partly due to a religious dialectic that intensified in the late 1970s. On the one hand, unofficial and partial religious forms proliferated. On the other hand, the New Christian Right grew in power and influence nationally. Schulman shows new religious forms to be largely personal rather than communal yet nonetheless connected to environmentalism and other political movements (78–91). Similarly, McClure examines the presence of "preterite spiritualities" in postmodern literature from the 1960s onward (20). On the surface, these largely "unofficial" religious beliefs and practices would seem to be at odds with the strong religion of Christian fundamentalists and other groups in the NCR. However, Susan Friend Harding shows that the NCR is a theologically diverse movement of fundamentalists, evangelicals, Pentecostals, and other groups united around the common label "born-again Christian" (xvi, 10–13). In a monograph on evangelist Billy Graham, however, Steven P. Miller shows that some of what unites the NCR is also what allows the movement to match up with the spiritual and individualized practices of the 1970s: a set of beliefs that Miller terms "evangelical universalism." Miller names three features of evangelical universalism: a belief in the individual as the primary theological and political unit of society; confidence in relational solutions more than legislative solutions to social problems; and a trust in law and order as governmental institutions maintain them (9–10). The rise of NCR power resulted in part from its pitching of stricter social control in terms of individual empowerment and relational solutions. Moreover, while the match is not perfect, NCR attitudes fit within neoliberalism: privatization and economic reward or punishment for individual action could easily erode protection for non-Christians.

The dramatic increase of power for the New Christian Right and the simultaneous and seemingly opposed proliferation of religious forms have provided material for utopian visions across the political spectrum with varied positions vis-à-vis neoliberal logics. To consider the roles played by religion within, outside, and against publics, I turn to theories of the secular to help understand how religion works in public life more broadly. Much work has been done taking apart any simplistic notion of secularization; indeed, while the shape of religion has changed dramatically, over the past couple of centuries of modernity, religion has neither declined nor retreated from public life to the private spaces of individual conscience, home, and house of worship.[10] Further, scholars debate whether the terms "religious" and "secular" can be separated in any useful way. Talal Asad thoroughly explicates the relation between the two, showing the frequent overlaps and dialogues, but nonetheless suggests that an anthropology of secularism would note that the secular is recognizable and can be studied in relation to but is not identical with its religious origins.[11] On the other hand, arguing for new approaches to studying religion and literature, Michael Kaufmann contends strongly that any attempt to separate the two falls apart under the slightest pressure, and he advocates treating the two as coterminous ("Religious"). Many scholars basically agree, though with the caveat that to some degree, the categories themselves are powerful, and defining them creates both discursive and institutional regimes of power. This power in definition usefully alerts us to the possible variations of seculars and secularisms, and how these can include and exclude some voices and possibilities of power and community.[12]

Given the complicated relations between religious and secular, the way the two terms easily slide into each other, defining what counts as "religion" and what as "secular" carries a great deal of power. Asad defines secular*ism* in concert with the Western definition of "freedom of religion," a term with ambition to spread around the world. But freedom of religion requires a definition of religion, as Asad points out, and therefore is a regime of power since what *counts* as religion becomes extremely important. Typically, in Western countries, all belief, internal to the conscience, is free, but practice may not be (147).[13] Asad defines "secularism" as a rhetorical and institutional regime of power; definition, policy, and practice work together.

Definitions of secular and religious exist together, circulate among publics, and provide rhetorical and material power that underwrites competing political projects. Given that the division between secular and religious is unclear and that scholars have definitively cast doubt on any easy narrative of secularization, whence comes the term "postsecularism"? That is, if there is no clear phenomenon that is secular, how can there be a postsecular? In an essay establishing the importance of American Judaism and other non-Christian traditions in postsecular scholarship, Kathryn Ludwig argues that in postsecular literature, "the religious isn't so much reaffirmed as it is engaged" (83). Ludwig's assertion applies more to the profession of literary scholarship than to anything else. Still, I think her definition is useful with an adjustment: postsecularism involves not just an engagement with religion (which would be nothing new) but a fresh layer of self-consciousness about secularism. Indeed, the willingness to examine the secular as a varied phenomenon shows some sort of meta-awareness that begins to transcend the secular even as it grows from it. In *A Secular Age*, a long history of secularization in the West, Charles Taylor argues that in contrast to premodern societies, modern societies have religion as a "choice among many"; in theory, in a modern society, one can lead public and private lives without encountering God or gods more than in passing. Further, in this environment, people have options in their pursuit of what he calls "fullness"; any choice made, however, has to be done self-reflectively. In the array of theist, atheist, and nontheist choices, naïve belief and practice are no longer possible (Taylor 12–13). Because one encounters so many options, one must be choosing—passively or actively—a religious standpoint of some kind.

I argue that, like Taylor's secularism, one can define "postsecularism" as a wide category capable of accommodating a varied set of intellectual approaches; their uniting characteristic lies in eschewing naïve or simplistic distinctions between the secular and the religious. That is, the insight that the secular and the religious are constantly mediated, redefined, and repositioned with respect to their historical circumstances and adjacent political projects informs all postsecular approaches. Moreover, the new phase of self-conscious mixing of religious and secular combines with the circulation of ideas and affects in new media and enters a neoliberal ideological landscape that makes everything unavoidably public in one sense or another. One interesting thing about the texts in this study lies in their redefinition and employment of publics in order to assert a broader vision, a hope that the whole world or some significant part of it might be remade into a social dream.

Organization of the Book

In the first two chapters of this volume, I explicate two politically opposed sets of texts to reveal a surprising convergence in American utopianism: similar approaches to defining authority within and against neoliberalism. The two sides of this battle hail publics based on contrasting utopian and dystopian visions. In his novel, nonfiction books, and television series, astronomer

Carl Sagan promises humankind a fulfillment of cultural and technological evolution with the joining of a utopian, multispecies galactic civilization. In the popular *Left Behind* series, the Antichrist rises to power in fulfillment of prophecy and imposes a nightmarish globalized society. While Sagan's work and *Left Behind* appear politically opposite, they both contrast proper and improper authority, asking readers to fulfill their religious duties by supporting and identifying with some authorities over others.

In chapter 1, "'The Way of the Machine': Carl Sagan's Faith in Science as Cosmic Citizenship," I argue that Sagan's television series, *Cosmos* (1980), and novel, *Contact* (1985), evangelize a public for science as a religion. *Cosmos* and *Contact* construct religious hierarchies and structures of feeling that hail a public looking simultaneously for cultural superiority and multicultural democracy. By mixing together scientific investigation, religious structures of feeling, and technological progression, Sagan invites his audience to participate in a secularized religion that promises membership in a galactic civilization characterized by cooperation, equality, and technological mastery. This galactic civilization contrasts sharply with the economization and fragmentation of the neoliberal United States of the 1980s. Sagan's work presents a challenge: neither secularized religion nor an entrée of religious dogma into politics, his equation of science as religion represents a powerful, mostly progressive rhetorical strategy contrary to militarism and neoliberal privatization and economization. At the same time, by aggressively contrasting its own scientific commitments with a largely undifferentiated mass of fundamentalisms, New Age practices, and ancient mythologies, Sagan's public religion relies on adherents' sharp contrast of themselves as legitimate and everyone else as foolish. In other words, in an effort to get past petty conflicts of twentieth-century Earth, Sagan helps to set the stage for the further fragmentation of the American public and the identitarian conflicts of the twenty-first century.

In chapter 2, "'Nobodies Trying to Be Somebodies': Restoring Authority in *Left Behind*," I argue that the popular Christian *Left Behind* series by Tim LaHaye and Jerry Jenkins embraces the cultural logics of neoliberalism to sacralize the global authority of American men. The novels hail a non-evangelical public in service of socially conservative goals both inside Christian reading publics and in broader nationwide debates. The series uses utopian literary conventions to map born-again modes of authority onto more secular conservative concerns about domestic politics, family life, and international politics. The resulting narrative evangelism invites non-born-again readers to identify with the correct people rather than with political interests or a common public sphere. Read together, Sagan's work and *Left Behind* reveal a neoliberal religious dialectic shaping the conflicts of the late twentieth century: while the works appear politically opposed, they both assert hierarchical authority structures wherein truth regimes (religious or secular) serve to support cultural hierarchies more than searches for truth. This relation challenges common conceptions of religious fundamentalism and secular science as straightforwardly opposed, and in so doing redefines the deep politics of public religions away from a simple right-left ideological binary and toward more global conceptions of religious rhetoric.

In chapters 3 and 4, I explicate the religious utopias of Octavia Butler's *Parable* novels (1993–1998) and Margaret Atwood's *MaddAddam* series (2003–2013). Whereas Sagan and *Left Behind* aim to construct redemptive hierarchies of authority, Butler's and Atwood's novels imagine religious publics built on solidarities among people, nonhuman species, and the environment. These works focus on characters who have no economic and cultural privilege to protect. Instead, for these people, their utopian visions begin with the modest goal of survival for them and the rest of the human species in the face of ruthless neoliberal economization and privatization. The religions in these novels refocus on the goal of long-term survival, creating disciplinary regimes for sustainable living among a diverse citizenry. This sustainability requires that these systems evolve as environmental and social conditions change, adjusting with thoughtful, communal intention rather than through the fragmented and unplanned patterns of an unregulated neoliberal economy.

In chapter 3, "Smooth Dinosaurs versus Adult Humans: Biosocial Adaptation as Religious Mission in Octavia Butler's *Parable* Novels," I argue that the characters in *Parable of the Sower* (1993) and *Parable of the Talents* (1998) create a "biosocial theology," Earthseed, that invites the evolution of the human species through extraterrestrial colonization. This recognition of the species as biological actor radically situates the characters within historical and material circumstances, requiring interventions in the social and the biological, the communal and the material. Earthseed makes the utopian goal into a transcendent commitment and holds together a contingent, evolving social organization. An evolutionary religious paradigm allows the characters to transcend the self-interested, short-term logics of neoliberalism in favor of ecologically sound practices better suited to future survival. For the novels' protagonist and religious leader, Lauren Olamina, models of the public evolve, but the central goal of long-term survival and adaptation to change remains constant. Like the work of Carl Sagan, Butler's novels reorient science and space away from economization and toward an ecologically sustainable, humanity-wide consciousness.

In the fourth chapter, "'Like Some Demented Theology Debate': Postapocalyptic Junk Religions in Margaret Atwood's *MaddAddam* Trilogy," I argue that Atwood's *MaddAddam* novels—*Oryx and Crake* (2003), *The Year of the Flood* (2009), *MaddAddam* (2013)—unlike Butler's *Parable* novels, reject intentional biological intervention as a method for (r)evolutionary change. Instead, these works incorporate the biological products of late capitalism (new species, gene splices, the products of ecological disaster) into an expanded notion of kinship in a "junk religion" made of the reassembled refuse of pre-apocalyptic religious ideas. The novels present a series of failed interventions: genetically engineered superhumans turn out to be quite human, a survivalist ecocult nearly thwarts its own survival, and bioengineered animal species threaten survivors of a plague. The continuous failures set up something new in the final novel: an interspecies cooperative convened for sustainable survival. As satire, the *MaddAddam* novels tend to make fun of religion; nonetheless, religious commitment helps to realize the modest utopian goal of survival and a real future outside the ruthless economic logics of neoliberalism. Thus, while Butler's and Atwood's series take different positions toward global intervention, they together suggest a model for enacting theological-political commitments that value justice and sustainability.

After having explored some of the socially and ecologically reparative possibilities of public religions in chapters 3 and 4, in the book's final chapter I examine a countersecular public against Western neoliberal globalization. In chapter 5, "'The World at an Angle': Islam and the Hope of the Arab Spring in G. Willow Wilson's *Alif the Unseen*," I explore possibilities for reinvigorating American public secularism by looking outside of it. I argue that Wilson's 2012 novel posits a Middle East–based, broadened secular energized by Islamic piety and democratic politics. Through a comparison between online dissidents and the world of jinn and other magical creatures, the novel imagines a secularism with room for Islamists, hackers, Communists, feminists, and social media citizens. Drawing on the hope of the Arab Spring, *Alif the Unseen* warns against religiously and technologically supported vertical power structures and urges an Islamic reverence that puts all beings of creation on the same level. Through Islamic tradition, the novel theorizes a digital public in the service of democracy rather than power. Islamicized secularism creates a public against the economization of neoliberalism, a public that recommits to international cooperation, scientific discovery, and democratic regulation of the political economy. This final chapter helps to define postsecularism not as the transcendence of secularism, but as the thoughtful employment of religion to realize the secular project of equality.

In the conclusion, I place my project in the context of Trumpism in the United States after 2016. I argue that utopian public religions in the novels I am studying produce a dialectic. On the one hand, the novels do the work of imagining genuine alternatives: tracing some sort of path to revolution and imagining a society with values in contrast to the economization of neoliberalism. On the other, despair over the possibility of genuine change haunts these works just as it haunts our public discourse around revolution. This dialectic, I argue, produces an unsustainable lack, a feeling that all possible courses of action are at best not good enough and at worst hasten the very destructiveness they seek to move away from. Religion in our current moment nonetheless offers utopian aspirations: the possibility of the radical other in history and the hope of revolutionary arrangements arising out of decidedly status quo conditions.

CHAPTER 1

"The Way of the Machine"
Carl Sagan's Faith in Science as Cosmic Citizenship

At the end of Carl Sagan's 1985 novel, *Contact*, the main character, an astronomer named Ellie Arroway, experiences a revelation from God: not through vision, prophecy, or ancient text, but with the aid of a computer with advanced calculation and artificial intelligence software. The revelation comes in a message hidden in pi, the ratio of the circumference of a circle to its diameter. As a geometrical property, pi applies equally to any circle in the universe, so a mathematical message within it can only have been left by the designer(s) of the universe: God or gods. As Ellie sees the obviously intentional pattern of ones and zeros revealed on her screen, she thinks, "in the fabric of space and in the nature of matter . . . there is, written small, the artist's signature. Standing over humans, gods, and demons . . . there is an intelligence that antedates the universe. The circle had closed. She had found what she had been searching for" (431).[1] These last words forcefully illustrate some of the key oppositions on which Sagan builds a proposed path to human citizenship in an advanced, cooperative cosmic collective: the revelation in pi suggests that science can answer the big questions of religion (such as the origin of creation). At the same time, this final passage equates the work of a scientist (Ellie finds the message in pi alone with the aid of a computer) with the assertion that science is fundamentally democratic: "In whatever galaxy you happen to find yourself, you take the circumference of a circle, divide by its diameter, measure closely enough, and uncover a miracle. . . . It doesn't matter what you look like, or what you're made of, or where you come from. As long as you live in this universe, and have a modest talent for mathematics, sooner or later you'll find it. It's already here. It's inside everything. You don't have to leave your planet to find it" (430–31). The novel contrasts this freely available revelation with the more esoteric and/or culturally specific knowledges of the world's religions.

Sagan presents science as a democratizing force capable of holding all of humanity together. Against fragmented, competitive interests under neoliberalism, Sagan's science unites and advances the entire human race. This presentation relies on the recursive building, collapsing, and rebuilding of a science-versus-human cultural paradigm. By manipulating this opposition, Sagan invites his audience to participate in a secularized religion that promises membership in a galactic civilization characterized by cooperation, equality, and technological mastery. Sagan builds a public based on a faith that science brings better, more complete revelations than organized religion does; that these revelations come to a public that supports scientists in their investigations and conclusions; and that these revelations speed along the progress of humankind toward a more technologically, culturally, and morally advanced state. This religious science opposed the militarization of scientific research and the alternative epistemologies of the New Christian Right (NCR) and various New Age forms popular in the 1970s and 1980s. He clearly separates legitimate applications of the scientific method from nonscientific regimes of knowledge coming from religion, mysticism, and pseudosciences like astrology. On the other hand, he appropriates the desires of these forms and suggests that science and scientists offer the true satisfaction of those desires. Further, unlike the culturally specific qualities of nonscientific knowledges, science, Sagan argues, offers access to truth that transcends cultural specificity and individual limitations. In making this argument, Sagan tries to combat neoliberal and nationalist logics that would deny science any public role beyond the manufacture of consumer technologies and weapons. He proposes a counter-economy in which science pays off through technological, cultural, and personal development.

Sagan's public religion consists of highly secularized yet recognizably religious conceptions of time, authority, and divine presence. It would be perfectly fair simply to consider it as a prime example of straightforward secularization, where nonreligious institutions and ideas substitute for traditionally religious ones. Despite this secular quality of his rhetoric, however, the scientism with which Sagan hails his reading and viewing publics constitutes a public religion for three reasons. First, through science, Sagan engages with traditionally religious questions: the origin and design of the universe (traditionally, the purview of "natural theology"), the origin of life, and the ultimate purposes of intelligent life vis-à-vis creation. Second, despite the absence of formal religious structures, Sagan creates rhetorical structures that parallel those of Western faiths: a priesthood, a laity, belief, education, relics, prophecy, and, most significantly, revelation. Third, by addressing history, the present, and the future, the political and the interpersonal, the natural and the supernatural, Sagan attempts to construct a master discourse under which all human experience and natural law fit together. Secularized or not, how Sagan attaches nonrational religious feelings to the scientific method is what's important here. Sagan imagines science as a religion backed by the epistemology of the scientific method while simultaneously laden with the religious elements of revelation, spirituality, priesthood, ritual, holy objects, and interconnection of life. This public religion forms the basis of his imagined multispecies galactic utopia in *Contact*; it also undergirds his invitations to readers to imagine themselves as progressive against the alliance of fundamentalists, nationalists, and nuclear hawks backing the Reagan administration. Sagan connects this progressive self-identification to the practice of astronomy, inviting the audience to see astronomical projects as key to making a united, morally and technologically advanced world.

It may seem strange to begin a discussion of public religion with Carl Sagan, an atheist who was at best skeptical and often openly contemptuous of religion, which he placed alongside astrology and other pseudoscientific systems.[2] But along with being worth examining as a highly influential—one might say ubiquitous—public intellectual, Sagan's work shows how religion pervades utopian politics beyond the Christian Right and other overtly, strongly religious forms.[3] Sagan's highly secularized religion serves simultaneously as a motivation for the individual pursuit of science and as a social glue that, through acts of imagination, invests in the elite pursuit of scientific investigation. This type of priestly scientific authority challenges the antielitism and neoliberal economization that underlies conservative power by reorienting toward a democratic faith that lends power to and expects leadership from elite authorities of science.

The Cultural Economy of Science in the 1970s and 1980s

Understanding how Sagan constructed a public eager to connect experimental science with progressive goals requires that I place him within some dramatic cultural shifts of the 1970s. For my purposes of understanding Sagan's public religion and its significance, three particular changes are important: the accelerated shift of experimental science away from university-centered exploration and toward military and commercial applications; the reorientation of countercultural energies away from political activism and toward self-oriented spirituality; and the rise of the NCR. While on the surface Sagan actively opposed these developments, he redefined science partly by appropriating the logics of all three: drawing sharp contrasts between legitimate and illegitimate science, on the one hand, and productive and unproductive belief, on the other.

By the time Ronald Reagan was elected president of the United States, the uneasy peace between the United States and the Soviet Union known as détente seemed to be dissolving; the increased likelihood of confrontation empowered Reagan and other conservatives to advocate for experimental science to focus mainly on military applications.[4] Reagan ran for president advocating the development of new weapons systems and the possibility of direct confrontation as responses to the Soviet invasion of Afghanistan and other conflicts. Coupled with Reagan's promise to cut government funding of scientific research without clear military benefit, possibilities materialized for dramatic changes in the administration of research funding and, more generally, the purpose of scientific research. For liberal scientists like Sagan, the Reaganite economization, militaristic nationalism, and the NCR represented threats to both the cultural prestige of scientists and the funding of scientific research.[5] In a 1977 interview published in the *New York Times*, Sagan somewhat self-deprecatingly admits that his impetus to publish nonfiction for a popular audience is partly "naked self-interest": if people don't understand science, they won't vote to fund it (Rensberger). As the 1980s wore on, Sagan and his writing partner and spouse, Ann Druyan, took a more active role in antinuclear protests and other opposition to the Reagan administration.

Sagan's political opposition to federal budget cuts for scientific research and to the exclusive military application of science drew on a mix of powerful cultural shifts in the 1970s. It's a somewhat glib commonplace that the radical energies of the 1960s countercultural movements dissipated and were tamed in various ways in the 1970s, an idea alternately lauded and lamented by commentators, scholars, and former 1960s activists. Bruce J. Schulman argues that in the 1970s and 1980s, political and cultural energies turned inward toward the self or toward smaller communities instead of more national or global identifications. His examples of this fragmentation include ethnically centered cultural movements; the formation of networks of feminist activists for advancement in private arenas rather than mass organization around, for example, abortion or the ERA; the preference of artists for "utopias within" rather than the reforming of broader societies; and the development of self-help and spiritualist movements (Schulman 14–18). One might significantly complicate Schulman's casual association of self-help with reparative activist nationalisms, but it appears that Sagan saw it similarly. He expressed sympathy for a variety of civil rights movements, but he also argued for changes to the society of the whole world. Interestingly, he argued for those changes largely in the language of self-discovery, faith, and spirituality. He was simply careful to draw distinctions between unacceptable spirituality (for example, astrology) and acceptable spirituality (feeling awe while looking through a telescope).

Sagan employed seeking, self-help, and spiritual rhetoric partly in opposition to the seemingly more aggressive and bureaucratic belief structures advocated by the New Christian Right. I go into much more detail about the NCR in chapter 2, and it's sufficient to say here that the NCR was a loosely coordinated, interdenominational set of organizations that advocated for political positions (for example, for the tax-exempt status of religious private schools, and against abortion) but, more influentially, for the cultural and political power of "Christians" writ large. For Carl Sagan and many others, the threat of this was twofold. First, most broadly, members of the NCR and their supporters normalized revelation and their interpretations of scripture as an equal or greater regime of knowledge compared to natural and social sciences. Thus, their arguments about policy tended to be much different than those of researchers. Second, more specifically, the NCR tended to make claims on educational institutions for equal time, placing "creation science" on an equal footing with evolution. The NCR was an important part of the rise of Sunbelt conservatism, which broadly rejected academic knowledge, elitism in culture, and the social movements of the 1960s. The NCR rhetoric and organizing represented a striking threat to the public authority of scientists and other researchers.[6]

At the same time that these tendencies challenged the practice of astronomy (for example, NASA-funded space exploration), they also provided a new opening for Sagan, who could sell his science popularization in multiple media, construct a public of truth-seekers, and easily appropriate the affects and organizing strategies of the religions he rejected. More important, he could hail a public of seekers by demarcating acceptable seeking, acceptable religion, and acceptable science over and against antielite nationalism, nonscientific claims to knowledge, and privatization. Sagan began this work through television appearances and nonfiction books for general audiences in the 1970s, but his most thorough attempt to hail this public came in the 1980 public television series *Cosmos*.

Cosmos: The Progress and Regression of Civilization

"We are made of star-stuff," Carl Sagan declares near the beginning of the first episode of *Cosmos*. Sagan makes physical and spiritual connections among people and everything else in the universe, and throughout the series he argues that, like varieties of religious revelation, these connections require things of the people who recognize them. While Sagan's fully realized vision of cosmic citizenship didn't come to fruition until 1985's *Contact*, he invited readers to international citizenship through his books and, most dramatically and with the greatest audience, through his TV show *Cosmos: A Personal Voyage*. A thirteen-episode series originally airing on Sunday nights from September 28 to December 21, 1980, *Cosmos* was PBS's highest-rated program for the entire 1980s (Sorensen 29–30).

As an educational program, *Cosmos* gives viewers a brief history of Western astronomy, telling stories of scientists such as Eratosthenes, Hypatia, Johannes Kepler, and Percival Lowell. The series features some accessible explanations of scientific principles and discoveries. More than this, *Cosmos* evangelizes its audience, asking them to make spiritual and material investments in astronomy. In her brief introduction to the 2000 rerelease of *Cosmos* on DVD, *Cosmos* cowriter Ann Druyan argues that *Cosmos* offers a "history of the scientific enterprise and an attempt to convey the soaring spiritual high of its central revelation: our oneness with the universe." She ends the introduction, "Now please, enjoy *Cosmos*, the proud saga of how through the searching of 40,000 generations of our ancestors, we have come to discover our coordinates in space and in time, and how, through the awesomely powerful method of science, we have been able to reconstruct the sweep of cosmic evolution and been able to find our own part in its great story."[7]

Druyan combines scientific language ("coordinates in time and space," "scientific enterprise," "cosmic evolution," "discovery") with a language of spiritual seeking and even religiosity familiar to audiences in 1980 ("soaring spiritual high," "awesomely powerful," "searching," "revelation," and most notably, "oneness with the universe"). This combination fits well with *Cosmos*'s rhetorical appeals, the religious qualities of which are a central focus of the small amount of scholarship available on Sagan's popular work. Indeed, despite twelve nonfiction books, one novel, one film, and countless appearances in popular media, it's *Cosmos* that has gotten the most attention from scholars. A few years after its initial airing, Thomas Lessl cleverly excavated the religious qualities of the rhetoric in *Cosmos*, showing how Sagan as host of the show occupies various religious roles of priest, seer, prophet, and teacher (Lessl, "Science"). In a different article, Lessl argues that science popularization is a form of priestly discourse: the rhetoric of the priest is didactic, attempting in both traditional and industrialized societies to mediate between the established conceptions of the general culture and those of an elite cognitive, religious, or aesthetic subculture (Lessl, "Priestly" 184). As a science popularizer, Lessl argues, Sagan mediates the elite knowledge of science and links it to viewers' everyday experiences, allowing them access not just to interesting information but to contact with the laws of the cosmos ("oneness with the universe," as Ann Druyan puts it). In *Cosmos and the Rhetoric of Popular Science* (2017), Karen Schroeder Sorensen extends these insights further, offering some illuminating rhetorical analysis of *Cosmos* to show how Sagan creates a mythos for the audience to share. In *Cosmos*, the authority of science rests on this mythos.

Lessl and Sorensen cleverly realize that whatever else it may be, *Cosmos* is an interesting rhetorical object that draws on religious forms to argue for the importance of science. Their arguments largely show analogies between the secular science of Sagan and Western religious structures of rhetoric and mediation. But I think *Cosmos* in the context of the rest of Sagan's work shows something religious beyond analogy: not just a religious appeal, but religious structures of faith, revelation, self-conception, and public cohesion. Across its episodes, *Cosmos* asks for something fairly straightforward from viewers: support for public money for astronomy research. The series, however, more subtly asks viewers to see themselves and others as people who know how to gain knowledge (natural and spiritual) through science. Rejecting religious fundamentalism, racism, sexism, and nationalism, the series argues that science transcends cultural differences and thus offers the key to progressive evolution toward a just, multicultural global society. Through stories of historical astronomers and mathematicians, Sagan suggests that while scientific discoveries happen within cultural contexts, science as an epistemology is transcultural and as such builds a bridge between cultures, the self, and the universe. Across thirteen episodes, *Cosmos* presents science this way by purifying culturally specific myth and religion from science. Correspondingly, Sagan reconfigures religious feeling so that it supports, rather than questions, scientific knowledges. Proper religious feeling, Sagan argues, drives adherents to see understanding nature as a duty and as the path toward a more just, moral world. Science, in this case, offers world-changing benefits far beyond any financial or national defense benefit. For Sagan, science offers the solution to all conflicts and therefore transcends financial calculations and demands a reversal to privatization.

At the end of his opening narration in episode 1, "The Shores of the Cosmic Ocean," Sagan makes a bold promise that signals the purification and hybridization that characterize the series: "We wish to pursue the truth no matter where it leads. But to find the truth, we need imagination and skepticism both. We will not be afraid to speculate, but we will be careful to distinguish speculation from fact" (Malone, "Shores"). The series, however, is full of speculation. Sagan delights in it, imagining, among other things, life forms floating in the clouds of Jupiter, the contemplation of the stars by early humans, and the reactions of extraterrestrial civilizations to Earth's sillier television programs (Malone, "One Voice," "Backbone," "Persistence"). Claiming at once the authority that comes with the rigorous evidentiary standards of scientific research and the fun of imaginative speculation allows Sagan to associate both rigor and enjoyment with science. Science answers the desires both for an unassailable truth regime and for imaginative freedom. This move lends cosmic significance to imagination (much like the religious and mythical stories to which Sagan denies equal status with scientific "fact") while it lends authority to the adherent to deny the legitimacy of other sources of imagination. In effect, Sagan less separates science from speculation and more separates good from bad imagination.

Through this differentiation, the series contrasts science with the illegitimate knowledge regimes popular at the time. In all of *Cosmos*, the most aggressive purification happens in episode 3, "The Harmony of the Worlds," where Sagan demonstrates the illegitimacy of astrology. The episode begins with some brief views (both telescopic and animated) of constellations and planets, but quickly moves to separate astronomy from astrology with such statements as "to the astronomers, Mars is a place as real as the Earth, a world awaiting exploration; but the astrologers see Mars as a warrior, the instigator of quarrels, violence, and destruction." As Sagan narrates in voiceover, a montage contrasts photographs of Martian landscapes with astrological paintings of the warrior Mars. Through most of the rest of the episode, Sagan historicizes the divergence of astronomy and astrology by describing the achievements of Johannes Kepler, a mathematician who discovered the elliptical motion of planets around the sun by abandoning mystical astrological beliefs about what the motions of the planets *should* be. Through Kepler, Sagan establishes astronomy as a superior truth regime to astrology, showing that the discovery of fact—Mars as a place, for example—requires a clear purification and protection of the methods of astronomy. In Kepler, one sees the qualities of the subject ideal for achieving this truth: a person obsessed with finding fact and willing to abandon incorrect belief to find it. The ideal seeker, the story of Kepler seems to suggest, is so committed to the progress of knowledge that they recognize the old knowledge—in Kepler's case, undifferentiated astrology and astronomy—as a hindrance to be overcome.

Through his criticisms of astrology, Sagan marks a distinction between scientific and nonscientific observations and conclusions. Subjected to rigorous examination, Sagan argues, astrology fails to offer a mechanism by which the planets might influence human destiny or any verifiable instances in which the planets have done so. He dramatically illustrates this point by reading two horoscopes next to each other and observing that they offer nothing specific enough to examine rigorously. Sagan links the nonscientific basis of astrology with regressive structures of power, suggesting that astrology belongs to an earlier phrase of civilizational development, including despots: "Astrologers became employed only by the state. In many countries, it became a capital offense for anyone but the official astrologer to read the portents in the skies. Why? Because a good way to overthrow a regime was to predict its downfall." He goes on, "Astrology developed into a strange discipline: a mixture of careful observation, mathematics, and record-keeping with fuzzy thinking and pious fraud." Other examples appear throughout the series. In episode 4, "Heaven and Hell," and in several of his books, Sagan takes on the theories of Immanuel Velikovsky, a psychologist who gathered ancient legends and put them together to conclude that the planet Venus emerged from Jupiter sometime in early human civilization, and its movement through the solar system to its present orbit was responsible for a number of scriptural and legendary occurrences (like Earth's spin ceasing in the book of Joshua). Sagan is deeply invested in showing why, according to observation and current scientific knowledge, that would be impossible. He also dips often into classical civilizations to draw distinctions between proper science (based on observation, experiment, and deduction) and thought experiments. In episode 7, "The Backbone of Night," Sagan contrasts the Ionian philosophers like Democritus, who conducted experiments and made observations, against the later Platonist philosophers, who were more committed to pure thought.

Sagan pairs the non-experimental stance of Plato, Aristotle, and Pythagoras with their epistemic secrecy, the restricting of knowledge to only a privileged few, whose conclusions never face scrutiny. Sagan presents this as both undemocratic and fracturing; if knowledge is limited to a relatively few people, cosmic citizenship is impossible. In contrast, Sagan presents the scientific method as a universal that bridges the gap between cultures and between individuals. To make this true, however, he starts by highlighting the proper consciousness of individuals. For example, Kepler's success at formulating the three laws of planetary motion, according to *Cosmos*, was based on his willingness to abandon astrology. Further, Kepler was convinced that the planets known at the time (Mercury, Venus, Earth, Mars, Jupiter, and Saturn) were the only planets and corresponded with the five perfect solids of geometry. Sagan argues that these sorts of personal pet theories have to be abandoned in order to find truth. Similarly, in episode 5, "Blues for a Red Planet," Sagan tells the story of Percival Lowell, an astronomer who studied Mars and was convinced he saw Martian-made canals on the surface. Lowell constructed a whole story of ecological crisis on Mars to explain these canals.[8] Lowell made several important discoveries regarding Mars and other areas of astronomy. While Sagan narrates them, he also establishes that Lowell's equipment was not powerful enough to see Mars as clearly as would have been needed to know that there are no Martian canals. Pet theories, Sagan seems to be arguing, are fine if the development of science can go forward, and more powerful space telescopes and eventually NASA probes would explore Mars more thoroughly.

Sagan is at his clearest as an explicator of scientific discoveries, and his descriptions of the inferiority of astrology and other pseudosciences as truth regimes are accessible and fairly persuasive. As Sagan separates science from pseudoscience, he also repurposes the kinds of seeking and wonder expressed in astrology, religion, and myth toward emotional and material investments in science. At the end of the anti-astrology segment in "The Harmony of the Worlds," Sagan contrasts astrology with the superior connections with the universe that science offers: "[Astrology] pretends to satisfy our longing to feel personally connected with the universe," but "we *are* connected; not in the trivial ways the pseudosciences promise, but in the deepest ways. Our little planet *is* under the influence of a star—the sun warms us; it drives the weather; it sustains all living things. Four billion years ago, it brought forth life on Earth. But our sun is only one among a billion trillion stars within the observable universe, and those countless suns all obey natural laws, some of which are already known to us" (Malone, "Harmony"). As Sagan speaks these words, a series of filmed scenes and technical diagrams appear on the screen.

While they are not still pictures, the form is a montage more than a film sequence: the images do not describe a process but show a series of moments associated with the overall theme. Sagan describes neither a technical process nor specific scientific laws; instead, he suggests that making physical laws "known to us" makes the "deepest" relationship achievable. Science both describes the relations among people and the universe and makes possible the proper experience of those relations.

In *Cosmos*, Sagan represents science as both a regime of truth and a mode of spiritual experience, one that brings the seeker to a feeling of oneness with the universe. The series attaches this spiritually inflected connection to the universe to a co-arising liberal, progressive vision of investment in the future and in multiculturalism. Sagan calls this progress toward a global, multicultural, democratic society "evolution" and sees it as related to biological evolution. Sagan's biographer Keay Davidson notes the contradiction in Sagan's deployment of the term "evolution" between a nonteleological biological evolution and a unidirectional, teleological cultural evolution. Sagan understood that biological evolution relied enormously on randomness, and he says in "The Harmony of the Worlds" that, were Earth to start again, life would evolve differently (Malone, "Harmony"; Davidson 274). On the other hand, he consistently espouses the idea that cultural evolution happens according to a determined path. For him, it was a foregone conclusion that all intelligence in the universe eventually develops along a technological path from the Stone Age through radio telescopes to space flight, and from tribalism to nationalism to cosmopolitanism.

In *Time and the Other*, Johannes Fabian explores how conceptions of time have developed and changed over the course of history and how competing conceptions of time help to structure cultural relationships, classifications, and power differentials. Sagan uses a conception of time recognizable to his audience as progressive, in which his viewers represent an acme of cultural and technological evolution. Behind them lies a past that led to their current state of development; this includes present-day people (largely in the Global South) who are still catching up, as it were. Simultaneously, Sagan shows his audience a future in which the human race can become higher, better, more advanced; in that timeline, present-day human civilization (including the audience) is backward and needs to choose to advance. At the end of episode 1, "The Shores of the Cosmic Ocean," Sagan introduces the "cosmic calendar"—also found in Sagan's book *The Dragons of Eden* (1977)—a special-effects-heavy one-year calendar that he can walk in, complete with square months and a familiar calendrical layout. With the cosmic calendar, Sagan condenses the approximately fifteen-billion-year history of the universe into the viscerally comprehensible format of one calendar year. For example, on Sagan's cosmic calendar, the big bang, represented by a bright glow at the top left-hand corner of the calendar, occurred at 12:00 a.m. on January 1; the Milky Way galaxy formed on May 1; life appeared on Earth on October 2; and modern *Homo sapiens* made their earliest appearances at 10:30 p.m. on December 31. While Sagan carefully explains the development of all these events, and he carefully emphasizes the inherent randomness of evolutionary processes, the randomness is overridden by a pervasive undercurrent of progressive evolution, the idea that the turning of time on the cosmic calendar leads inexorably to those final seconds of December 31—leads, in other words, inevitably to the current state of human civilization and culture. As the segment ends, he declares, "We are the legacy of 15 billion years of cosmic evolution. We have a choice. We can enhance life and come to know the universe that made us, or we can squander our 15-billion-year heritage in meaningless self-destruction. What happens in the first second of the next cosmic year depends upon what we do" (Malone, "Shores").

I could spend pages discussing the implications of this conception of time—its colonialist quality, for example. For my purposes, though, what's interesting is how Sagan combines progressivism with a flavor of apocalyptic millennialism in order to attach a world-shaking significance to the audience's investment in science. Given the frequent repetition of his anti–nuclear arms stance (it's peppered throughout the series, and the final episode, "Who Speaks for Earth?," is devoted solely to it), it would have been easy for the audience to recognize what he means by "we can enhance life and come to know the universe that made us, or we can squander our 15-billion-year heritage in meaningless self-destruction." The stark choice—destruction or knowledge— accesses both a liberal rejection of war and a belief in the liberatory potentials of knowledge. The cosmic calendar relies entirely on secular knowledge (the big bang, the evolution of the human species), but it nonetheless accesses a sacred history and duty, positing this moment as the decisive turning point in the fulfillment of the true purpose of the human species.

Cultural advancement is possible, *Cosmos* insists, and Sagan argues that faith in science and its revelations produces that advancement better than faith in religion, myth, nationalism, or any other antiprogressive force. He further shows some ideas of what a public sphere that supports this scientific, sacred, progressive timeline would look like. This progressive public is characterized, on the one hand, by individuals with a sense of wonder and delight in discovery and, on the other hand, by public and private financial investment in discovery. "The Backbone of Night" dramatizes the relation between these two across a wide-ranging hour. Early in the episode, Sagan visits students in a classroom at the elementary school in Brooklyn he attended as a child. As the children cheer, smile, and enjoy, he passes out photos taken of moons and planets by NASA's space probes. The sound of the classroom fades, and a series of shots, lasting only a few seconds each, shows the children's faces as they look at the photos. "Every one of us begins life with an open mind, a driving curiosity, a sense of wonder," Sagan narrates, and then the sound returns to the classroom as he answers kids' questions—such as why the Earth is round—while referring to some of the photos he brought. The images and his narration suggest an uncomplicated, joyful desire to understand. Sagan answers the students' questions with scientific knowledge—a short lecture about how gravity shapes planets, an explanation of what is and isn't in the Milky Way galaxy. Science, he suggests, produces delight and fulfillment just as worship or faith might. Right after this segment, Sagan argues that the current moment in the history of knowledge especially offers this delight: we would not have known, only a few hundred years ago, what planets and stars were. He considers early people wondering about stars, including the myths they invented, alongside their lack of scientific knowledge. The ancients had to make do with myth; science, he suggests, is the modern and best way to satisfy our curiosity.

Along with the childlike curiosity of the individual, societies more broadly support or hinder the satisfaction of this curiosity and its concomitant technological and cultural advancement. In the previous week's episode, "Traveler's Tales," Sagan makes a similar historical progress argument when talking about the European age of exploration. He focuses especially on the sixteenth-century Dutch republic, arguing that the newly democratic, commerce-driven society encouraged exploration, invention, and trade, goals that he takes for granted are positive because of their production of knowledge. (The problems of colonialism are briefly acknowledged, but then largely left out of the discussion.) The Dutch republic, he claims, had a broad investment in the advancement of knowledge.

Cosmos's presentation of the wonder-filled classroom in Brooklyn and the sixteenth-century Dutch republic provides glimpses of Sagan's utopia—a society aimed correctly toward advancement and discovery. His discussion of the Ionian philosophers and the Library of Alexandria in episodes 1, 7, and 13 offer similar hints. The full development of a perfectly advanced society would have to wait five years for his novel, *Contact*, but in the meantime, Sagan presents the nightmarish, dystopian vision of a society that fails to follow discoveries and denies the advancements of science and its corresponding liberal, progressive values. In the final episode, "Who Speaks for Earth?," Sagan makes an extended, one-hour argument against nuclear proliferation and confrontation. In it, he flies in his "spaceship of the imagination," which takes him to other worlds suddenly silenced by nuclear conflagration. Most movingly, he imagines traveling toward Earth and listening to its radio signals, which suddenly go silent as the United States and the USSR destroy the world in nuclear war. The camera shows Sagan's profile in close-up as he bows his head in mourning. This nightmarish vision wasn't new to much of Sagan's audience, who had witnessed public debates about nuclear proliferation especially in the run-up to the 1980 U.S. presidential election. Additionally, the post–nuclear apocalypse science-fiction novel had been popular for decades. For example, Sagan himself had been deeply influenced as a young person by Nevil Schute's 1957 novel, *On the Beach* (Davidson). The vision is not new, but Sagan invites his audience to share his knowing sadness at the folly of nuclear war. The childlike sense of wonder that he advocates and a reverence for creation would lead in exactly the opposite direction, toward disarmament, the loosening of national borders, and increased international cooperation in the pursuit of nonmilitary science and technology. The improper use of science for the basest causes (that is, science to produce weaponry) and a lack of true spiritual understanding of the purpose of science lead to destruction, the opposite of future hope.

What's interesting here is not just that Sagan ties some of the questions of religion (How did all this come to be? How are we related to each other? How do things work and why?) to science, but how Sagan makes a spiritual science that ties to self, community, God, and the universe. As an all-encompassing matrix of personal, cultural, and universal, Sagan's science goes beyond the careful methods he urges and the interesting results he discusses; science provides a master discourse that ties together human experience (historical and personal) with the sweep of cosmological history. Science's potential to encompass everything transcends any narrow economic or individual interest. Its history, *Cosmos* implies, shows the potential of a public sphere built around public investment in science. In *Contact*, Sagan makes this connection more explicit, holding out a promise to readers who see the cosmic significance of science: a whole universe teeming with cooperative, multispecies intelligence waits to welcome humans to investigation and the control of nature and its deepest mysteries. In other words, humans can know and maybe even become God.

Contact: The Revelation of Cosmic Citizenship

Cosmos establishes some of the chief terms of Sagan's public religion, which connects a personal sense of wonder with a progressive vision of peace and international cooperation. His 1985 novel, *Contact*, shows in more detail what this public religion makes possible, both imagining progressive ends on a cosmological scale and suggesting ways that present-day humankind can move into that better future by transcending fragmentation and self-interest. *Contact* takes place on a very near future Earth characterized by nationalism, suspicion, injustice, nuclear arms, and environmental waste. Through revelation brought by scientific practice and a faith that continued investigation will yield yet greater revelations, the main characters imagine citizenship in an already integrated, well-engineered cosmos, utopian in its multicultural equality, cooperation, and mastery of nature. The move from the fractured present to the joining of the cosmic collective in the future involves not just a (mostly secular) commitment to scientific discovery but a recognition of the extraterrestrials as morally and technologically superior and a wish to emulate them through technological development. *Contact*'s encounter with extraterrestrials calls for a humbling of humans before superior intelligence and a trust that science will bring humankind closer to the godlike alien beings.

Two connected articles of faith anchor Sagan's public religion: faith that investigation will yield significant revelations, and faith that these revelations will advance the human race along a relatively narrow line of technocultural development. The Search for Extraterrestrial Intelligence (SETI) provides the perfect investigation for this faith.[9] "Christians await the Second Coming," says Sagan biographer Davidson. "SETI scientists await the first message from the stars. They are brothers under the skin" (260). SETI requires extraordinary patience in scanning the entire sky with radio telescopes, and it keeps faith that this investigation will yield contact with extraterrestrials who will be much more technologically and culturally advanced than humans.[10]

Contact centers on Dr. Ellie Arroway, an astronomer and the director of a SETI project at a radio telescope array in New Mexico. The novel explores its themes through Ellie's development from childhood to adulthood, showing her abiding commitment to scientific skepticism, driving curiosity, and contempt for nonscientific truth regimes like religion. Ellie maintains this mindset as she leads an international effort to decode a message from extraterrestrials. The message contains instructions for building a machine, the function of which is not clear. An international group named the World Machine Consortium (made up of scientists and officials from most countries of the world) builds the machine and determines that representatives from the United States, the USSR, India, China, and Nigeria will sit in the machine when it is activated. As the U.S. representative, Ellie travels in the machine with the international scientist team through a series of wormholes to a giant station at the center of the galaxy, home to an infinitely advanced, multispecies galactic civilization. Ellie speaks to an alien being who appears to her in the guise of her long-deceased, beloved father. The extraterrestrial reveals the existence of a vast, multigalactic, multispecies cooperative using highly advanced technology to "cultivate" the universe. He also tells her of messages hidden in transcendental numbers, which were clearly left by the designing intelligence of the universe.[11]

When they return to the machine, the scientists reappear on Earth at the same instant they had left, and their recording equipment has failed to document anything. Very few people believe their story, and the scientists are all accused of having faked the message and the machine. At the end of the novel,

Ellie uses a computer program to discover a message hidden in the number pi. She shares her experience with Palmer Joss, a fundamentalist Christian leader whose mystical investment in truth prepares him to make a conversion from Christianity to Ellie's scientism. At the same time, Ellie understands that, due to the absence of evidence, her experience at the galactic center is now an impetus to faith. The novel ends, then, with a self-conscious hybridizing of religion and science, of faith and skeptical inquiry. This new, religiously inflected science, the novel promises, will yield greater discoveries in the future.[12]

Readers responded positively to *Contact*, and it was the seventh highest-selling novel in 1985 ("What Were We Reading"). Like *Cosmos* and all of Sagan's nonfiction books, *Contact* self-consciously if somewhat clumsily enters the political conflicts of its era, taking time to express sympathy for civil rights and feminist activists, to decry nuclear armament, and to express frustration with the machinations of military establishments and nationalist politicians. It also takes for granted that the building of the machine would be a public effort, a detail that especially annoyed conservative reviewers.[13]

Contact spends less effort than does *Cosmos* in separating good science from bad science and instead draws sharp distinctions between proper and improper mixes of science and culture. The novel does not offer an argument against religion or the political regulation of science; rather, it presents science as the proper expression of religious feeling over and against religious fundamentalism. In *Formations of the Secular*, Talal Asad argues that "secularism is not simply an intellectual answer to a question about enduring social peace and toleration. It is an enactment in which a *political medium* (representation of citizenship) redefines and transcends particular and differentiating practices of the self that are articulated through class, gender, and religion" (5, emphasis in original). Secularism, in other words, is a discursive site of conflicts over political legitimacy. Fighting the use of science for militaristic application and the limitation of the power of scientists by religious missions, such as the teaching of creationism in schools, Sagan presents science both as the way to answer religious questions and as the religion that can unite all people and, indeed, other intelligent life in the universe.

Whereas *Cosmos* is about the seeking of truth through astronomy research, *Contact* is about revelation—how people should find it, how they should react to it, and what the social impacts of it should be. The first task in pitching the novel's science-as-religion argument is to show very clearly what sort of combinations are harmful to society. Primarily, the novel decries the influence or power over science of any interest not driven by discovery, and this comes in two forms: the desire of religious belief to stop any discovery that would contradict such belief, and the use of science for the waging of international conflict. While the novel never successfully portrays the two as connected, it does classify them in the same category of wastefulness. Throughout the novel, military and national concerns interfere with the scientists' attempts to decode and use the message. Shortly after the reception of the message, for example, Michael Kitz, a member of the U.S. Department of Defense and the novel's chief antagonist, appears in Ellie's office and threatens to classify the entire operation, such that no information about the message could be shared with the U.S. public or with scientists from other countries (80–82). Kitz objects throughout the novel to international cooperation, and other governments have similar characters with similar objections. One Russian representative to the World Machine Consortium suggests ignoring the message and ceasing all further radio astronomy so that the new technologies offered in the message will not create competition and conflict among nations (187–90). At the end of the novel, when Ellie and the other scientists return from their galactic voyage, each country's defense establishment attempts to discredit their story and suppress it. Kitz spins a conspiracy theory wherein Ellie and the other scientists invented both the message and the machine as a hoax; he threatens to release false, damaging information about her psychological state should she ever tell anyone of her experiences (380–91). Ellie sees Kitz's paranoid fantasies as the result of two connected cultural and personal pathologies: a commitment to militarism and conflict that the extraterrestrials showed was obsolete ("an amalgam of diverse species from separate worlds working together in concert. Their very existence was an unspoken rebuke" [388]), and a personal paranoia driven by fear ("Kitz's rendition of events was so malign that it revealed, she thought, someone truly wounded, afraid, in pain" [387]).

Through Kitz, *Contact* presents militaristic nationalism as a paranoid obstacle that prevents not only international peace but also the recognition of truth coming from revelation and the search for further revelation. Similarly, the fundamentalist Christian characters reject the revelations of science because of their possible conflicts with the revelations of scripture. Through them, Sagan argues that religion prevents the pursuit of truth and offers shallow personal fulfillment compared with scientific investigation. While Christopher Douglas argues that *Contact* aims "for a fictional détente between science and religion" (185), in my view the novel seems to reject anything like organized religion based on its epistemic limitations.

The trouble with religion, according to *Contact*, is not simply that it aims people toward the wrong truths but that fundamentalist leaders create publics that influence policy away from the support of science by undermining both the epistemic truth claims of science and the authority of scientists. The novel features only two fundamentalist characters, both of whom are national public personalities who command large followings of Christian believers. Billy Jo Rankin, a Jerry Falwell–type televangelist character with an extra dose of faith-healing hucksterism, denounces the satanic undermining of biblical truth and accuses scientists of all varieties of moral iniquity. The novel gives a more sympathetic portrayal of the fundamentalist believers in Palmer Joss. An autodidact with a taste for classical texts and a distaste for the snake-oil elements of televangelism, Joss makes more intellectual objections to Ellie and the other scientists, questioning the moral neutrality of the scientific method and observing the limitations of the scientists' faith in their own practices. Joss also comes across as less afraid of new discoveries, and his intellectual curiosity and willingness to listen form the basis of his friendship with Ellie. In Joss's first appearance in the novel, Ellie watches him in a relatively calm television appearance. He questions whether advanced science and technology have brought a happier or more moral world; given the novel's constant denunciation of the military dominance of science, it seems by this point in the book like a fair question. Joss argues that scientists form an elite population, overestimate their own knowledge, and underestimate other truth regimes. He further argues that decoding the message should be both a scientific and a moral effort, led in part by religious leaders in concert with scientists. "Science," he concludes, "is too important to be left to the scientists" (130–31). Joss challenges the scientific method and the authority of scientists, but instead of simply portraying science as evil and nonbiblical, he articulates a vision of a public religion that checks possible abuses of technological development.

In part through *Contact*'s sympathetic portrayal of Joss (he is a seeker like Ellie and a thoughtful listener), the book invites the reader to consider Joss's challenges of morality and of access: what in science makes a happier, more moral population, and shouldn't science open truth to common, non-elite people, rather than making it the sole province of elite scientists? Fortunately, through its proposed scientific public religion, *Contact* has prepared answers to these questions. Due to Rankin's and Joss's popularity, the president of the United States and her science advisor become concerned about their objection to the message project, and they arrange a meeting of the two preachers, Ellie, and another scientist on the project. Their discussion is rancorous (and a bit shallow).[14] Rankin and Joss challenge Ellie's authority directly, suggesting that the willingness of scientists to change their mind in light of new evidence undermines public trust in important matters of faith: "Right from the beginning you rule out almost everything religion is about. I mistrust scientists because the scientists mistrust everything" (160). In challenging the changeability of science, Rankin helps the case for science in the book: religion, he seems to be suggesting, is unchanging and therefore regressive. He sets up Ellie to make the novel's most important arguments about science: that scientific skepticism and development allow it to evolve progressively and upwardly, and it is therefore a superior truth regime, a superior means to social cohesion, and a superior method to satisfy spiritual leanings. Ellie starts simply by contrasting the revelations of science with the revelations of scripture. Whereas science progressively discovers new truths, the revelations of scripture do not evolve nor do they offer unambiguous confirmation of their own authority over time. Ellie argues, "Imagine if your kind of god . . . really wanted to leave a record for future generations, to make his existence unmistakable to, say, the remote descendants of Moses. It's easy, trivial. Just a few enigmatic phrases . . . such as, 'the sun is a star.' Or 'Mars is a rusty place with deserts and volcanoes, like Sinai.' Or 'a body in motion tends to remain in motion'" (163). According to Ellie, the trouble with scripture isn't so much that it isn't scientific but that its revelations do not change with the development of new methods and technologies.

The argument for science, then, begins with its changeability: with change, the book argues, comes progress. Addressing a reading public in 1985, a time of the rise of conservatism, a redirection of public resources toward defense spending, and related reactions against civil rights, feminism, and internationalism, the appeal to progress over and against fundamentalism is clear. Nonmilitary science, *Contact* claims, offers both a superior truth regime and a better means toward social progress. The problem isn't the existence of religion—Ellie is careful to declare the right of all people to religion and says she considers herself Christian because of Christ's message of love and peace (167–68)—but the antiprogressive intrusion of religious thought on scientific investigation. The novel links this retardation of scientific progress with the opposition by the New Right to the reparative social movements of the time. As a liberal progressive, Sagan was aware of injustices, particularly those of race- and gender-based discrimination, and of anticolonial movements (for example, those against apartheid in South Africa). While he shows a direct impediment of scientific investigation by militarism, nationalism, and fundamentalism (212), he only hints that these same forces prevent the growth of equity and justice. Nonetheless, through Ellie, the connection is made: the same misunderstandings of truth drive political regression as they drive technoscientific regression. Flying high above Earth on a plane, Ellie imagines how superior extraterrestrial beings would view racism, and she thinks about protestors in Washington, D.C.: a "massive rally of black Americans protesting economic disparities and educational inequities. Considering the justice of their grievances, she thought, they had been very patient" (92). Earlier, the novel narrates Ellie's encounters with sexism in graduate school, as she has to learn to speak in certain authoritative ways ("a physics voice, a professional voice") to get male scientists to listen to her even when such ways of speaking put her "in danger of bursting out laughing" (22). The connections between the need for socially progressive movements and the novel's main antagonists of militarism and fundamentalism, however, are unsatisfactorily made.

Contact does make clear, however, that the petty suspicions of nationalism and the regressive faith of fundamentalism prevent the discovery and revelation of truth and the social progress brought by such revelation. Nationalism, militarism, and fundamentalism, the novel testifies, improperly mix knowledge with social practices and religious beliefs. *Contact* offers an alternative mix, one that reverses the direction. Whereas Ellie decries the expectation that science serve faith or government, the novel presents an ideal in which religious feelings and states serve science, which holds the key to the linked goals of personal fulfillment and social progress. Two things simultaneously characterize a public based in this proper hybridization: the individual who pursues revelation and religious feeling through science, and the social and political structures that actively support scientific investigation. This faithful support of science, the book argues, produces more revelations and properly understands them. This in turn satisfies the curiosity of seekers and propels the human race in an ideal progressive evolution.

Through stories of Ellie's youth, the novel describes the ideal faithful seekers who will be fulfilled through scientific investigation. Ellie is a seeker in the sense of the post-1960s counterculture; she is from a young age suspicious of organized religion, curious about the world, and willing to defy authority in order to pursue her passions. Ellie's "sense of wonder" before the universe serves throughout the novel both as motivation for her actions and as a central subject of dialogue between Ellie and the other characters. The novel opens with Ellie's childhood curiosity; in one of the first passages, she clandestinely disassembles a broken radio:

> Guiltily, she let herself into the spare room. The old Motorola radio was on the shelf where she remembered it. It was very big and heavy and, hugging it to her chest, she almost dropped it. . . . with her tongue between her lips, she removed the screws and exposed the innards. As she had suspected, there were no tiny orchestras and miniature announcers quietly living out their small lives in anticipation of the moment when the toggle switch would be clicked to "on." Instead, there were beautiful glass tubes, a little like light bulbs. Some resembled the churches of Moscow she had seen pictured in a book. The prongs at their bases were perfectly designed for the receptacles they were fitted into. (5)

After young Ellie fixes a broken vacuum tube, the tubes all begin to glow, and static comes from the radio. "Glancing toward the closed door with a start, she lowered the volume" (6). After listening to an announcement about *Sputnik* (which dates this incident to late 1957), Ellie, "fearful of being discovered," puts the radio away, emerges from the room "a little out of breath," and startles when her mother walks by (6).

This passage early in the novel establishes several crucial elements of the seeker-reader Sagan hails throughout. First, intellectual curiosity needs little stimulation from other people: at younger than ten years old, Ellie wants to look inside machines to see how they work. Second, innate intelligence: by simply looking at the insides of a radio for a few minutes, she understands at least basically how it works and fixes it. Third, a complex affective dimension to this curiosity makes it into a "sense of wonder." This is seen in the guilty pleasure she gets by clandestinely working on the machine in a spare room with the door closed, emerging "a little out of breath" as the episode ends. The narrator gives little indication that Ellie's family discourages her, but she "sneaks away" nonetheless to experience a private, embodied pleasure at understanding things. Similarly, the next pages recount a family vacation where Ellie escapes two hated cousins and lies on her back on the ground: "She looked up at the brilliant spangled sky and found her heart racing" (7). Alone, thrilled, she tries to picture Earth from a cosmic perspective: "the world only looks flat, she thought to herself. Really it's round. This is all one big ball ... turning in the middle of the sky ... once a day. She tried to imagine it spinning, with millions of people glued to it, talking different languages, wearing funny clothes, all stuck to the same ball" (7, ellipses in original). She thinks about Earth's rapid spin, and "gratifyingly, she was overtaken by the giddy sense that she had better clutch the clumps of grass on either side of her and hold on for dear life, or else fall up into the sky, her tiny tumbling body dwarfed by the huge darkened sphere below. She actually cried out before she managed to stifle the scream with her wrist" (8). These early life stories begin the connection between religious feeling and scientific investigation. Ellie experiences bodily feelings and non-intellectual impressions, including powerful impressions of sublime smallness. She connects those sensations, though, to material knowledge (what she knows about Earth and its size, and what she can touch and fix in the radio). Young Ellie experiences these religious feelings, and she turns to scientific knowledge and technological development to satisfy them.

As an adult and an accomplished scientist, Ellie extends these notions into a more thorough philosophy of religious feeling and science, which once again hails a public of religious skeptics with spiritual desires. Ellie makes an argument for the religious quality of her sense of wonder to her lover, presidential science advisor Ken der Heer, after the message has been received. Lying in bed, Ellie and Ken have a wide-ranging discussion about the distance between language, feelings, and reality. Ellie considers her own grief over her long-deceased father and then connects that grief to religious feeling and the desire to believe, especially in heaven with "nice moms and dads floating about or flapping to a nearby cloud. It would have to be a commodious place to accommodate all the tens of billions of people who had lived and died since the emergence of the human species. It might be very crowded, she was thinking, unless the religious heaven was built on a scale something like the astronomical heaven. Then there'd be room to spare" (152). The move from fantasy heaven to astronomical heaven begins the substitution of scientific investigation for religion, and she continues this move in musing aloud to Ken about large numbers—the vastness of space, the number of possible intelligent beings in the galaxy, the number of stars in the universe, and other viscerally intimidating numbers. In this private, intimate conversation, Ellie makes a step-by-step connection from religious desire to science through scale, considering how science and math help people understand the vastness of the universe both in size and in possibility. This substitution of the scale of the universe for religious desire ties the individual person to the vast cosmos through nonrational, affective desire.

Ellie uses early twentieth-century Protestant theology to connect this nonrational feeling to science and mathematics defined over and against organized religion. Reading from an encyclopedia entry marked "Sacred or Holy," Ellie explains to der Heer:

> The theologians seem to have recognized a special, nonrational—I wouldn't call it irrational—aspect of the feeling of sacred or holy. They call it "numinous." The term was first used by . . . let's see . . . somebody named Rudolph [*sic*] Otto in a 1923 book, *The Idea of the Holy*. He believed that humans were predisposed to detect and revere the numinous. He called it the *misterium* [*sic*] *tremendum*. Even *my* Latin is good enough for that.
>
> In the presence of the *misterium tremendum*, people feel utterly insignificant, but, if I read this right, not personally alienated. He thought of the numinous as a thing "wholly other," and the human response to it as "absolute astonishment." Now, if that's what religious people talk about when they use words like sacred or holy, I'm with them. I felt something like that just *listening* for a signal, never mind in actually receiving it. I think all of science elicits this sense of awe. (153)

Ellie's recognition of herself in Otto's definition of the holy appears to make an overture: scientific and religious experience, she claims, share a nonrational dimension, a sense of wonder. This redefinition of what counts as religious experience (it could include scanning the sky with radio telescopes, according to Ellie) makes an overture less to churchgoers or members of traditional religious communities and more to the seekers of the 1970s. She pays off this overture with a promise that such a spiritual-scientific move offers a promise of cultural rebirth. She reads from the entry: "whether or not man is now in a new situation for developing structures of ultimate values radically different from those provided in the traditionally affirmed awareness of the sacred is a vital question" (153). By dipping in and out of Protestant theology and countercultural spirituality, Ellie seamlessly arrives at an anti-institutional yet religious conclusion: "I think the bureaucratic religions try to institutionalize your perception of the numinous instead of providing means so you can perceive the numinous directly—like looking through a six-inch telescope. If sensing the numinous is at the heart of religion, who's more religious would you say—the people who follow the bureaucratic religions or the people who teach themselves science?" (153–54). Ellie suggests that science and religion both provide methods of access to the wonder produced by the universe, and methods for understanding that universe, but science, Ellie suggests rhetorically, is better. Tying this viewpoint to an intimate moment (a conversation had as Ellie and Ken lie in bed) suggests that proper affective relations with the universe also underlie interpersonal relationships. Ellie's rejection of "bureaucratic religion" is the first signal of a recurring argument in *Contact* that science provides the proper method for accessing a universal "numinousness" and that science, despite its imbrication in the politics and culture of modernity, resists "bureaucracy" in an antiauthoritarian way.

Indeed, for *Contact*, science provides the primary means of transcending historically specific conflicts and inequities. Through this conversation and several others in the novel, Ellie makes a case for science as the most satisfying form of religious faith for people with curiosity and intelligence. Her quotation of Rudolf Otto (along with many of the epigraphs that begin each chapter of *Contact*) places this argument in a long tradition of religious thinking. The novel, however, does not remain within the realm of individual therapeutic fulfillment; it is a utopian work with a vision of what these religious-scientific feelings do for the whole world and beyond. Ellie's arguments about religious feeling are almost entirely confined to individuals and seem to make sense for those wanting to become theoretical scientists. What of the broader publics hailed by the novel, and what of the rest of the society the novel wants to change? To make this move, Sagan presents scientists as the key to international cooperation, the practice of science as the key to world-changing revelation, and the development of technology as the key to a peaceful and productive universe. Through Ellie's friendship with Vasily Gregorovich "Vaygay" Lunacharsky, a Soviet astronomer, the book suggests that Cold War animosities do not interest genuine scientists, who connect over their love of science and lament that their governments prevent them from working together more closely. Ellie and Vaygay have political and social debates and lament the infrequency of their visits (110–13).[15]

The other scientists who enter the machine with Ellie and Vaygay come from India, China, and Nigeria; they have diverse beliefs and customs, but they all share an eerily similar commitment to the scientific satisfaction of their religious feelings. Devi Sukhavati of India talks at length with Ellie about the contrasts between ancient mythical stories of the constellations and what scientists know in the present (199). Abonnema Eda of Nigeria practices a form of Sufism. When Ellie asks him if he ever feels religious feelings not connected to the practice of science, he answers unequivocally "never" (315–16). Through the scientists with whom Ellie works, *Contact* connects its scientific religion with a transcendence of cultural differences that, the novel seems to suggest, otherwise cause conflict. Beyond the interpersonal connections among scientists advanced enough to rise above cultural differences, the novel also promises material benefits from international scientific cooperation. As Ellie patiently explains to Kitz, the violently suspicious defense establishment operative, the message cannot be decoded and the machine cannot be built without international cooperation if for no other reason than the fact that because of Earth's rotation, all of the signal cannot be gathered by one nation (105–6). The nations of the world are largely convinced, however, by the promise of new industries and new technological knowledge that will come with the machine (205).

These material reasons, the novel makes clear, merely provide arguments to convince the doubters. The real reason for the cooperation grows out of the desire for discovery that the novel calls "religious" and out of the faith that the signaling aliens will be morally as well as technologically superior. Sagan contrasts the scientific response to the revelation with the religious and nationalistic one, and the novel makes clear that science produces and responds to revelations in more personally fulfilling and publicly productive ways than do organized religions. Scientific revelations, the novel argues, help produce a more just, unified public than religious revelations can, but only if people see science as religious. In *Saint Paul: The Foundation of Universalism*, Alain Badiou provides a means by which to understand a religion as a social structure responding to a "truth event." Badiou reads Paul as a "poet-thinker of the event, as well as one who practices and states the invariant traits of what can be called the militant figure. He brings forth the entirely human connection . . . between the general idea of a rupture, an overturning, and that of a thought-practice that is this rupture's subjective materiality" (2). Paul articulates a truth that "overturns" the prevailing subjective orders of his time, and he enacts the resulting subjectivity. According to Badiou, Paul's event—the resurrection of Christ—happens in a particular context, but it is universal, addressed to all people (14). In *Contact*, the extraterrestrial signal is a revelation, a truth event that overturns the subjective order of nation-states, the economization of science, and the regressive forces of religion.

The event, however, does not produce this effect universally; the question for the novel is how a new, postnational, postfundamentalist symbolic order will emerge and who will bring it about. The signal produces immediate public effects, which the novel gives in lists with clear judgments of correct and incorrect responses. Early in the process of decoding the message, its mere existence stimulates ideological ferment: "Zealotry, fanaticism, fear, hope, fervent debate, quiet prayer, agonizing reappraisal, exemplary selflessness, closed-minded bigotry, and a zest for dramatically new ideas were epidemic, rushing feverishly over the surface of the tiny planet Earth" (129). In this list is a clear binary between the good responses (hope, selflessness, zest for the new) and the bad (zealotry, fanaticism, bigotry). The important thing here is that the reception of the signal creates not just change but a revolutionary moment, an event that could lead dramatically forward in social progress or stimulate regressive social and philosophical moves. Given Sagan's recurring theme in his nonfiction work of a precarious moment between regression and progress, it's unsurprising that this same idea surfaces repeatedly in *Contact*. Shortly before the team embarks on the journey, the novel returns to this, coining a Japanese neologism, *machinado*, or the way of the machine: "the increasingly common perspective of the Earth as a planet and of all humans sharing a stake in its future" (315). The progressive element of this becomes clear when an American newspaper commentator opines, "'Mankind has been promoted to high school.' ... There was a widespread anticipation of imminent secular revelation ... there was also a notable decline in many quarters of the world of jingoistic rhetoric and puerile self-congratulatory nationalism" (180–81). The proper response to revelation, then, lies in the rejection of borders, bigotry, and jingoism. For the novel, advancement is cosmopolitan—recognizing Earth as one planet with one destiny—and cosmopolitanism can only be produced by the study of and engagement with the cosmos.

While the narrator of *Contact* refers to "secular revelation," the religious quality of the novel's rhetoric solidifies in Ellie's conversation with one of the alien beings, who appears to her in the guise of her deceased father. Ellie thinks about the super-advanced extraterrestrials as godlike figures: "How ... theological ... the circumstances had become. Here were beings who live in the sky, beings enormously knowledgeable and powerful, beings concerned for our survival, beings with a set of expectations on how we should behave. They disclaim such a role, but they could clearly visit reward and punishment, life and death, on the puny inhabitants of the Earth. Now how is that different, she asked herself, from the old-time religion? The answer occurred to her immediately: It was a matter of evidence" (371, ellipses in original). Ellie convinces herself that the video evidence she has gathered will offer unambiguous proof, the same kind she had demanded from scripture in her earlier encounter with Rankin and Joss. In a dramatic twist, however, all of the evidence evaporates for Ellie and the other scientists. When they return, their tapes are blank, and due to some sort of alien space-time trick, they arrive back at the same instant they departed Earth. Ellie and the other scientists carry a revelation without proof, one that others will or will not believe. The suspicious defense establishments of the United States and the Soviet Union do not believe it, and in Kitz's interrogation of Ellie, he pointedly asks the same question she had asked of Rankin and Joss: "if the extraterrestrials wanted to make it unambiguously clear you'd really gone somewhere, they would've brought you back a day later, or a week. Right?" (389). Ellie and the others suddenly have a matter of faith rather than evidence.

Rather than an attempt by Sagan to inject epistemic humility into the narrative or show that religious leaders and scientists are on the same level, these events suggest two things: first, parochialism and pettiness still limit science; the defense establishments will suppress the stories and restrict further discussion. Second, and more important, these events show that continued scientific investigation requires faith, but that proof exists if one pursues it. Like the (second) coming of the messiah, or the day of judgment, or the resurrection, scientific faith requires confidence that revelation will arrive in the future, given continued pursuance. The difference lies in seeking, rather than waiting, for it.

An Intergalactic Imperial Utopia

For *Contact*, proper faith produces personal passion and public support for scientific investigation. The alien beings at the center of the galaxy show Ellie and the others the utopia made possible by this faith. The first element of the intergalactic utopia is the joining of a multispecies collective of technologically and socially advanced species. *Contact* presents this as a matter of dramatic progress, for humanity lacks the advancement to do so in Ellie's present. The book expresses this through nineteenth- and twentieth-century imperialist metaphors: the advanced extraterrestrials lead a galactic civilization at multispecies imperial metropoles, and humankind is too "backward" to yet emerge from the periphery because, the novel suggests, people have not grown beyond religious dogmatism and nationalism. The backwardness of humankind as compared with extraterrestrial civilizations comes up again and again in the novel and, indeed, in all of Sagan's work. In a 1975 article on extraterrestrial intelligence, Sagan and coauthor Frank Drake write: "Since we have achieved the capability for interstellar radio communication only in the past few decades, there is virtually no chance that any civilization we come into contact with will be as backward as we are" (Sagan and Drake 83). The assertion here relies partly on a fairly straightforward scientific argument: if many civilizations on planets throughout the galaxy develop radio broadcast technology, they will do so at different times, and a civilization would broadcast for a long time before Earth scientists discovered it. In other words, if Earth scientists made contact with broadcasters elsewhere, it would be very unlikely that *both* species were relatively new to radio technology. However, this conclusion also relies on a narrow conception of the progressive advancement of technologies: that all surviving civilizations eventually develop radio technology, and that such technology continues to develop in basically the same way that radio technology has evolved on Earth. Given the complex formations influencing the development of radio on Earth—commercial interests, scientific accidents, and so on—this is a big assumption.

Through comparison between extraterrestrials and humans along a progressive timeline, the novel makes civilizational appraisals key to understanding the cultural development of humanity. In assuring politicians that the alien beings sending the message are unlikely to attack Earth, scientist Devi Sukhavati states, "It is unlikely in the extreme that beings on a planet of the star Vega are exactly at our level of technological advance. Even on our planet, cultures do not evolve in lockstep. Some start earlier, others later. I recognize that some cultures can catch up at least technologically. When there were high civilizations in India, China, Iraq, and Egypt, there were, at best, iron-age nomads in Europe and Russia and stone-age cultures in America" (191). Here, the novel's temporality inserts extraterrestrials into a progressivist reading of Earth history. The idea of "levels of technology" expressed in terms of Iron Age, Stone Age, and Space Age absorbs any hypothetical aliens and signals that they are in some way just like peoples of Earth—that is, they are simply a more "advanced" form of human civilization (no matter how often scientists, including Sagan, warn that alien beings are not likely to be anything like humans).

While *Contact* espouses a progressive politics of racial and gender equality, the characters imagine the galaxy in imperial metaphors. The galaxy is organized and governed like a modern Euro-American empire. Throughout the novel, characters speculate on the motivations of the extraterrestrials who sent the message and the instructions for building the machine. In a particularly telling answer to the alien motivation question, Ellie's friend Vaygay, the Soviet scientist, offers: "The Earth is a . . . ghetto. Yes, a ghetto. All human beings are trapped here" (209, ellipsis in original). He continues, "The cities are too far away, and we are too poor ever to go there, even the richest of us. Anyway, we know they don't want us. That's why they've left us in this pathetic little village in the first place. And now along comes an invitation. . . . There will always be people who are flattered by the invitation, or who think it is a way to escape our shabby village" (209–10). Vaygay uses a nineteenth-century European imperial analogy: Earth is peripheral, and its people are backward. The analogy continues later as the five scientists travel inside the machine through tunnels in space. First, the machine moves through a tunnel from Earth to the area of space near the star Vega. Ellie and the others are surprised that they cannot see any planets or extraterrestrial spacecraft, and Ellie wonders, "was a delegation from the provinces so unremarkable that no one had been assigned even to note their arrival?" (335). The machine in which they ride finally passes an alien device—an array of radio telescopes. Xi Qiaomu, a physicist from China, compares the telescopes to "watchtowers of the Great Wall. If you are limited by the speed of light, it is difficult to hold a galactic empire together. You order the garrison to put down a rebellion. Ten thousand years later you find out what happened. Not good. Too slow. So you give autonomy to the garrison commanders" (335). He goes on to compare the tunnels from one star system to the next to "imperial roads. Persia had them. Rome had them. China had them. Then you are not restricted to the speed of light. With roads you can hold an empire together" (335–36). Vaygay and Xi imagine the galactic organization as a premodern empire—ancient in the case of Rome, Persia, and China and fairly old in terms of Russia and France. Earthlings are provincial imperial subjects.

A sudden shift occurs in the imperial metaphor, however, only a few pages later; the novel still imagines the galaxy as part of an imperialist geography, but it becomes a modern, seemingly benevolent domain that imitates the rhetorical strategies of the U.S. empire in the late twentieth century. The analogies change as the machine takes them through several other tunnels and past other stars. Whereas Xi spoke of "imperial roads" and Vaygay earlier of "droshkys," Eda, the Nigerian scientist, says, "I think this is an underground . . . a Metro. A subway. These are the stations. The stops" (338). The shift to an urban metaphor sets up a different kind of travel networking, a more modern one that still preserves distinctions between center and periphery but changes their nature to something more like a city and suburbs. They wonder why, through all the subway stops, they do not see any signs of habitation. Ellie and Sukhavati speculate that the extraterrestrials do not want them to be scared by seeing alien beings: "There's some sort of ethic of noninterference with primitive planets. They know that every now and then some of the primitives might use the subway . . . so you let them ride only on subways that go to the sticks" (340–41). This "ethic of noninterference" represents the kind of enlightened imperialist thinking found in other science fiction of the late twentieth century; it supposes an extraordinarily powerful but benevolent empire, one that swears noninterference so that other cultures might "develop" into something similar to the empire.

When the scientists arrive at their destination, they find a metropole infused with the spirit of late twentieth-century multiculturalism. This spirit comes through specifically in the absence of any actual extraterrestrial beings. As the space vehicle arrives at the center of the galaxy, they encounter an amazing spaceport:

> And swimming into her field of view as the dodec [space capsule] rotated was . . . a prodigy, a wonder, a miracle. . . . On its surface were hundreds, perhaps thousands, of illuminated doorways, each a different shape. Many were polygonal or circular or with an elliptical cross section, some had projecting appendages or a sequence of overlapping off-center circles. She realized they were docking ports, thousands of different docking ports—some perhaps only meters in size, others clearly kilometers across, or larger. Every one of them she decided, was the template of some interstellar machine like this one. . . . It was a democratic arrangement, with no hint of particularly privileged civilizations. The diversity of ports suggested few social distinctions among the sundry civilizations,

but it implied a breathtaking diversity of beings and cultures. Talk about Grand Central Station! she thought. The vision of a populated galaxy, of a universe spilling over with life and intelligence, made her want to cry for joy. (341–42)

Diversity here is expressed in terms of size and shape, and Ellie infers it from docking ports. Physiological, rather than cultural, difference is presented here. The scientists, however, encounter no further extraterrestrial difference; when they disembark, they find themselves on a simulation of an Earth beach, and later they talk to extraterrestrials who appear in the guise of loved ones.

Further, the advancements of extraterrestrial cultures look remarkably like the advancements of Euro-American modernization extended to a greater scale: they have infinitely advanced technologies, but the multispecies, democratic collective uses them for the sake of exploration and stewardship on a universal scale. The comparison is made between Earth and the universe. Early in the novel, Ellie looks out the window of an airplane at the landscape of the United States and wonders what it would signify to an extraterrestrial observer: "There were vast areas of the Midwest intricately geometrized with squares, rectangles, and circles by those with agricultural or urban predilections; and, as here, vast areas of the Southwest in which the only sign of intelligent life was an occasional straight line heading between mountains and across deserts. Are the worlds of more advanced civilizations totally geometrized, entirely rebuilt by their inhabitants? Or would the signature of a *really* advanced civilization be that they left no sign at all?" (91). Later, the shapes Ellie sees in the spaceport provide examples of exactly the "geometrization" she expects from advanced civilizations. The comparison between the alien base at the center of the galaxy and a later version of a modernized and mechanized Earth continues in the details of the plot and even in subtle throwaway lines. As their space vehicle docks in an opening of the giant spaceport, Ellie says aloud, "well, it isn't Bridgeport" (342). This offhand reference to Mark Twain's *A Connecticut Yankee in King Arthur's Court* is a joke that alludes to the "Yankee" Hank's travel backward through time to Camelot—only in a kind of reversal. Rather than being transported to a cultural landscape awaiting modernization (a modernization that eventually leads to mass death in *Connecticut Yankee*), Ellie and the others have been transported *forward* in time to something that looks like completed modernization. This modernization is so complete that it networks not only the world, but the entire universe.

The extraterrestrials have technologies so advanced as to be indistinguishable from magic, including a nearly divine power over nature and culture. The extraterrestrials use this power not for dominance, but for shepherding new civilizations (like Earth's) into cosmic citizenship and, more significantly, for responsible ecological stewardship of the universe. Through this infinitely advanced civilization, in other words, Sagan demarcates the correct uses of technology and hails a liberal public becoming increasingly concerned about eco-logical damage to Earth. The alien being disguised as Ellie's father tells her of the grandest engineering project ever conceived. As they speak, he shows El-lie in their simulated sky a supermassive black hole at the center of the Milky Way galaxy; large quantities of matter flow into it. She asks the alien being if the mass of the matter goes anywhere, and he tells her it goes to Cygnus A, a very bright object in the sky that puts out energy in jets of superheated gas.[16] Ellie, incredulous, asks, "you're *making* Cygnus A?" Her "father" answers her, "oh, it's not just us. This is a ... cooperative project of many galaxies. That's mainly what we do—engineering. Only a ... few of us are involved with emerg-ing civilizations" (363–64, ellipses in original). Ellie expresses astonishment: "'There are cooperative projects between galaxies?' she asked. 'Lots of galax-ies, each with a kind of Central Administration? With hundreds of billions of stars in each galaxy. And then those administrations cooperate. To pour mil-lions of suns into ... sorry, Cygnus A? The ... forgive me, but I'm just staggered by the scale. Why would you do all this? Whatever for?'" (364, ellipses in origi-nal). The alien's answer is telling:

> "You mustn't think of the universe as a wilderness. It hasn't been that for billions of years," he said. "Think of it more as ... cultivated."
>
> "But what for? What's there to cultivate?"
>
> "The basic problem is easily stated. Now don't get scared off by the scale. You're an astronomer, after all. The problem is that the universe is expanding, and there's not enough matter in it to stop the expansion. After a while, no new galaxies, no new stars, no new planets, no newly arisen lifeforms—just the same old crowd. Everything's getting run-down. It'll be boring. So in Cygnus A we're testing out the technology to make something new. You might call it an experi-ment in urban renewal. It's not our only trial run. Sometime later we might want to close off a piece of the universe and prevent space from getting more and more empty as the aeons pass. Increasing the local matter density's the way to do it, of course. It's good honest work." (364, ellipsis in original)

The extraterrestrial frames the explanation with two statements that serve to anchor this project squarely in human terms.[17] "The basic problem is eas-ily stated. Now don't get scared off by the scale" suggests that this endeavor echoes the kind of massive engineering projects undertaken at various times on Earth, including the building of modern communication and travel net-works and the construction achievements of ancient empires—like the build-ing of the Great Wall of China. Calling it "good honest work" identifies it with a working-class sense of useful production. The fact that this is cooperative work between "Central Administrations" of galaxies suggests a model for Earth-based cooperation between nations and cultures, a kind of bureaucratic rather than democratic Earth empire, complete with central administrations, garrisons, and imperial roads. The goal of the cooperation, moreover, is not so much democratic as aesthetic; the cooperation happens in engineering enterprises for the beautification of the universe. The problem with the deadness of the expanding universe is "boredom," and the solution lies in a kind of "urban renewal"—a project of modernization to deal with the effects of modernization or, in this case, to deal with the inevitable effects of geologic evolution over time. Just as cultures evolve in historical time, the universe evolves in geological time. The cooperating extraterrestrial races throughout a group of galaxies, then, pull off the ultimate engineering project and, in so doing, *become gods*—they control not just individuals in experiential time, nor cultures in historical time, but the universe in geological time. "You've been pouring matter into Cygnus A for the last six hundred million years?" Ellie asks. The answer she receives suggests an even longer time scale: "Well, what you've detected by radio astronomy was just some of our early feasibility testing. We're much farther along now" (365).[18]

The general imperialist ethos lies in the execution of control over nature, but it is clearly coupled in the book with racial hierarchies. Ellie muses, "There was a hierarchy of beings on a scale she had not imagined. But the Earth had a place, a significance in that hierarchy; they would not have gone to all this trouble for nothing" (365). The engineering achievements of the intergalactic civilization confirm what the novel has emphasized all along: the human race is relatively backward. The problem lies in the expression of that backwardness. Through Vaygay's and Xi's imperial metaphors and through the very cultivation of the universe by the wielding of Western technoscience, the extraterrestrials (multispecies, multigalaxy, and diverse as they may be) represent the acme of Euro-American civilization. Humankind (with its dogmatic religions, incomplete modernization, and relative newness to empirical science) becomes, in contrast, non-European. The conversations Ellie's companions have with their respective extraterrestrial "family" members are not presented in the book. It is only to Ellie, a white American, that the existence of this multispecies cooperative is a relative shock, and only her understanding of it is represented within the novel's imaginative space.

The imperialist temporality of Sagan's "hierarchy of beings" undercuts his argument that science provides the democratic knowledge regime over and against the mediated, hierarchical qualities of religion. The assumptions that underlie the novel's definitions of progress lead to a final, surprising conclusion near the end of Ellie's conversation with the alien being. Indeed, there is a God or gods, and the backward are not just less culturally and technologically advanced than the aliens; they are farther from God. With this move, Sagan links scientific development with a crucial part of Western religion: the knowledge of and communion with God. The religious dimension of the vast engineering project becomes clear when the extraterrestrial moves from his description of the cultivation of the universe to telling Ellie about the mysterious presence of messages in transcendental numbers. He begins by revealing that the tunnel system that the five scientists traveled through was not constructed by the intergalactic civilization—it was found by them already built, but with no sign of the civilization that constructed it. Coupled with his description of the messages in transcendental numbers, the implication becomes clear: the universe was created by an intelligence akin to that of a Western God, but that intelligence is described as an engineer. These creators, in other words, are yet another step above the extraterrestrials in technological evolution: they engineered a universe. The cultivation of this universe, then, becomes a project in religious stewardship; as people are to cultivate God's Earth, all intelligent beings are to steward the universe.

Further, people can experience the numinousness Ellie described earlier simply through investigation—looking at the sky or taking apart a radio like young Ellie. The extraterrestrials show, however, that people *enact* the numinous through technological manipulations of nature. The novel makes this link through a somewhat abrupt transition. Right after she learns of the engineering project, she asks whether the extraterrestrials "feel the numinous": "I want to know about your myths, your religions. What fills you with awe? Or are those who make the numinous unable to feel it?" (367). The alien responds by suggesting that human beings make the numinous too and confirms that the extraterrestrials feel it. He locates the extraterrestrial sense of the numinous in just one place—mathematics. He suggests that messages of some kind lie within transcendental numbers. The alien explains: "Well, eventually—let's say it's in the ten-to-the-twentieth-power place—something happens. The randomly varying digits disappear, and for an unbelievably long time there's nothing but ones and zeros" (367). The ones and zeros, he says, cannot be random because they contain an eleven-dimensional "picture" of sorts. Ellie objects: "Mathematics isn't arbitrary. I mean pi has to have the same value everywhere. How can you hide a message inside pi? It's built into the fabric of the universe." "Exactly," the extraterrestrial answers (368). Through this scenario, the extraterrestrial suggests an answer to Ellie's earlier challenge to Joss: why didn't God leave an unambiguous message confirming his existence in the Bible, like saying "the sun is a star" or "Mars is a rusty place with deserts and volcanoes, like Sinai"? (163). The extraterrestrial's talk with Ellie confirms that such messages do exist: the hidden message he talks about in pi confirms that the universe was intentionally, thoughtfully designed by something akin to a Creator God. In the very last pages of the novel, Ellie confirms that a pattern does lie deep in pi (430–31). The kind of god revealed here, however, mimics the gods of revealed religion only in limited ways. This is God the engineer, not God the ethicist, not God the Father, nor even God the Creator—this God requires nothing and demands nothing.

Because God the engineer is revealed through mathematics rather than scripture, the novel suggests, the designers reveal themselves in a democratic way, not concerned with time, place, language, or other culturally specific paradigms. Unlike in institutional religions, which always include some type of authority, these divine revelations are available to anyone: "As long as you live in the universe, and have a modest talent for mathematics, sooner or later you'll find it" (431). In this, the novel's final statement, is found the strongest statement of *Contact*'s politics. It suggests the democratizing power of science and mathematics in the style of old arguments about Enlightenment rationalism: science and mathematics work in tandem with democratic government to undermine old dogmas, unseat tyrants, and enshrine individual rights. The kind of Western privilege required by this subject, however, is not buried very deeply. The mathematical concept of pi is fairly elementary and, while not universal, requires in theory only a "modest talent for mathematics." However, Ellie arrives at this secret message in pi not with mere calculation, but with calculation carried out by computer technology.

The conception of science and math as a great democratic leveler presents a problem: relatively few people have anything beyond a high school science education. What, then, does the novel demand of a general public without expertise? Through Ellie's continued relationship with the fundamentalist leader Palmer Joss, the novel answers that a nonscientist public must invest their religious feelings in a faith that science has yielded and will continue to yield world-changing revelations. After the five scientists are threatened to maintain secrecy, they struggle together with whether they should tell anyone. Vaygay Lunacharsky opines, "In their hearts, they wonder, 'Could it be true?' A few even want it to be true. But it is a risky truth. They need something close to certainty ... And perhaps we can provide it. We can refine gravitational theory. We can make new astronomical observations to confirm what we were told—especially for the galactic center and Cygnus A" (403, ellipsis in original). While Vaygay speaks of the government officials who have refused to believe them, his argument reveals a central idea about a proper scientifically faithful public: they want to believe. Like good scientists, they require strong evidence, and scientific investigation (in this case, astronomical observation) will provide. The public, then, need not be scientists, but they need have Ellie's religious feelings before the universe, basic scientific skepticism, and faith that science will satisfy those requirements in the future. When Ellie tells Joss about her experiences in the center of the galaxy, he believes her immediately. Although she is being threatened by the U.S. government, he does not quite understand why she does not simply tell her story; being a man of faith, he does not naturally accept scientific standards of evidence. He also resists when she tells him about the divine mathematical messages. After several pages of explaining the mathematical basics to him, he says, "You're looking for Revelation in arithmetic. I know a better way." Ellie answers, "Palmer, this is the *only* way. This is the only thing that would convince a skeptic" (419). She comments on the reversal of their positions—she with a "profound religious experience [she] can't prove" and him a skeptic—and he answers, "I'm not a skeptic. I'm a believer. . . . [Ellie's experiences make] God very big" (420). Joss and Ellie meet less in epistemic paradigms and more in a sense of wonder for the sheer size of the universe. Only a "very big" God could create it, in contrast to the small God who expresses the kinds of concerns for human affairs found in scripture.

It's tempting to read Joss's movement toward science and Ellie's movement toward faith in something she cannot prove as a sort of middle ground, a détente between rigorously secular science and rigorously unscientific faith. The meeting, however, is far from in the middle. While Joss does not repudiate scripture or faith, he does accept the terms by which Ellie defines religion: as a conception of God as the designer of the laws of the universe, one who can be found with continued scientific investigation. Joss represents the ideal public here: a nonspecialist who invests religious feeling in scientific investigation and has faith that it will yield more revelation. Ellie has only moved in the sense that she has begun to believe in the intentional design of the universe and in an intelligence that created it. Her method of investigation involves mathematics and computers instead of scripture. The end of the novel features the discovery already discussed: a message left in pi and therefore in the design of the universe. Given that the message from God is in math, rather than in any scripture that comes in a particular language and from a particular context, Ellie thinks of this message as equally available to all: "As long as you live in the universe, and have a modest talent for mathematics, sooner or later you'll find it" (431). But Ellie is a scientist; she has been told of the message in pi by the alien being she met after having participated in decoding and answering the first message; and she has a computer. Essentially, she knows how and where to look. As Thomas Lessl argued about *Cosmos* ("Priestly"), in this view scientists are like priests: they decode the revelation for the faithful public and continue to analyze text. As Ellie looks at the message in pi, she thinks, "There would be richer messages farther in" (*Contact* 431).

Conclusion: Hope for a Progressive Future

Contact's final religious gesture, then, is a dual promise that can be recognized especially in Western religions: more revelations and a better world are coming in an unspecified future. Further, this promise is prophetic in the sense of the prophetic tradition of the Hebrew Bible—that is, the promise of revelation and a better world hinge on the good, proper actions of "the people" as a whole. It asks for identification with the authority of scientists, both as researchers and as philosophical and moral guides. In short, *Contact*'s conception of science does not merely mimic some of the forms of religion; it actively appropriates them to make a religion out of astronomy, a public religion that aims individual affect and public belief toward support for experimental, non-military science.[19] It is, in other words, a hope for a set of outcomes in the future, ones that Sagan has attached somewhat loosely to progressive politics.

Sagan attempts to find universality in science and mathematics, and in doing so, he pushes strongly against the privatization, economization, and nationalism of Reagan-era scientific investment. However, Sagan hails a public based on a somewhat exclusivist model; he invites the audience to identify with the progressive and the academically knowledgeable over and against the backward and regressive political and religious conservatives aligned with Ronald Reagan. Further, while *Contact* and Sagan elsewhere identify the justified grievances of historically disempowered peoples, his universalism does little to remedy those issues beyond some very focused objections to nationalistic and military dominance. In his pitch for science against the regressive, in other words, Sagan wages a relatively narrow culture war against a not particularly well-understood adversary. That adversary, in the form of the New Christian Right, was busy prosecuting a much wider-ranging, influential culture war of its own. In the 1980s and 1990s, the NCR was gearing up to make its own push for popularization and mainstreaming to complement its already effective political organizing. While the NCR had its own objections to neoliberal ideology and a conception of authority not unlike Sagan's, its vision of public and private differed significantly from his.

CHAPTER 2

"Nobodies Trying to Be Somebodies"

Restoring Authority in *Left Behind*

It's easy enough to place the *Left Behind* series (1995–2007) in the utopia genre. The series narrativizes the fundamentalist theology of premillennial dispensationalism, which, interpreting a set of prophecies across the Hebrew and Christian Bibles, predicts great suffering (dystopia) before the return of Christ for a millennium of just and perfect rule (utopia).[1] Whereas Carl Sagan turns science into a religion that unites humankind in the godlike powers of infinite technological advancement, the *Left Behind* series turns to organized, fundamentalist religion for the source material of its utopia. The books show an uneasy relationship between Christian fundamentalism and neoliberalism. On the one hand, *Left Behind* presents a diversity of interests and identities as threatening. On the other, the series presents responsibilization and globalization as opportunities to confirm the superiority of fundamentalism.

Left Behind rejects elitism, modern science, and multicultural liberal progressivism; instead, it promises utopia through a patriarchal populism characterized by proper hierarchies of people and knowledges. Moreover, the series equates true, born-again Christianity with a global hierarchy in which American Christian men are on top, and God punishes everyone who does not acquiesce to this hierarchy. In *Left Behind*, the Antichrist's dystopian global government is statist, multicultural, and pacifist. The Antichrist's progressive politics, however, are merely a deception: shallow notions of justice providing cover for a war against God. *Left Behind*'s utopia restores a believed-lost sharp line between truth and falsehood, connecting that truth less to factual or theological accuracy and more to the Christian identity of those who believe it. To be saved is to identify correctly as Christian, and to be Christian is to occupy the correct position within cultural hierarchies. The series' utopian vision looks forward to the end of a fragmented culture and economic competition through the final defeat of all competitors.

That *Left Behind* has a political agenda is hardly surprising. As many scholars have shown, it fits comfortably into a long tradition of apocalyptic fiction, evangelistic cultural products, and even dispensationalist end-times fiction.[2] Moreover, that it aligns with late twentieth-century conservative ideas (antifeminism, white privilege, and anti-intellectualism) is equally unsurprising.[3] Despite its obvious politics, the series interestingly bridges the gap between a born-again Christian reading public and the broader public sphere it seeks to evangelize. Scholarship on *Left Behind* has shown acute awareness of the series' multivalent audiences. Some scholars have interpreted *Left Behind* as "mainstreaming," an attempt to evangelize the broader public for fundamentalist Christianity, conservative domestic politics, patriarchal family arrangements, pro-Israel policy, and imperialist international politics.[4] Others have written insightfully on *Left Behind* as addressing primarily Christian reading publics. *Left Behind* addresses all these reading publics at once by using utopian literary conventions to map born-again ways of reading and conceptions of authority onto more secular conservative concerns about domestic politics, family life, and international politics.[5] The series accomplishes all of this through a utopian triple formation that contrasts the dystopia of the Antichrist, the utopia of Christ's millennial rule, and the implied utopia of pre-Rapture Christian family life. In doing so, the series grants narrative power to the New Christian Right among born-again Christians and a more religiously diverse public. But deliberately or otherwise, its power goes beyond the specific political goals of the NCR.[6] The series joins a broader cultural shift toward dualistic apocalyptic thinking, enclave politics, and the waging of cultural conflict as a method for gaining political power. While it shows some discomfort with logics of neoliberalism, the series invests deeply in a competitive cultural economy in which Christians must dominate others. Thus, the series helps to exacerbate the identitarian conflicts of the early twenty-first century.

Left Behind appeals to evangelical and secular readerships through a utopia that embraces, and then settles, neoliberal competition. To show how these Christian and secular readerships come together, I first examine *Left Behind* as texts entering the conflicts among evangelical Christians around global mission. Drawing especially on the work of Melani McAlister, I show how *Left Behind* denies liberal evangelical engagement in global social problems in favor of a globally dominant Christianity led by American fundamentalist men. I then show how the novels argue for American Christian dominance by creating a definition of authority that combines fundamentalist modes of reading with secular notions of verifiable truth, common sense, and masculine activeness. Armed with a reoriented authority, the novels imagine a utopia for that authority to create. In the third section of the chapter, I show how the series contrasts proper and improper relations between the state and Christians. In a globalized world, the best states protect the privilege of Christian men; dystopian states try to equalize different, fragmented groups in public participation. Finally, I consider how *Left Behind*'s properly structured utopian public rewards Christians and punishes enemies of God economically and materially. Unlike the other works I examine in this volume, *Left Behind* seeks not to fix cultural fragmentation, but to win it.

Whither Christian Globalization?

From an outsider perspective, evangelical Christianity might appear fairly uniform ideologically. However, from its inception in the late nineteenth century, many theological and political positions comprised the movement.[7] Moreover, global neoliberalism lent greater urgency to some of these ongoing intramovement debates. Globalization provided new opportunities for evangelical Christians to evangelize people in missions all over the world. At the same time, globalization brought to the forefront a pressing debate over mission: what, if any, responsibilities do Christians have to non-Christians beyond evangelization? Myriad theological and political questions lie at the root of this debate. When St. Paul urges Christians to be "in the world, but not of it," what does he mean? What is the relationship between the Christian requirement to evangelize and social and political injustice?[8]

Christians mostly agree that Jesus commanded his followers to spread the gospel. Among evangelicals, however, the question of how to spread the gospel spurs strong disagreement that engages race, internationalism, and authority generally. In *The Kingdom of God Has No Borders*, Melani McAlister studies the records of Christian mission organizations, the proceedings of significant mission-centered conferences, and the writings of leaders in and around the movement. Drawing on a varied archive, McAlister argues that American evangelicals understand themselves through identification with global Christians through enchanted internationalism (nonwhite Christians are simple, enchanted, closer to early Christians) and through victim identification (nonwhite Christians, poor and oppressed, are linked with American Christians in response to a global rejection of Christianity) (11–12). While this identification has made American evangelicals acutely aware of the experiences of nonwhite Christians, it also causes a problem when Christians from the Global South want to participate equally in international Christian mission organizations. Christians from Congo, for example, expressed anger in international meetings over the representation of helpless, backward, persecuted Africans. Further, with some American allies, they argued that it was part of Christian mission to oppose oppression (political and economic), whereas more conservative American Christians have focused on saving souls and on controlling the narrative (1–16).

This ongoing conflict entered a new phase in the second half of the twentieth century with the emergence of Global South Christians in mission organizations. Conservative, evangelism-focused Christians faced off with socially focused Christians at the International Congress on World Evangelization in Lausanne, Switzerland, in 1974, where Global South Christians challenged "the rigid equation of social conservatism with evangelism" as a "form of conformity to the world, rather than a way of speaking prophetically about the needs of that world" (McAlister, *Kingdom* 86). A racially diverse group of Christians "spoke forcefully at the meeting as equals, not as missionary objects" (87). Out of the Lausanne conference came continued conflicts among right-wing and more liberal evangelical Christians but also a new consciousness of non-U.S. cultures among evangelical Christians who came to see themselves as part of the world (91).[9] The conflict in the twentieth century over what ideas and which people represent Christianity in the world was increasingly fought in public, among non-evangelicals, and within efforts at evangelism and political activism. Christ and the Bible, they all seemed to be saying, offered not only individual fulfillment, but the model for an ideal society. But whose Christian model would be *the* Christian model?

Left Behind represents a public foray into those conflicts, but the series is also, through the recruitment of a broader, more secular, and religiously diverse sphere of readers and actors, an attempt to settle the disputes through force of narrative and number. Unlike the other works I examine in this book, *Left Behind*'s utopia seeks to *use* rather than oppose neoliberal fragmentation, responsibilization, and economization. The series does not seek a way forward; it seeks a victory. The series' methods, however, are more subtle than they at first appear. *Left Behind* sides with those in the debate who believe that Christian duty lies in evangelism and not in addressing any social ill beyond religious persecution. Poverty, injustice, and oppression are not within the realm of Christian concern; indeed, they are merely signs of the coming end times, and the Antichrist will exacerbate these problems under cover of trying to solve them. Surprisingly, *Left Behind* further sides with those who welcome nonwhite, non-American Christians to participate in Christian organizations—but there is a clear sense that white male Christians remain in control.

The series advances these positions by engaging global Christianity. The Antichrist's machinations are global, and so are the Christian responses. The main characters travel throughout the world to fight the Antichrist; one is even an international commercial pilot. At every turn, nonwhite Christian allies appear in important places to help the characters. They occupy important roles in a network aimed at combating the Antichrist, protecting Christians, and saving as many souls as possible. These characters, however, play primarily supporting roles to the white American Christian heroes. Tsion Ben-Judah, an Israeli rabbi and convert to Christianity, becomes the chief theologian of the series. The non-American characters, in short, serve to confirm the wisdom and authority of the American Christians. The series engages globally with all peoples of the world as participants, but insists on the proper cultural hierarchies.

From Biblical Reading to Masculine Action

In response to conflicts over mission among evangelical Christians, *Left Behind* makes the authority of American male Christians paramount over other Christians and far above anyone else in the world. The series uses this authority to hail more secular conservative publics in an economized, fragmented neoliberal public environment. This translation from evangelical public to broader public, however, requires an uneasy, sometimes contradictory combination of theological and cultural positions. In *The Book of Jerry Falwell*, Susan Harding argues that Falwell and other NCR preachers "stand in the gap" between scripture and contemporary experience, "[converting] the ancient recorded speech of the Bible once again into spoken language, translating it into local theological and cultural idioms and placing present events inside the sequence of Bible stories" (12). She argues further that this gap changes the way listeners understand NCR rhetoric: not as literally true but, like the Bible, as always *coming* true. It is generative, not factual (26–27). The insight that figurative truth forms the basis of NCR reading practices helps mark a difference between NCR and more secular rhetorics. Harding builds on this to show in part how big these gaps can be and how these gaps constitute the authority of NCR speakers, whose testimony on all matters (biblical or otherwise) is backed up by being "saved." In contrast, the "lost" must enter a passive state, ready to listen and ultimately believe the testimony of the saved speakers. There is no position, Harding specifies, from which one seeks information. One is lost (in which case one listens), or one is saved (in which case one speaks) (39–42). For the saved, the infallible truth of the Bible extends to their own speech: they are always correct at some level; they must be listened to (and ultimately obeyed); and their authority assumes that of the Bible through its continual interaction with scripture (88). This flexible authority of the saved speaking men allows an easy extension; while the Bible and the Holy Spirit provide the basis of their authority, it's relatively easy to subsume other sources of authority (for example, secular science and everyday common sense) into a modernized, conservative, identity-based authority. The series itself performs these maneuvers, constantly moving among the everyday lives of characters (supposedly) like its readers, the generic conventions of fiction, geopolitical relations, and the Bible.

The Bible provides the chief source of religious authority for the *Left Behind* books. The series is a novelization of a nineteenth-century Christian theology called "premillennial dispensationalism," a set of interpretations of the Old and New Testaments. Dispensationalism, a view held by a small yet influential group of Christians in the United States and Europe, divides history into distinct periods ("dispensations" or "ages") and predicts the coming of the final dispensation, which will be preceded by a series of horrifying events prophesied mostly in the book of Revelation.[10] These events begin with the disappearance of "true" Christians in the Rapture, continue with seven years of earthly suffering through the demonic world dictatorship of the Antichrist, and end with the glorious return of Jesus Christ, who will rule over the earth directly for one thousand years.[11] The novels begin with the Rapture and then follow a group of new Christians as they fight against the Antichrist and evangelize others who were left behind. While the series features many characters, it begins with three based in suburban Chicago and remains with them through most of the series: a "left behind husband" and commercial pilot named Rayford Steele; his daughter, a college student named Chloe; and Cameron "Buck" Williams, a world-traveling journalist. With help from others, these three form the "tribulation force," leaders of a global network of evangelization and resistance to the Antichrist's rule. The first two novels, Tim LaHaye and Jerry B. Jenkins's *Left Behind* (1995) and *Tribulation Force* (1996), narrate the characters coming to understand their new faith and end-times prophecy, monitoring the rise of the Antichrist, and beginning to build their network of resistance. In the third novel, *Nicolae* (1997), their battles with the Antichrist begin in earnest.

Out of the dispensationalist interpretations of the Bible, the series constructs an uneasy intellectual authority meant to satisfy empirical and largely secular standards. In *Fundamentalism and American Culture*, a study of late nineteenth- and early twentieth-century American fundamentalist writers, George Marsden notes a long history of "tension between trust and distrust of the intellect" among fundamentalist Christians (7). Fundamentalists' insistence on close, complex readings of scripture across the books of the Bible requires intense, sustained study and ongoing discussions among professional interpreters. However, Glenn Shuck describes late nineteenth- and early twentieth-century American dispensationalism as a populist movement that expressed suspicion of cultural and theological elites, which included academics and their processes of textual interpretation (71–75). According to Harding, fundamentalists partly resolved this tension in the 1980s through the construction of "creation science," a quasi-scientific set of arguments deployed to combat the teaching of evolution and modern social science in public schools: "creation scientists seized the forces of representation, and with their fusion of religion, science, and politics, turned left-liberal clichés about equal time, pluralism, advocacy politics, participatory democracy, and tyranny of experts inside out. For those who followed their lead, they occupied the terrain of science, reason, and education with the Bible and thus recaptured cultural ground lost during the earlier Fundamentalist movement. They were Davids slaying the Goliath of secular science, expertise, and the nation's cultural elite with their slingshot, the counterdiscourse of creation science" (217–18). Harding argues further, through a reading of a hoax exhibit about Noah's ark in a creationist museum at Liberty University, that creation science—and the use of empirical discourses by the NCR more generally—involves self-conscious gaps and problems that invite the believing subject to reconcile them as an act of faith.

Harding's interpretation of the Liberty museum exhibit begins with what many critics of NCR science argue: the empiricism of the NCR contains contradictions and irresolvable problems. Harding reveals, however, that these gaps offer a discourse that seems to meet secular standards of empirical evidence while simultaneously inviting believers to exercise their own faith in reconciling the discourse's tensions. In doing so, believers affirm their special faith. *Left Behind* performs a similar uneasy reconciliation: first, through its empirical confirmation of dispensationalist prophecy interpretation; and second, by suturing the intellectualism of prophecy interpretation to an explicitly masculine subject of militant public activism. In *Left Behind*'s world, the first reconciliation is easy: every dispensationalist prediction comes true in the narrative. The second, however, remains uneasy: the populist discomfort with intellectual work remains, and to resolve it, *Left Behind* splits the masculine subjectivity it idealizes in two. On the one hand, the *interpreting* subject possesses the insight needed to read the Bible and systematize the prophecies within; on the other, the *activist* subject moves through the world working to thwart the Antichrist, often operating with seemingly un-Christian deception and violence. For *Left Behind*, the interpreting subject lends both theological and secular scientific authority and, thus, moral sanction to the actions of the activist subjects, freeing them from moral codes or broader cultural responsibility. This allows the series to maintain the split between the active, testifying Christian and the passive, listening unsaved. Once saved, the activist subjects of *Left Behind* need to combat the Antichrist through espionage and militant action rather than merely testimony, which would save souls. The saving continues, however, through the interpreting subject.

A populist notion of common sense unites interpretation and activism in the narrative, reconciling the intellectual complexity of dispensationalism with the appeal to biblical literalism. Made up of key passages scattered across the books of the Bible, dispensationalist readings of scripture rely on complex heuristics. For many dispensationalist writers, detailed charts and illustrations indicate that their interpretations of scripture carefully employ scientific principles. Paul Boyer explains that many dispensationalist writers particularly in the nineteenth century insisted on the empirical nature of their textual hermeneutics, proving their interpretive rubrics to be valid by pointing to biblical prophecies that have already come true: "Far from demanding a blind leap of faith, prophecy belief was presented as a logical inference from the evidence of prophecies already fulfilled" (294). Marsden, drawing on the work of Ernest Sandeen in *The Roots of Fundamentalism* (1970), traces this insistence to a commitment to an intellectual paradigm called Scottish common sense realism, which rejects the modern idea that interpretation and subjectivity affect perception of reality in meaningful ways. For writers invested in this form of common sense, "basic truths are much the same for all persons in all times and places" (Marsden 111). Further, rejecting modern scientific processes of hypothesizing and evidence gathering (the processes that led to the development of paradigms such as Darwinian evolution and quantum physics), adherents of Scottish common sense realism follow Francis Bacon, beginning with "known facts" (for example, the facts revealed in scripture) and working backward to understand how they came to be or how they work (Marsden 55–56). Fundamentalist writers insist that "the role of the interpreter ... [is] not to impose hypotheses or theories, but to reach conclusions on the basis of careful classification and generalization alone" (59). This insistence on Baconian scientific paradigms allow fundamentalists to claim a scientific authority alternative to modern science rather than simply rejecting science out of hand.

Presenting dispensationalism as a scientifically validated narrative helps extend it within the realm of secular science by suggesting that prophetic scriptures are understood through empirical analysis. However, the supposedly verifiable, transparent quality of dispensationalism also allows the series to make a relatively new rhetorical move: the secular standard of evidence met by the prophetic interpretation legitimizes the authority of a male subject who meets both fundamentalist and secular standards for authority. As Buck muses to himself late in LaHaye and Jenkins's *Tribulation Force*, "Jesus was either the Messiah ... or he could not stand up to the scrutiny of the record" (391). Through two preacher-intellectuals, *Left Behind* builds an authority based on careful, scientific interpretation of prophetic scripture and a sacred commitment to God and the Bible. First, Bruce Barnes, the pastor of Rayford Steele's church, and later, Ben-Judah, the Israeli biblical scholar who converts to Christianity in the second novel, provide the moral and intellectual authority needed by all the characters to fight against the Antichrist. For the rest of the characters, conversion and evangelizing remain the only crucial spiritual moves. Rayford's conversion occurs not so much from reading scripture as from receiving the proper impressions from the network of people around him: his disappeared wife, his disappeared wife's pastor, and eventually, the church that he joins. The novel presents the final consequence of this conversion, however, as a matter of personal conscience. Through Chloe Steele, Rayford's daughter, the authors mark a crucial contrast between the new post-Rapture Christian (Rayford), who surrenders his doubts and embraces the obvious truth of the premillennial dispensationalist narrative, and the potential new Christian who indulges doubt and refuses to "be saved." Chloe, like Rayford, is a model potential convert: she is kind, analytical, smart, and passionate. Chloe speaks in parodies of academic analysis that Rayford calls "pseudosophisticated" (*Left Behind* 237), talking of "intellectual honesty" and even telling Rayford that his new faith makes "a lot of sense if you buy into all that. I mean, you have to start with it as a foundation" (230). The novel describes Rayford as analytical as well; he's proud of his detached skepticism, and this pride is one of the first sins he confesses as he prays for the first time (216).

The contrast between these two forms of intellectual engagement dramatizes the rejection of modern biblical criticism that helped give rise to the fundamentalist-versus-modernist controversy in the late nineteenth century (Marsden 43–125). More important, it also lends sacred weight to Rayford's version of common sense. The reader, in on the secret that the end times have begun, sees Rayford's born-again belief as scientifically valid and morally just, and Chloe's resistance as stubborn and silly. The validity of the narrative, then, has already been established before the explications of the end times really begin. The novels present scriptural exegesis as a scientific process, yet it is a process that takes place as a private, obscured act that the inspired interpreter then conveys to an audience. The richest scriptural exegeses occur in the second novel, *Tribulation Force*. Bruce delivers the first in a sermon to a packed church (63–75), and Tsion gives the second in a televised revelation that his study of messianic prophecy has confirmed that Jesus was the Jewish messiah (390–97). In his sermon, Bruce presents a textual reading of Revelation 6 (the famous passage about the four horsemen of the apocalypse). The sermon features a warning of events to come. Both Rayford and Buck see that Bruce appears "inspired"—he is disheveled and exhausted, and he tells his friends that "God has weighed heavily upon me this week" (63)—but they are impressed by the fluency of his readings and the age of the commentaries and biblical text he cites (67). As Bruce lectures on the Antichrist, Rayford sees some audience members take notes, and "everyone [followed] along in a Bible" (63–64). Rayford wonders, "Would he tell this body that he believed he knew who the Antichrist was . . . or would Bruce simply tell them what the Bible said and let the people come to their own conclusions?" (65).

Rayford's musings highlight a recurring tension in the representation of interpretation in the series: assembling these impressive readings has been an exhausting task for Bruce because he extensively studied the scripture and commentaries. However, Bruce simply tells them "what the Bible said and let[s] the people come to their own conclusions" (*Tribulation* 65). There is only one correct conclusion, and the reading is difficult but not hidden. Just as important, the novel narrates the sermon through Rayford, who already knows the identity of the Antichrist and has already been told by Bruce much of the information in the sermon. The narrative becomes focused, then, on Bruce's impressive authority as an interpreter; his authority comes from his ability to explicate the text in a convincing, charismatic presentation rather than from the biblical text itself. The interpreting subject, then, has an inspired authority that comes from neither the text (which is supposedly transparent) nor the church community, which will perform its own acts of interpretation to confirm the interpreter's. For the novels, reading scripture is an intense and personal act that reveals to the close reader not only events to come, but the meaning of all of human history. The transparency of scriptural prophecy endows the careful, insightful reader with both scientific and religious authority. In this conceptual gesture, the novels reconcile American fundamentalism with secular modernity.

As the novels continue, the authority of the scriptural interpreters transfers to the activist characters, who will fight the Antichrist through their wielding of technological prowess and privileged global mobility. The second scriptural exegesis in *Tribulation Force* dramatizes the conferral of the interpreting subject's authority onto the activist subject. Tsion Ben-Judah, sponsored by the Israeli government, delivers the results of a lengthy study of the Hebrew scriptural prophecies regarding the Jewish messiah; Tsion's exegesis (broadcast worldwide by CNN) follows much the same pattern as Bruce's sermon. Delivered by an Israeli rabbinical scholar but confined to the vocabulary of American dispensationalism, the lecture reveals what most of the characters already know: Jesus was the messiah predicted in the Hebrew Bible. Tsion's lecture implies that his identification of Jesus as messiah confirms dispensationalist interpretations of the Bible. Tsion carries out the entire study in isolation, and when he delivers his conclusions on television, "Orthodox Jews"—a category that evidently includes everyone in Israel who has not already converted to Christianity—try to attack him in the TV studio.[12] Buck helps Tsion escape, and Tsion, while active in evangelizing the world in later novels, also spends much of his time in hiding.

Buck's dramatic effort to rescue Tsion in *Tribulation Force* affirms the importance of intellectual interpreters like Tsion and Bruce: through their careful readings of scripture and their spiritual leadership, they help establish the mix of religious and secular authority that the novels idealize. At the same time, Buck's rescue of Tsion suggests that the interpreters rely on the actions of the activist subjects. The need to protect the interpreters lends moral legitimacy to the activist subjects, while the interpretations themselves help give the broader actions of the activist subjects meaning and authority. Armed with all necessary faith and foresight, the characters can pursue their fights against the Antichrist. Interpretation is an individual, obscured act; the knowledge it brings does not vary, but it must be imparted to others. Agency for the listeners does not come from participating in acts of interpretation, but in responding to them either wrongly (as in the violent attacks on Tsion and his family) or rightly; the latter involves being, as Bruce tells his congregation, "ready this time. Be ready. I will tell you how to get ready" (*Tribulation* 67). What it means to be ready, however, is complicated in the novels. To combat the Antichrist, spread Christianity, and wait for the return of Christ through the seven-year tribulation period, the activist characters will need technological competence and a privileged position in a globalized world.

The *Left Behind* series locates authority in individual subjects depending on their social identity positions. Saved Christian men seize the authority not just of scripture and its interpretation but also of the proper responses to events, conditions, beliefs, and so on. They get to determine truth, speak it, and act on it. The job of unsaved men is to listen, be receptive, and come to the correct conclusion not merely about Christ being the savior but also about the truth of the dispensationalist prophecy narrative. Once they are saved, they can move from passive to active. Everyone else—nonwhite men and women both white and nonwhite—experience a similar transformation from reception to action. They, however, arrive at the truth simply by trusting the testimony they hear from others. Their own testimony and action (once saved) must be undertaken not so much in support of God in the battle against Satan, but in support of the white men and how they are undertaking action in support of God. This demand for trust in authority is dramatized shortly before Rayford's conversion in the first novel. In a videotape left by the now-Raptured pastor of his wife, Irene's, church, Rayford sees the pastor conclude his explanation with "you don't need to understand all this theologically. You can become a child of God right now by praying as I lead you" (*Left Behind* 215). While *Left Behind*'s conception of authority offers people the power of understanding, it also suggests that truth requires faith not so much in God as in the men who would act for him. This conception of authority combines secular and fundamentalist modes, and it allows the reassertion of cultural hierarchy. This hierarchy predates the dominance of neoliberalism, but the series makes it fit well.

The Political Economy of *Left Behind*

Left Behind uses its unique conception of authority to connect fundamentalist hermeneutics, identity-based hierarchies, and secular conceptions of truth. This hierarchical, text-based authority, however, also interacts effectively (if somewhat awkwardly) with emergent American ideas of globalization. *Left Behind* draws on an intersection of neoliberalism, conservatism, and U.S. global supremacy that was emerging in the 1990s. In *Life between Two Deaths, 1989–2001*, Phillip E. Wegner argues that after the destruction of the Berlin Wall, the absence of the global symbolic order of the Cold War opened the world to the imagination of radical new collectivities (9–10). The 9/11 attacks in 2001, however, helped to establish a dominant symbolic order characterized by the spread of ruthless global capitalism and the containment of cultural others in the war on terror (24–25). *Left Behind* indulges a utopian hope that injustice might be opposed and finally ended with the return of Christ. Its vision of utopia, however, relies on U.S. military power coupled with a neoliberal economics that concentrates power and wealth in few hands. The series legitimizes this order by yoking a born-again-leaning secularism to an emergent neoliberal American dominance. In this version of utopia, neoliberal competition rewards Christians as the natural leaders who triumph over everyone else theologically, militarily, and economically. A society of peace and beneficence can only happen once enemies have been defeated. And that triumph must be continually refreshed as enemies repeatedly must be combated. An ideal society rewards good guys, punishes bad guys, and prevents bad guys from doing any more damage. In this way, *Left Behind* promotes a fundamentalist version of militant morality that predetermines the results of global competition.

Left Behind's political-economic vision rests at the confluence of two concepts: responsibilization and apocalyptic dualism. Wendy Brown defines neoliberalism as a "normative order of reason" that "transmogrifies every human domain . . . according to a specific image of the economic" (9–10). She argues that classical liberal logics tend to privilege citizens as political actors with rights, responsibilities, interests, and conflicts. Neoliberal institutions and logics, on the other hand, center human citizens as economic actors whose worth is determined by their economic activity. Under neoliberalism, individual citizens are responsible for investment (individuals invest in themselves entrepreneurially) and economic growth (it is the duty of citizens to sacrifice for the sake of economic, rather than political, health) (32–35). The neoliberal political economy does damage to the least protected people; however, the neoliberal concept of responsibilization places moral responsibility squarely at the feet of those whom neoliberalism has harmed: "Responsibilization tasks the worker, student, consumer, or indigent person with discerning and undertaking the correct strategies of self-investment and entrepreneurship for thriving and surviving" (132–33). For Brown, responsibilization conceptually drives neoliberal discourse and policy. Her concern is that the concept turns power upside down, obscuring the larger flows of economic, cultural, and political power.

In *Left Behind*'s political economy, responsibilization performs not only the work of flipping, but the work of sorting individual people and their associated identity groups according to moral choices (part of "investment," in Brown's terms). The best economy allows the best, smartest choice-makers to acquire social power; at the same time, in whatever economy one happens to be, those with the most power are those who have made the best decisions morally and economically. The direction, in other words, cuts both ways so as to allow those with power to justify inequality. Responsibilization potentially obscures inequality in a supposedly equal field of players, and the fundamentalist version of responsibilization similarly puts responsibility on relatively powerless individuals and obscures broader relations of money and power. However, in a fairly easy move, *Left Behind* adds apocalyptic dualism to this formula; in a justly administered economy, success and failure wouldn't simply be a matter of good, moral choices. Success would go to people who are objectively good, and failure to those who are evil. The two are sharply separated, and while people can choose to *do* good or evil, these choices are merely evidence of the already-made choice to be of God's people or of Satan's. The only real "investment" choice is to side with one or the other.

Through contrast between dystopia, actual utopia, and implied utopia, *Left Behind* draws on popular notions of masculinity, evangelical ideas of family, and apocalyptic conventions of dualism. Like its forerunners in prophecy fiction, *Left Behind* rails against the social and cultural phenomena its authors despise. But while *Left Behind* certainly features ungenerous representations of abortion, popular culture, and liberal activism, its deeper politics reveals something a little more subtle: the series envisions a globalized world interconnected through unofficial economic relationships that are policed almost entirely by cultural hierarchies. In *Left Behind*'s implied utopia, the properly identified Christian individuals receive economic and cultural power as recognition of their proper positions and actions. In *Left Behind*'s actual, Christ-ruled utopia, those properly identified individuals receive recognition from Christ. Through this, the series stakes a claim on neoliberalism. It echoes responsibilization logic, but its version of reward is not merely economic and not merely behavior based; rather, reward lies in trusting the right authorities for one's proper position. In this sense, the series is genuinely conservative, but it is a modernized conservatism that looks forward to what will become the dominant conservative notions of the early twenty-first century. Just as Bible reading combines faith and secular authority, *Left Behind*'s neoliberal logic renders as biblical the conservative notion of hierarchy in globalization. The careful dance between biblical, Christian, and secular ideas allows the series to create a careful notion of hierarchy.

Left Behind features a triple formation: the dystopia created by the global rule of the Antichrist, Nicolae Carpathia; the utopia implied through opposition to that dystopia and glimpsed in the interactions of the Christian characters; and the actual utopia implemented by the returned Christ in the twelfth novel, *Glorious Appearing* (2004), and the sequel to the twelve-book series, *Kingdom Come* (2007). While the Antichrist's dystopia has received the most attention from scholars in part because the novels' presentation of it so cleverly draws on dystopian conventions, it's only the first part of the *Left Behind* utopian vision. Unsurprisingly, the dystopia heavily features late twentieth-century conservative bugaboos. As Crawford Gribben says in his study of prophecy fiction, *Writing the Rapture* (2009), Rapture novels across the twentieth century imagine a post-Rapture tribulation wherein "the resources of history's most advanced regime will be directed toward the final eradication of Christians and Jews. But throughout the genre, that regime has become a palimpsest routinely identified with the social trends of the present that authors find most objectionable" (13).[13] In the dystopia, however, lie fairly strong arguments for societal arrangements that would be most amenable to the spread of God's word and godly action. In *Left Behind*, the worst society is the one in which natural boundaries between good people and bad people, between moral and immoral, are flattened and reversed. The best society allows social hierarchies to form based on identity and individual interaction.

It's worth looking, therefore, at some of the details of the Antichrist's world system to see how the series' relational logic works. Like its forerunners in twentieth-century Rapture fiction, the series dramatizes events the authors believe are depicted in the biblical book of Revelation. Some of these events come in the form of disasters like plagues, earthquakes, and supernatural locusts. Others feature descriptions of actions of the evil Antichrist, world powers, and military forces. Imagining how these somewhat vague prophecies might play out provides some of the fun of prophecy fiction and helps to explain how it can appeal across audiences. *Left Behind*'s dystopia presents many horrors and injustices. Beyond the natural disasters, the series claims that the true horror of the global system of the Antichrist is that it upends social and moral distinctions, such that immoral behavior and immoral people gain power, which is then denied to moral people and behavior. This happens in four basic ways in *Left Behind*'s dystopia: the global consolidation of political entities and economies; the redistribution of money and power; multicultural and ecumenical cooperation, which for the series equates to moral relativism; and finally, deception, which lies underneath all of the Antichrist's liberal rhetoric. All four of these elements in the series turn authority upside down, locating it in scientific and philosophical discourse instead of in the common sense of Christian men.

When the Antichrist, Nicolae Carpathia, appears in the first novel, the main characters find him exciting: he talks of international peace and justice. Before these characters discover near the end of the novel that Nicolae is the Antichrist, he begins to consolidate power. Nicolae becomes secretary-general of the United Nations and, with help from some powerful financiers, moves every country in the world to one currency so that all economies can be more easily consolidated into one global economy.[14] The plot to install Nicolae in the United Nations includes his disingenuous refusal to become secretary-general unless the members of the United Nations agree to a set of improbable international demands focused on political-economic consolidation. These demands include the destruction of 90 percent of every nation's military arsenal (the remainder to be donated to the United Nations for peace-keeping missions), a reorganization of the U.N. Security Council (which would be stacked with Nicolae's allies), a move of U.N. headquarters from New York to a rebuilt city of Babylon in Iraq, a treaty with Israel so that Nicolae might control a powerful agricultural fertilizer, and "the establishment of one religion for the world, probably headquartered in Italy" (*Left Behind* 350–53). The demand for a consolidated religion perhaps seems most strange to nondispensationalist readers, given that it's hard to imagine a United Nations that could mandate the religious beliefs of the world's citizens. In part, it's simply a reading of a passage in Revelation that predicts such a religion. In this context, however, it shows how the series links political economy with culture; to consolidate politically is to flatten cultural distinctions.

The Antichrist's solidification of power is a staple of prophecy popularization, but *Left Behind* emphasizes that this consolidation is based on a satanic cultural relativism that rewards theological and moral incorrectness more than good. The one world religion (headed by a Catholic bishop named Peter Mathews, who is elevated by Nicolae to the position of pontifex maximus) parodies ecumenicism and multiculturalism. In a conversation with Buck Williams, Mathews denies biblical truth in a way that not only contrasts Catholic and Protestant ideas, but denies the virgin birth of Christ, the creation of the world as described in Genesis, and even the existence of God: "Hardly anyone today would imagine a supreme spirit-being full of goodness and light subjecting the entire Earth ... to a calamity like an earthquake" (*Nicolae* 359). Mathews refers to himself as a "former" Catholic and says, "I must, in the spirit of unity and conciliation and ecumenicism, be prepared to admit that much Catholic thought and scholarship was just as rigid and narrow-minded as [fundamentalist Protestant literalism]" (360). More subtly, this collapse of boundaries is dramatized in the first novel when, after the Steele house is burgled, one character declares, "it's as if the inner city has moved to the suburbs. We're no safer here anymore" (*Left Behind* 265). In the dystopia of *Left Behind*, boundaries come down: all religions are equally true, people step out of their proper places, and private property and conscience are invaded by the wrong people and wrong ideas. The series links this relativism with scientific discourses. It's already obvious to readers what the truth is, and that truth collapses together evidence-based science and scriptural prophecy. Nicolae, however, uses the discourses of science as deception, just as his efforts to help the poor, establish peace, and redistribute power are deceptions aimed at consolidating power. For example, in the first few novels, the narrative sometimes pauses to address all of the incorrect, nondispensationalist theories for people's disappearances in the Rapture. Nicolae talks about the "stockpiling of nuclear weapons" as a cause (*Left Behind* 253), while others suggest a "cosmic evolutionary cleansing, a survival-of-the-fittest adjustment in the world's population" (*Tribulation* 53).

Nicolae's deceptions undermine hierarchies, and in the series that undermining is identical with the bigger goal of the Antichrist: to make war on Christians and Jews as a way of making war on God. The war on truth through the flattening of hierarchies undermines the truth of God, which is both biblical and based on the common sense of the good characters. Nicolae's government continues this war through controlling mass media (though this control is often broken by the use of the internet by Christians), the application of military power (including a nuclear strike on the city of Chicago near the end of *Tribulation Force*), and at last, in the final battle in *Glorious Appearing* in which the military forces of the Antichrist close in on the faithful taking shelter in the ancient city of Petra. Nicolae's control of media begins with him trying to take over the *Global Weekly* magazine that Buck Williams works for by recruiting its top editors. His need to control the media is dramatized in *Tribulation Force* when Tsion Ben-Judah delivers the results of his official Israel-sponsored study concluding that Jesus was the Jewish messiah. As Tsion delivers his address, Nicolae watches on television and mocks him (*Tribulation* 391–97). Throughout the series, the Global Community government seizes and consolidates media, making all mass media mouthpieces for Nicolae's government. Military force comes in the form of putting down revolts and of pursuing enemies like Ben-Judah and eventually, in the later novels, all of the Christian characters in one way or another.

In this way, the series marks a strong equivalency: Nicolae's liberal discourse about justice and global cooperation is not merely deception, but its mere presence is an act of war against Christians. The series thus presents its identitarian dystopia: liberal discourse is war on the good people. The main characters' responses to the chaos of the Rapture, the machinations of the Antichrist, and the oppressions of the Global Community government suggest a utopian opposite. The problem with the world system instituted by the Antichrist isn't simply reduced to communism versus capitalism, nor can it simply be described as antiscience or antimodernity. The anxiety about global modernity is that its technologies and discourses reverse natural, godly authority by taking it away from American men. The series' implied utopia reasserts that authority not simply through scripture, but in contrasting the knowledges of the main characters with the actions of the relatively faceless characters who aren't Christian.

This contrast between right and wrong people does not always lie in an easy good versus evil but also includes important versus unimportant. A particularly telling moment happens in the opening pages of the third novel, *Nicolae*. Rayford, Buck, and Chloe have just unsuccessfully tried to rescue their pastor, Bruce Barnes, who dies early in *Nicolae* when Global Community forces bomb a Chicago hospital as part of putting down a rebellion led by a former U.S. president. As they drive toward their church, they get stuck in chaotic traffic caused by the attack. Police officers attempt to direct traffic, a development Rayford finds annoying, telling the others in the car, "I'm trying to ignore them ... all these nobodies-trying-to-be-somebodies think they have a better idea about where the traffic should go. If we listen to them, we'll be here for hours. I just want to get to the church" (*Nicolae* 3–4). This exasperated expression—"nobodies trying to be somebodies"—being applied to government officials trying to manage chaos strongly indicates some of *Left Behind*'s deeper politics. Rayford speaks with angry contempt to a police officer who talks to him, which amuses Buck (5). Stuck in the car, Buck thinks about the power of their vehicle: "inching along in near gridlock made the huge automotive power plant feel like a stallion that wanted to run free" (9). Unlike the police officers, Rayford and Buck are *somebodies*, though whether they are somebodies because of their knowledge of prophecy or because of their possession of a powerful car is not quite clear. Here, the series highlights its social hierarchy: just as Rayford and Buck are to be believed when they speak about the Bible, they are to be allowed, unlike everyone else, to drive however they see fit. The attempted management of people in cars by well-intentioned authorities just shows the laughably false authority of those police officers.

There are somebodies, and there are nobodies, and unsurprisingly for any piece of fiction, the main characters are somebodies. This distinction lies at the heart of mapping the series' secular biblical authority onto the emergent neoliberal cultures of the time. How, then, does the series show more broadly who are somebodies and who are nobodies? In *Left Behind*, the important people are those who recognize the truth of the dispensationalist narrative; evangelize others in an attempt to win souls for Christ; and wield technological and financial power. There is also a second category of somebodies: those who aid in the missions decided upon by the truth-speaking Christian men who wield financial and technological power. In a utopian society, the somebodies have the power to do what's best; a dystopian society empowers the nobodies to direct traffic, to rearrange natural power relations in the name of an equality that falsely flattens the natural hierarchies.

To create this picture, the series relies on a common ideological conception that transcends evangelical and non-evangelical Christians in the United States after World War II. In *Billy Graham and the Rise of the Republican South*, Steven P. Miller identifies evangelist Billy Graham as an important figure in spreading some of the central concepts of what would become southern-identified conservatism. This book-length study takes a detailed look at Graham's writing, programs, and reception particularly around issues of integration and gender. Miller identifies two rhetorical concepts particularly key to Graham's cultural influence: evangelical universalism and the politics of decency. Miller defines the former as an "evangelical social ethic centered on the individual soul and will, and predicated on the universal commonality of divinely created humans. This ethic . . . viewed *the individual soul as the primary theological and political unit in society, prioritized relational over legislative solutions to social problems, and . . . tended to acquiesce to the ultimately inscrutable realm of ordained legal authority*" (S. Miller 44, ellipses and emphasis added). Miller specifies that these ideas were hardly new—only that Graham had particular success at using them to unite people of various persuasions into a Republican South.

The *Left Behind* series presents the three constituents of evangelical universalism as key to a good society, but ultimately shows them to be in conflict: in order for the individual soul to be the primary unit, and for solutions to be relational rather than legislative, acquiescence to "ordained" legal authority requires identification of that which is ordained and that which is not. In other words, *Left Behind* relies on a constant separation of legitimate from illegitimate authority. Nobodies are still nobodies even if they claim legal authority. Miller echoes this last element when he identifies Graham's politics of decency, which asked Americans and Christians to support that which is right, but not to speak too loudly for it or to offend good people's sensibilities in doing so. Graham, for example, integrated his crusades and generally privately opposed segregation. He did so, however, without open support for civil rights marches and other such unquiet activity (S. Miller 68).

The Antichrist's government in the series represents a breakdown of both evangelical universalism and the politics of decency. Attempts by the government to legislate morality and equality both supersede more "relational" solutions (for example, local church communities giving to the poor) and treat individuals as parts of broader social and economic patterns rather than as individual actors responsible for themselves. This treatment of individuals as part of broader patterns makes liberal economic and social policy initiatives laughable. Moreover, quiet, unobtrusive activism under the politics of decency cannot happen post-Rapture; indeed, it's without a doubt a fight between good and evil, one in which liberal policies and social movements are not merely incorrect, not merely threatening, but satanic. The result of this is interesting: *Left Behind*'s main characters can claim to be avatars of right, of decency, of relational over legislative or mass action. Due to their own authority being superior to that of others, however, and due to the end-times context of the novels, they do not need to act this way. Instead, they can form militant groups, perform their own political and even military actions, and do everything to undermine the legal authority of governments. Because these governments are a priori illegitimate—"nobodies trying to be somebodies"—they can be ignored or opposed without violation of the principles claimed.

The series shows this a priori superiority by drawing on a convention of apocalypse identified by Michael Barkun as the "righteous microcosm v. the evil macrocosm" (91). For *Left Behind*, the righteous microcosm is located almost entirely within the suburban home. After his wife's disappearance in the Rapture, Rayford remembers Irene's fastidious and detailed housekeeping routine, featuring a clean and well-decorated house, daily coffee, and surprises like homemade cookies mailed to him at his workplace (*Left Behind* 66–68). Rayford realizes he wasn't worthy of his wife, which the series connects both to Rayford's romantic interest in Hattie Durham and to his refusal to listen to Irene's attempts to evangelize him (100). Much of the series' utopian hope lies in an ideal domestic home relation, wherein Rayford would not merely have appreciated his wife's enactment of feminine roles, he would have matched it with his own attention and, most important, would have accepted the dispensationalist gospel and led the family in the practice of Christianity. Most strikingly, Rayford remedies this failure by reasserting his own authority as speaker and leader of his family first. After his conversion, he turns immediately to leading his daughter, Chloe, to the same conclusion. To be a good Christian is to testify and convert the home before the world. The novels connect this to the proper enactment of love both through evangelization and through home-centered care. In genuinely moving passages, family members and friends express concern for each other and provide material comfort in the form of food, transportation, and physical touch. Rayford cooks dinner for Chloe and muses on the joy of preparing food with and for loved ones (162–63). In the second novel, he makes sure to provide fatherly guidance about marriage and other matters to his daughter and son-in-law. For *Left Behind*, the best functioning of a society is when men lead families in private homes, and absent the invasion of the Antichrist, problems are for individual men to solve. In this way, individuals make choices that are either rewarded or punished culturally and economically—as they should be.

Proselytization is the greatest act of interpersonal love and the relational solution to all societal problems. In the series, though, logical arguments about the dispensationalist narrative are ineffective; proper affective relationships work much better. As the leader of a family, Rayford must convert his loved ones; as the followers of a father, they should believe him because of who he is and not because of what he says. The first novel makes clear that it is Rayford's job to proselytize and Chloe's job to believe. As he tries to persuade Chloe and she resists, he muses that it is logical that he and Chloe were left behind, while the two who believed (his wife and son) were Raptured (*Left Behind* 163–65). Rayford's success as a new Christian relies on Chloe's acceptance of the dispensationalist narrative, and his arguments don't sway her. But Rayford's concern for her changes her mind. One night as he lies in bed, he worries so intensely for his daughter's soul that he cries out, causing her to come to his door and reassure him (299). Rayford recalls an argument with Chloe when she was in high school about drinking at parties. It was his concern for her, not his argument, that led her to promise not to drink (161). Chloe's decision to say the salvation prayer comes when she sits on a commercial flight that Rayford is piloting. She sends a message to her father in the cockpit, and he comes back, and they pray together, weeping for joy. While Rayford's salvation prayer happens when, alone, a videotape recorded by Irene's Raptured pastor persuades him, Chloe's prayer happens as an act of communing with—and ultimately believing—her father. Similarly, having been persuaded by Rayford, Buck's prayer happens when he is alone in a public restroom in the U.N. building before he enters a meeting with Nicolae (*Left Behind* 446–47). Buck and Rayford are persuaded by other men and by the evidence of events they have witnessed; Chloe believes her father. And Hattie Durham clearly makes the wrong choice by not believing Rayford nor accepting his friendly concern for her.

Proselytization allows individuals to make the most important choice, and then those who make the best choices find each other and self-organize into family and church units. Buck and Chloe both eventually receive Rayford's evangelist efforts according to their relative positions. Buck, a man, a global traveler, and clearly about to marry Chloe, is persuaded by the logic of the argument and makes that decision by himself. Chloe is persuaded by her father's concern for her and prays together with her father. Buck and Chloe form their own family unit, and in initially awkward but kindly conversations find that they already more or less look at the world in the same way. For example, they have an early conversation in *Tribulation Force* in which they discover that despite having been thoroughly secular people, neither of them have had sexual partners (198–202). This may seem like a minor point, but it underlines *Left Behind*'s notion of essential identity. Unlike Christian narratives that privilege conversion not merely of soul but of behavior, *Left Behind*'s Christians, while flawed people (witness Rayford's inclination toward infidelity), already more or less behave as good Christians are supposed to. Becoming Christian is merely a confirmation.

The series, then, not only opposes the righteous microcosm with the evil macrocosm, but the authors have very specific ideas about the unwritten social hierarchies that govern that righteous microcosm and how biblical truth and authority fit within it. The contrasting evil macrocosm, however, threatens to change that well-structured Christian home and upend the "natural" hierarchies. Ideally, adherents of what Miller calls "evangelical universalism" and the "politics of decency" hope for an environment where challenges to these natural hierarchies are socially and even legally punished. The Antichrist's dystopia, however, upends this, pushing liberal policies that would not treat the individual as the basic unit of society and would seemingly mandate relations through legislation. How, then, can Christian authority be harnessed to set things to rights? How should Christians behave, depending on their identitarian positions within the evil macrocosm? What is a government for? And what would an ideal globalization look like?

Rewards and Punishments

Left Behind's main characters engage in military action and espionage throughout the series. The books make clear that this is necessary to oppose the Antichrist, but it's also the job of a government: not to solve social problems, but to protect against threats to the righteous microcosm. A government can exercise state violence and thus be supported by its citizens as part of what Miller calls "evangelical universalism." A state that cedes that militant power ceases to be a state worth having. The prologue of *Nicolae* emphasizes this when it reviews the events at the end of *Tribulation Force.* "World War III" began when the former president of the United States, "Carpathia-emasculated" (*Nicolae* viii), leads an unsuccessful rebellion against Global Community and the Antichrist's authority. The word "emasculated" equates the loss of presidential and national authority with the loss of exactly the military-technological power that the novel privileges again and again. This power must be reseized by a private, apolitical citizen who stands up to an invasive threat. Rayford muses that he had always thought that American "militias" were full of criminals, but the seizure of power by Global Community made him think otherwise (20). Published just two years after the bombing of the Alfred P. Murrah Federal Building in Oklahoma City by militia sympathizers concerned with the increasing intrusion of the federal government into private lives, *Nicolae* makes clear the "proper" function of government in the novel's political world: a government should protect the inviolability of the private conscience and private domestic space. For the government to invade this space is for it to emasculate its citizens; for the government to cede the power of protecting this space is for it and its leaders to be emasculated. At this point, it is necessary for the virile, masculine, private, apolitical citizen to take charge by utilizing the same apparatuses and networks that the government should have used to protect its citizens.

Interestingly, this presentation of the proper role of the state (to exert violence on behalf of the freedoms of its male citizens) underlies a striking element of *Left Behind*'s actual and implied utopias: violence is a crucial part of utopia. While there's a clear role for military and police power, incredibly the presence of Satan and his forces remains even during the millennial rule of Christ. LaHaye and Jenkins's reading of the book of Revelation suggests that after the millennial rule of Christ, Satan will escape from the pit and once again battle God and the faithful. Even in Christ's millennial kingdom, then, there is the presence of an underground organization called the Other Light, which is made up of children born during the millennial kingdom who have the ability to choose not to accept Christ's salvation and be saved. Members of the Other Light follow Satan. Even as leopards cuddle with people like house cats do

(*Kingdom* 1–2), the main characters of *Left Behind* must combat the forces of the Other Light in preparation to face Satan again in battle. The peaceful millennial utopia still features a role for state and nonstate violence.

Whether exercised by the state or by individuals in paramilitary arrangements working in place of a derelict state, order-imposing violence occupies an important part of *Left Behind*'s social dream. This violence restores natural identity hierarchies, but the presence of evil makes up an important part of that natural order. Thus, the series pairs the neoliberal logic of responsibilization with the political-theological logic of state and parastate violence. Under responsibilization, the rewards for acting properly within identity hierarchies begin with material things. *Left Behind*'s main characters occupy financially comfortable, mobile, middle-class positions, and their economic security provides a sign of both their pre-Christian potential and their post-Christian rewards. Alongside the material rewards of properly occupying one's place in the moralistic identity hierarchy, and the state violence that helps to maintain it, a third element of this formation—recognition—provides a final confirmation of the order. This recognition goes beyond material and discursive power and becomes theological because it comes from God directly. Through these three elements, the series creates its own new politics of decency, which imagines a utopia wherein economic rewards and punishments are matched by divine rewards and punishments.

The *Left Behind* characters in many ways live a middle-class dream of the late twentieth century characterized by suburban homeownership, financial security, and especially global mobility and consumerism. The financial power of the characters in *Left Behind* has received quite a bit of attention from scholars, who have read this partly as the marketing of the New Christian Right as a modern, worldly movement (McAlister, *Kingdom*) or as a parasitic orientation toward an opposed mainstream secular economy (Shuck). Andrew Strombeck has explicated the series' neoliberal logic of Christianity as an investment that pays off theologically and materially. The *Left Behind* novels show discomfort with many aspects of the modern world, but they show little discomfort with wealth. The novels even seem to connect luxury with evangelizing; each of Rayford's attempts to convert people in the first two novels happens in settings that highlight his wealth. He proselytizes his daughter in their well-appointed suburban Chicago home (*Left Behind* 162–64), a copilot while the two are flying a 747 (*Tribulation* 1–5), and his friends Hattie and Buck in the Carlisle Hotel's dining room in New York. In the last setting, Rayford "press[es] a large bill into the waiter's palm" to let them stay after dinner ("and the water glasses were always full") (*Left Behind* 382). The tone of the passage suggests little discomfort with this wielding of wealth; indeed, it seems to invite admiration.

This seeming contradiction between devotion to Christian ideals and material wealth provides a fundamental aspect of the characters' authority: just as the dispensationalist narrative passes both religious tests of faith and secular tests of rational empiricism, the wielding of economic privilege confirms both faithful devotion and secular, middle-class definitions of success. Further, the first three novels maintain their mainstreamed, middle-class appeal through the sharp division of domestic from public space, which allows the characters to preserve special separateness while fully engaging in the public sphere. This clear separation between private and public spaces allows the characters to have, in their purified private spaces, something to protect through their public actions. The novels' representation of middle-class privilege goes beyond suggesting commensurability between the enjoyment of modern, worldly luxuries and a fundamentalist commitment to God. The characters of *Left Behind* have conservative commitments to gender roles, doctrinal purity, and separation from a fallen world, but the narrative ties these commitments to signs of secular authority. For *Left Behind*, evangelizing means enjoying privilege in an exploitative economic system while securing the boundaries between privileged insider and threatening other.

The novels pitch fundamentalism as modern by emotionally tying together the dispensationalist narrative, American consumer products, and a home life built around the performance of rigidly defined gender roles. The novels show this triple affective formation to be opposed to a corrupt, globalized public world of satanically driven consolidation. *Left Behind* idealizes an apolitical, private, domestic space characterized by properly gendered behaviors. A sharp distinction between domestic (in both senses of the word) and international divides the structure and the underlying ideology of the first novel, *Left Behind*. This book features two almost entirely separate plots. In the first, Rayford Steele sets his house in order and learns to be a good born-again Christian after his wife and young son disappear in the Rapture. The novel locates Barkun's righteous microcosm in this domestic space; in fact, this private space is at first inseparable from the private decisions of conscience Rayford must make regarding the truth of the born-again salvation narrative. In the other plot, the dashing young reporter, Buck Williams, unearths the cosmic conspiracy whereby the Antichrist rises to power by manipulating world finance structures and the United Nations. Buck moves within the evil macrocosm, and this experience leads him eventually to become born-again and to retreat temporarily, at the end of the first novel, into the domestic space of suburban Chicago to prepare for further fights against the Antichrist. The purification of the domestic space according to the standards of what Linda Kintz calls "tender, but virile" Christian masculinity (3) prepares the masculine subject for combat within the evil macrocosm.

In *Between Jesus and the Market*, Kintz explores the ways conservative Christian writers use emotional resonance to make corporate interests and antifeminist gender politics feel familiar and emotionally appealing. According to Kintz, this resonance helps to explain how political linkages that might otherwise seem absurd—between, for example, Christian faith and entrepreneurial initiative—are sutured together in conservative discourse. For conservatives, this means linking political positions to an emotionally familiar "plain folks Americanism," a combination of specific values, gendered behaviors, and beliefs common among small towns in the Midwest and suburbs throughout the United States (Kintz 17–25). *Left Behind* creates a similar resonance through its construction of family relationships—in Rayford's concern for his daughter's and friends' salvation, his recollections of his now-disappeared wife's perfectly kept house, and, in the second novel, his provision of guidance to his daughter and future son-in-law.

Early on, the first novel establishes the primacy of the domestic sphere by locating the performance of born-again faith mostly in domestic behaviors; the saved individual expresses piety through gendered actions in private spaces, which include the home and church. The conversion of the remnant of the Steele family—to born-again Christianity and to properly gendered, suburban, domestic subjects—foregrounds the power of a born-again suburban lifestyle enclave in the novel. In their noted 1985 study of white American individualism, *Habits of the Heart: Individualism and Commitment in American Life*, Robert Bellah and colleagues make a useful distinction between community and "lifestyle": "Whereas a community attempts to be an inclusive whole, celebrating the interdependence of public and private life and of the different callings of all, *lifestyle is fundamentally segmental and celebrates the narcissism of similarity*" (72, emphasis added). A group of people bound by similar interests, tastes, and values make up a "lifestyle enclave." Christians in the books unite across the world in a spread-out, aggressive lifestyle enclave. The Rapture signals the "fundamentally segmental" nature of born-again Christians: it marks with absolute certainty who belongs and who does not, which is also signaled by specific domestic behaviors. The changes in Rayford and Chloe after their conversions—in the way they treat each other and remember their departed family members—also testify to their suddenly common interests and values. In *Left Behind*, born-again Christianity makes up one crucial element of broader similarities that set the protagonists apart from everyone else in the world.

Christian salvation and properly gendered behaviors help establish the fundamentally segmental nature of born-again Christians in *Left Behind*. Nonetheless, the born-again lifestyle enclave is situated within a broader, normative, middle-class picture of economic security and commodity consumption.

Over the course of the first three novels, Buck purchases with surprising frequency some highly expensive goods and services, including chartered flights (*Left Behind* 115–20; *Nicolae* 208–9), multiple cars (*Nicolae* 17), computers, and cell phones. Andrew Strombeck reads this wielding of consumer power as part of the deeper neoliberal politics of *Left Behind*, which, he argues, presents the decision to become Christian as a purchase in a marketplace of religions and values. The novels portray this choice as an investment that pays off with eternal life, just as skill and investment pay off with material rewards in neoliberal logic (Strombeck 161–62). Buck's economic privilege, however, does not grow directly out of his Christianity; instead, the people willing to convert to born-again Christianity, the novels imply, are the same as those who are successful and financially privileged.

Purchasing power grants *Left Behind*'s male characters the mobility necessary to combat the Antichrist's forces, but it also signals their ability to dominate multiple overlapping forces that affect their lives. That is, as highly skilled, intelligent, committed men, the characters succeed in the global economy of the 1990s. Rayford, an international pilot, plays a crucial role in maintaining global networks of travel, and Buck, a reporter, deals in the new global economy's most important commodity: information. Kintz examines the application of historian Frederick Jackson Turner's frontier thesis to the "fragmented, global, digitalized economy and the decentered postmodern electronic resources of financial speculation" in the writings of selected conservative political and economic writers, such as Newt Gingrich and Richard White (188–89). In this narrative, for the "cowboys of American conservativism" (Kintz 186), making money in the new economy is an American masculine imperative to tame a new frontier. *Left Behind* remains deeply ambivalent to the information economy; indeed, it is largely by seizing control of information and travel networks that the Antichrist seizes global control. Nonetheless, before the first novel's action even begins, the main characters have accrued the benefits of the global economy.

Through driving cars, flying planes, and using computers, the novels connect economic privilege with a paramilitary fantasy popularized in the 1980s and 1990s. For example, just four years prior to *Left Behind*, during Operation Desert Storm, news reports of precise and powerful weaponry constructed a military masculinity characterized by technical expertise and overwhelming force. Rather than showing soldiers engaging in battlefield operations, television news focused on young military personnel operating computers in remote places and driving armored vehicles, conducting low-risk warfare. This high-tech presentation helped construct a masculinity based in part on technological competence. In the *Left Behind* novels, Rayford and Buck construct a fantasy of male subjectivity wherein private citizens get to use impressive technologies to fight against evil and protect their loved ones. In *Nicolae*, Buck orders several high-tech laptop computers with "virtually no limitations" from a member of his church (46). He also orders "universal cell phones" for himself, Chloe, and Rayford, which function properly in the middle of the Sinai Desert (264).[15] Rayford's training as a pilot allows him almost unlimited access to the inner circle of the Antichrist; he becomes the Antichrist's personal pilot, flying a newly designed super-plane (*Nicolae* 16) reminiscent of a 757, which Rayford earlier compared to driving a Porsche or a Jaguar (*Tribulation* 89). He uses a specially installed device to listen in on the Antichrist's cabin conversations from the cockpit. Buck rescues his wife in suburban Chicago after an attack by Antichrist forces, driving on one occasion a "junky old import" (*Nicolae* 74) and on another a "fully-loaded Range Rover" he had just purchased (17), but both times off-road and in violation of traffic instructions given by police officers and other authorities. Also in *Nicolae*, Buck rescues Tsion by driving a school bus on a high-speed chase through the Sinai Desert, which ends in a harrowing run to a waiting Learjet at the Cairo airport (272–73).

Even before their conversions to Christianity, the characters already have what the novels value: good intentions, privilege, and technological competence. When they become Christians, however, they receive added benefits: family closeness, church community, and most of all, a clear knowledge of the sweep of cosmic history and their expected roles within it. Curiously, the series adds another element of neoliberal economic logic: jealousy, which is portrayed at the individual, international, and cosmic levels. It begins subtly in the first novel when, after the social chaos of the Rapture, people burgle the Steeles' house, upending the economic and social order. This theft shows an attempt to *take*, an envy-driven lack of respect for property. This logic extends internationally regarding Israel, which throughout the first novel and beyond is subjected to attacks from others. Israel enjoys record prosperity due to a fertilizer formula invented by Chaim Rosenzweig, a character who remains important throughout the series as a representation of Jewish people who will convert to Christianity. Near the beginning of that novel, in fulfillment of a prophecy found in Ezekiel 38–40, Russia and allies from "middle eastern nations" attack Israel not to steal the formula or control the country, but to destroy it out of jealousy (*Left Behind* 13–14). Divine intervention stops this attack. Later in the first novel, Nicolae's rise to power involves making a treaty between the United Nations and Israel so that the Antichrist's Global Community government can control and distribute the special fertilizer. Israel is vulnerable, the authors explain, because "the rest of the world resents its prosperity" (*Left Behind* 307). This resentment extends to the cosmic with Satan's and Nicolae's desire for God's power and their jealous war against God's followers. They want the throne of God and will continue to try to seize it.

Whether it's from the devil or people without privilege, this jealousy provides part of the moral basis of the series' neoliberal logic. Divine recognition is a second important element that follows the same economic logic but adds extra resonance. At the end of the twelfth novel, *Glorious Appearing*, the enemies of God get their just comeuppance from the returned Christ. In this moment, state violence and economic logic meet as the good and bad people will finally receive confirmation of their rightness or wrongness. *Glorious Appearing* dramatizes the descriptions of the visions of John of Patmos in the book of Revelation of a man on a throne (Christ) and the angels and martyrs of heaven around him, wherein Christ punishes his enemies. In a particularly lurid passage drawn almost word-for-word from Revelation (with some additions addressing the series' characters directly), the enemies and the "goats" (the people who tried not to take a side) scream and beg for mercy, but Christ passes judgment, and they are swallowed by the Earth (LaHaye and Jenkins, *Glorious* 379). After the enemies have been swallowed by the Earth, Christ formally recognizes his allies, both those still living (like Rayford) and those "who had died in faith," who now emerge "from everywhere, from the Earth and beyond the clouds" (383).

In a long passage that resembles a celebratory awards ceremony, Christ brings onto the platform one by one all of the biblical patriarchs and others who prefigured his arrival in the Old Testament; he gives a short description of how each aided God in the cosmic conflict against the devil. It's implied that many people are recognized, though the narrative only presents Abel, Noah, Abraham, Sarah, Jacob, Joseph, Moses, and Rahab and names several others briefly (384–87). The assembled people acknowledge this in identitarian fashion, as, for example, "Jews [begin] to stand" when Joseph and Moses receive recognition (386). A miraculous moment follows in which each person in the crowd witnesses their own friends and loved ones who have been martyred by the Antichrist acknowledged for their sacrifice. Christ gives each a moment of recognition (391–93).

This curious passage plays three important roles. First, it places contemporary Christians within the framework of the ancient biblical narrative. For fundamentalist readers, the Bible does not merely feature a record of what happened long ago; it features a description of themselves and their own lives with God. Abraham and the other biblical patriarchs prefigure the experiences of Christians like Rayford, and when Christ recognizes them together, they all become part of the same thread. Second, by showing each saved person their own friends and relatives, Christ links the divine and universal to the immediate and resonant. Just as the books have always shown, the individual, family, and church community are the basic units of society and beyond. Third, this passage adds divine endorsement to neoliberal economic logic: goodness in the form of proper behavior is not just materially rewarded, it is divinely recognized, and when that material reward is reversed, Christ will reverse it back. The morality of the market is the morality of God.

Conclusion: Christian Neoliberalism

For understandable reasons, scholars interested in religion who read *Left Behind* start with the dispensationalist prophecy narrative and study from one perspective or another how the books represent it and how readers interact with it. From the perspective of Christian publishing, this makes perfect sense, as novelization of dispensationalist eschatology always starts with, well, dispensationalist eschatology. When thinking about the broader utopian politics of *Left Behind* and its addresses to a broader readership, it makes sense to reverse this: why is the dispensationalist narrative necessary to perform the series' meshing of secular neoliberal logics and conservative theology? Or perhaps more accurately, what does the dispensationalist eschatological narrative *do* for conservative versions of emergent neoliberalism? In theory, the "free market" basis of neoliberalism suggests that power and material prosperity are open to anyone who makes the right choices of self-investment and action. *Left Behind*'s brand of Christian conservatism, however, cannot easily reconcile the possibility of success achieved by the wrong type of people, whether they are the Antichrist or simply people who are not white American men. The series, then, uses the end-times narrative to perform three maneuvers to reconcile the supposedly equal opportunity of neoliberal economics with the cultural hierarchies of twentieth-century conservatism. First, it offers a framework of authority that transcends the simple appearance of old-fashioned identity hierarchies as arising out of the desires of white men like those who wrote the novels. Instead, the hierarchies are biblical. Second, the dualism of the apocalyptic narrative takes the messy cultural logics of neoliberalism (wherein, for example, one could reap economic rewards despite undesirable moral traits) and flattens and sorts them, making clear that good and evil may be in part a matter of behavior, but they are also something deeper, more transcendent. This excess goodness and evil lend an affective righteousness to what might otherwise be political disagreements and cultural differences. Third, the relations between scripture and contemporary events allow for a reimagining and reconstitution of traditional authority. This authority oscillates between the sacred and the secular in a way difficult to understand, and that ambivalence allows for identity to settle it.

Left Behind may primarily be concerned with the saved and the unsaved, but its cultural politics ends up supporting the antifeminist and anti–civil rights reactions among conservatives of its times. Interestingly, it's this play between text and events, between history and the present, between authority and obedience that sets up the conservatism we know today, which is openly defiant of secular, scholarly authorities and of demands for equality for nonwhite people. So how does one recognize identity politics and imagine a utopian way around them rather than through them? How can knowledge be reclaimed without reinscribing either technocratic hierarchy or patriarchal white supremacist hierarchy? Only a religion can do it! But what if the invocation of religion for secular ends or the colonizing of the secular for religious ends won't do it? What will? In the next chapters, I turn to texts that situate identity politics within broader ecological, biological, and cultural frameworks to find religious and secular alternatives to the ruthless logics of neoliberalism.

CHAPTER 3

Smooth Dinosaurs versus Adult Humans

Biosocial Adaptation as Religious Mission in Octavia Butler's *Parable* Novels

Octavia Butler excites and discomfits literary critics. Her imagined futures and pasts feature strong, intelligent, and best of all, fully drawn characters who are people of color, women, and people with disabilities. Like all good speculative fiction, her stories estrange the conditions of the present and ask readers to imagine them in new and different ways (see Suvin). For critics invested in social justice, Butler provides both accurate, confrontational diagnoses of contemporary injustices and stories that imagine conflicted alternatives.[1] At the same time, despite powerfully rejecting so many conservative and neoliberal ideas of the 1980s and 1990s, Butler's stories come dangerously close on the surface to accepting some others. In her stories, race, gender, sexuality, and disability still are sites of conflict. Particularly in the *Parable* novels, crime and drug use drive terrible problems, as Los Angeles is, in Laurence Olamina's words, a "carcass covered with too many maggots" (*Sower* 9) and is overrun by the kind of "supercriminals" so feared in white discourse about cities.[2] In short, for Butler, people dominate, abuse, and fight each other not merely for socioeconomic reasons but because human biology drives them to do so, a position that veers uncomfortably close to essentialism.[3]

While Butler absorbs some of the common, problematic ideas of the 1990s, her ideas about the relationship between biology and social interaction go far beyond reactionary essentialism and rethink the "biosocial"—the ways human biology and social interaction relate to each other—in order to envision an evolving human future. In this chapter, I read the novels *Parable of the Sower* (1993) and *Parable of the Talents* (1998) as explorations of biosocial diversity and adaptation. Through the creation of an evolving, ambivalent religion called Earthseed, the novels' characters work toward the radical goal of emigration to other planets, non-eugenic biological change, and adaptation to (rather than elimination of) human hierarchical behavior. Progress toward this goal offers a critical utopia that suggests not the perfectibility of social relations but thoughtfully evolving social relations embedded in co-evolving environmental conditions. The religion Earthseed drives people—individuals, communities, and the entire human species—to change in light of evolving conditions and, in so doing, to see diversity, justice, and ecology as matters of faithful survival.

Across her fiction, essays, and countless interviews, Butler expressed interest in one complicated question, simultaneously urgent and mundane: How can the human race survive its own violent nature, or what an alien character in *Adulthood Rites* calls the "human contradiction" between intelligence and hierarchy? (442).[4] Butler became steadily more interested in religion as socially powerful. In one notable discussion, Butler argued against fellow panelist Harlan Ellison's denunciation of religion as vestigial and antiprogressive. Social phenomena like religion, politics, and economic self-interest, she argued, provide "brakes" to destructive ambition: "without them, we're likely to go charging off and do terrible things to ourselves" ("Octavia Butler: Science Future, Science Fiction"). Butler explores possible utopian roles for religion in the *Parable* series, where religion provides the central social means to pursue long-term human survival. *Parable of the Sower* (1993) and *Parable of the Talents* (1998) imaginatively extend the conditions of 1990s California: ecological disaster, economic devastation, and degradation of the public sphere. The novel's main character, Lauren Olamina, invents a utopian alternative: a religion that works toward non-eugenic human biosocial evolution. In Olamina's hope, this new religion will spur biosocial diversification and adaptation so that humanity might not destroy itself through ecological ruin or nuclear war. Based on the simple maxim "God is change," Earthseed encourages its adherents to embrace change and difference. Earthseed does not offer permanent solutions to anything, nor does it imagine a future utopia as a perfect society. Instead, Earthseed argues that change is inevitable, and because of that, change is possible. Butler pushes back against religious fundamentalisms that enshrine hierarchy and technocratic neoliberalism as natural and unavoidable. Seeing economization and fragmentation as antipathetic to long-term survival, Earthseed rejects the values of neoliberalism and embraces species-wide adaptation instead.

The *Left Behind* series and the work of Carl Sagan both appropriate neoliberal logics to specific political ends that fit (uncomfortably) within both transhistorical and immediate political visions. Butler offers something different: a religion that suggests utopia as a tool for the far more mundane matter of long-term survival of the human species. In doing so, Butler addresses multiple, overlapping reading publics familiar with some of the pressing problems of the 1990s: racial and sexual injustice, poverty, crime, and global warming. She reframes these problems as manifestations of broader transhistorical realities and, in so doing, invites her readers to imagine justice through a thoughtful engagement with human nature. I argue that by theologizing change and its companion concept, adaptation, the novels consider the relations among individuals, communities, and the whole human species. Earthseed envisions an adaptable utopia that eschews permanent social arrangements in service of a goal simultaneously radical and mundane: human survival within changing ecologies. The religion provides both the basic principles and the social glue that allows people to stick together through disaster and change.

While with others I'd like to read these novels as straightforward rejections of the fragmentation, economization, and wasteful consumption of neoliberalism, I suggest that Earthseed provides only a partial response to neoliberalism, seeking to adapt it and to adapt to it. Earthseed rejects responsibilization and ruthless economization; it also transmutes the responsibilized economics of self-investment into an economics of both communal and humanity-wide investment. Earthseed's theologizing of adaptation and diversification imagines a possibility not for a fundamental change to the human contradiction but for an adaptation to it so that people might not necessarily be so destructive. I begin this chapter with a brief reading of how the *Parable* novels connect neoliberal economics, Christian nationalism, and human sociobiology. Butler's novels carefully embed their biological critiques in particular historical and environmental conditions. This embedding provides the basis of the novels' most central utopian intervention: the idea that no permanently ideal social relationships exist, and everything must adapt to new conditions. I then consider how Earthseed's most radical project—"the Destiny," the emigration of people to other planets—provides the theological and social bases of hope for a just future. The Destiny provides a social glue for communities united around a goal. Even more important, the Destiny invites conditions wherein human adaptation and diversification become requirements of immediate and long-term survival. Finally, I consider the implied futures of Earthseed as a religion that will develop outside the control of its founders with both intended and unintended results. This tension between intended and unintended changes brings the novels back around to the pessimism and hope of the series. For Butler, human conflict is natural, and the possibility that humanity's hierarchies, conflicts, and injustices will return never goes away.

Dystopia, Biosocially

Parable of the Sower and *Parable of the Talents* both engage in the relations between hardwired biological tendencies and specific social situations. The two novels show two different dangerous, unsustainable biosocial relations: *Sower* presents a dystopia of unrestrained neoliberalism, and *Talents* shows a dystopia of aggressive religious fundamentalism. Moreover, the novels emphasize the embodied, biological experiences of both dystopias through the characters' experiences with disaster and suffering, and especially through Olamina's hyperempathy. Likewise, Earthseed's utopian program responds to these dystopias biosocially—that is, it presents biosocial evolutionary adaptation and diversification as the keys to sustainable, just societies in the long term. This controlling relation between the biological and the social, hardwired human nature and historically contingent circumstance, remains constant as Earthseed changes.

Both *Parable* novels qualify as "critical dystopias," which Tom Moylan defines as texts that "in order to bring utopian and dystopian tendencies to bear on their exposé of the present moment . . . linger in the terrors of the present even as they exemplify what is needed to transform it" (198–99). Like in most of the other novels I examine in this volume, the dystopian elements of the narrative contrast with implied and proposed utopias. As Jeffrey Allen Tucker observes, *Parable of the Sower* "is clearly dystopian in its setting; however, it is utopian in its themes, represented by the hope for humanity's future expressed in Olamina's journal writings" ("Dear Octavia Butler" 172). Gerry Canavan suggests that while Butler insisted that "[she didn't] write utopian science fiction . . . because [she didn't] believe imperfect humans can form a perfect society," she "*longed* to write utopian fiction, 'fix-the-world scenarios'" (*Masters* 120, emphasis in original). Understanding Earthseed's utopia requires a closer look at the dystopias of both novels.

Parable of the Sower opens with a fifteen-year-old Lauren Olamina living with her family in a walled neighborhood (a "cul-de-sac") in Robledo, a suburb of Los Angeles. *Sower* presents the exacerbated social, economic, and environmental problems of 1980s and 1990s neoliberal economic policies, particularly as they were felt in Southern California. The public sphere as such no longer exists. Public services are largely absent; everything—even firefighters and police—is available only for fees and largely unreliable. Public schools no longer exist. What's left of the middle class has retreated behind often ineffective walls and security, while the "outside" is a place of danger, crime, drug addiction, and endless cruel exploitation. Power and money have retreated, and in a not particularly exaggerated version of the LA riots that had occurred just a year before *Sower*'s publication, everyone left turns on each other. As Butler herself observes, "ecology, especially global warming, is almost a character in *Parable of the Sower*" (Rowell 61). Olamina and her family hold out behind the walls, but as a series of terrible things happen (burglaries, her younger half brother's murder, the disappearance of her father), Olamina plans to leave as she develops her new religious beliefs of Earthseed. Before she can get out, the neighborhood is destroyed in a fire by addicts who use a drug that makes it enjoyable to set fires. Olamina and two other young survivors—Harry, a white middle-class man, and Zahra, a young Black woman who had been married to a polygamist who purchased her as a teenager—head north in the hope of finding cooler temperatures and a safe place to live. Homeless migrants heading north on foot fill the abandoned highways of California, and Olamina slowly gains a group of converts and fellow travelers, including her future husband, an older man named Bankole. Through a series of hard trials, including attacks, the death of a fellow traveler, and a terrible wildfire, the group arrives at land Bankole owns near Eureka, California. As the novel closes, they form an Earthseed community there called Acorn, where they can practice sustainable communal living in preparation to fulfill the Destiny.

In her diary entries, Olamina reports much of what she sees and experiences and how her family and community react to events. These include seeing hungry and suffering people outside the walls of her community, responding to robberies and killings outside the walls, drug addiction, the absence of rain, the ubiquitous presence of fire (both arson and wild), gang fights and attacks on the road, and eventually the attack on and enslavement of their Acorn community in *Talents*. *Sower* connects this to neoliberalism through Olamina's hyperempathy. Thanks to a "smart drug" that their parents took to raise their ability to compete for jobs, Olamina and others feel the pain and pleasure of others (*Talents* 18). Further, at the beginning of *Sower*, the new U.S. president parrots neoliberal slogans around economization and privatization. He promises to do away with "'overly-restrictive' minimum wage, environmental, and worker protection laws for those employers willing to take on homeless employees and provide them with training and adequate room and board" (*Sower* 27). Olamina and her companions especially see the effects of privatization as they migrate north; they can only acquire necessities in exploitative private spaces like commercial water stations (201) and incredibly well-armed shopping complexes (173, 217). Economization and privatization have destroyed public services and spaces. As a result, the characters rarely experience safety; only through banding together for mutual aid can they find some security. However, as the second novel shows, that security remains precarious at best.

Parable of the Talents connects neoliberal degradation with misogynistic, exploitative religious fundamentalism. The novel opens with a thriving Acorn community. Olamina (now eighteen years old) and Bankole have a child they name Larkin. Olamina also finds her long-lost half brother, Marc, and rescues him from a slave trader. The community grows, but danger appears as a fundamentalist preacher, Andrew Steele Jarret, is elected president of the United States with fascist rhetoric about outsiders and heathens. A group of religious fanatics called Jarret's Crusaders attacks Acorn, kills many of its residents, and enslaves the rest to "reeducate them" using electronic collars. In a long section of the novel, Olamina recounts in her diary their horrifying torture for more than a year. Jarret's Crusaders, a branch of the nationalistic Christian America

Church, attack "cultists," though this typically involves killing people in farms in the hills, enslaving, and torturing. Christian fundamentalism in the novel is characterized by a combination of nostalgia and the rhetoric of purification, as the leader of Christian America, President Jarret, frequently says such things as "we are God's people, or we are filth!" while referring to all nonfundamentalists as an infestation to be uprooted (*Talents* 88–89). Christian America sets up horrifying versions of public services, including prisons (once occupied, Acorn officially becomes a prison that functions as a concentration camp crossed with an antebellum plantation), homeless shelters (where people are sometimes arrested for vagrancy and other invented crimes) (229–30), and adoption practices in which children are frequently removed from parents whose only crime is not conforming to fundamentalism (263).

Eventually, an accident deactivates the slave collars, and the remaining Earthseed members and other prisoners incarcerated at Acorn kill their captors and escape. At this point, Olamina breaks up Earthseed, and everyone goes to different places in order to escape further attention, to find their kidnapped children, and to grow Earthseed as a nonlocalized movement. The degraded public sphere of neoliberalism leaves Earthseed too open to violence and the country too open to conning by fundamentalists. Instead of forming Earthseed communities like she had originally planned, Olamina begins to evangelize people in their homes and slowly grows her movement. Framed by the narrative of Olamina's estranged daughter, Larkin, *Talents* suddenly jumps ahead to the future, in which Earthseed has wealth and power and can begin to send people to other planets. The novel ends with the first Earthseed ships leaving Earth.

Throughout both books, Olamina documents both the everyday, banal stress of social collapse and the horrifying abuses of religious fanaticism and slavery. To this, she adds visceral experiences of the embodied suffering of the system, brought to her (and to readers) through her hyperempathy. Sami Schalk gives an excellent review of the way many scholars have addressed Olamina's hyperempathy. She breaks the analyses into four categories: many ignore Olamina's disability altogether; others see it as a superpower, an advantage of some kind; others see it straightforwardly as a negative for Olamina due to her visceral suffering and difficulty; and others read it as a metaphor for social problems (Schalk 90–95). While Schalk does not simply reject all of these readings, she does convincingly argue for a different approach. Drawing on disability studies and Black feminist theory, Schalk argues for a dual move: first, to treat disabilities as they are experienced by people, and second, to understand that those experiences are inextricable from their sociocultural environments (3). In other words, while hyperempathy is a "non-realist disability," Olamina and other characters experience it in a sociocultural environment saturated with multiple kinds of pain and lacking anything like disability accommodation. Butler observes in an interview that hyperempathy "is a rough disability for [Olamina's] time" (Schalk 95–98).

While Olamina's hyperempathy often debilitates her, it also allows her to narrate the visceral suffering around her, moving big philosophical questions of theology and political economy out of the abstract and into the characters' everyday embodied experiences. *Sower* foregrounds this embodiment early. Olamina recounts traveling outside the walled community with a group of adults and children so that they may be baptized in a real church (rather than in Olamina's living room, where her Baptist minister father, Laurence, normally holds services). In this passage, Olamina connects her rejection of her father's Christianity to her developing beliefs in Earthseed and her sharing of other people's pain. As Olamina narrates feeling others' suffering, she connects that suffering repeatedly to multiple kinds of failure. The signs of decay are everywhere, but Olamina draws a stark contrast between this suffering and the relatively lesser suffering she encounters inside the walls. Her father, an ambivalent character from whom Olamina learns much about leadership, fails to understand the character of her disability, telling her that she can control her hyperempathy, that it's all in her head (*Sower* 11). Olamina associates this misunderstanding with her father's religion, which features what she calls a "big-daddy-God or a big-cop-God or a big-king-God" (15). Here, Butler draws together several things at the same time: historically contingent socioeconomic collapse, ideologies of authority, theology, and embodied experience. Still young, Olamina experiences a dawning awareness of the inadequacies of the available responses to suffering. She's starting to look for something bigger but is dissatisfied with any available doctrines. Hyperempathy allows her to connect large questions about human nature to immediate experiences.

Olamina adapts to the everyday experience of hyperempathy. In her diary entries, she embeds her own life within both her contemporary context and a broader, biological human experience. Even as Olamina and her friends suffer, she considers the larger conditions that frame her experiences. For example, the abuses perpetrated by fundamentalists in the novels are historically contingent: they flourish in the social disorder of the pox and feed off the reactionary nationalism, misogyny, and xenophobia of the late twentieth and early twenty-first centuries. Olamina connects them to the novels' sociobiological arguments in two ways. First, the books highlight the ecological wastefulness of Jarret's Crusaders. When they cut down all the trees at Acorn under the misapprehension that Earthseed worships trees, a resulting mudslide demolishes the slave collar control equipment. After the newly freed prisoners overthrow their captors, they note that Acorn had been reduced to a muddy pit where garbage blows in the wind (*Talents* 255). Second, through the running commentary in the novels, Olamina connects her violent oppression to the human impulse to dominate, and the fact that Acorn is so easily destroyed gives more credence to her argument that Earthseed needs to spread and diversify. At the same time, Olamina does not excuse the behavior of individuals, whether they be the guards who enslave the Acorn community or the demagogue president, Andrew Steele Jarret, whose rhetoric enables and encourages the actions of the crusaders.

Hyperempathy (or "sharing," as several of the characters call it) causes debilitating pain, and treating it as a superpower or merely as a metaphor requires ignoring Olamina's self-reported experiences. Nonetheless, for Olamina and the other sharers, hyperempathy underscores one of the novels' central ideas: the importance of adaptation. Carefully, thoughtfully, Olamina over a lifetime adapts to her hyperempathy to minimize its incapacitating effects and learn from it. When Olamina is young, hyperempathy puts her at a distinct disadvantage compared with the other kids in the neighborhood. She even sympathetically bleeds, which her brother uses against her by faking wounds on his own body (*Sower* 11). Olamina learns from a young age either to avoid fighting because "I felt every blow that I struck, just as though I'd hit myself," or to "hurt the other kid more than kids usually hurt one another" in order to discourage people from fighting her (11). Due to the disability's origin in the drug use of Olamina's deceased mother, her father insists that it remain a secret. Olamina largely does keep it a secret so that people cannot use it against her, an instinct confirmed when on the road she meets other sharers who tell her that sharers are often sought as slaves because they are easier to control (305). After the community in Robledo is destroyed, Olamina faces a challenge: outside the walls, hyperempathy could potentially make it difficult to defend herself and her companions. She adapts to this in two ways. First, Olamina has to kill any attacker in pain so that the pain will end and she will not feel it. Second, she must tell her companions so that they might help protect her. Both of these adaptations are difficult: she doesn't want to kill, and her companion and longtime friend Harry Balter takes the news rather poorly, feeling deceived and shocked by Olamina's combat ruthlessness (189–91). However, in future fights, the other travelers protect Olamina as best they can. Later in *Sower*, in fights involving guns, Olamina learns she must kneel before firing so that when she feels the shot person's pain, she won't fall (296).

Olamina's hyperempathy thus embodies the cruelty of neoliberalism and links her experiences to the broader evolutionary biology that underlies Earthseed's theology. Throughout the novels, Olamina gives a steady commentary that associates what she and her friends experience with a permanent sociobiological problem: the human contradiction, as a character in *Dawn* puts it, that people are both hierarchical and intelligent. Olamina sees this contradiction as repeatedly destructive throughout human history, and she declares that humanity "keeps falling into the same ditches" (*Sower* 260–

63; *Talents* 321–22). Earthseed tries to address—without necessarily solving—this human contradiction by trying to imagine processes by which humanity might adapt to its own destructive nature.

Inviting Evolution

Human nature, fundamentalism, and ecological and economic disaster all urgently dovetail at Olamina's time and place to demand new modes of social organization. Given Olamina's skepticism not just of religious fundamentalism but of her father's African American Baptism, it's surprising that the key to human survival lies in a religion. How, then, does Earthseed address both historically contingent social relations and the biological, material conditions of humanity? And how can wrapping these all together help Butler rethink the basic problems of late twentieth-century society? While Olamina designs Earthseed to evolve according to new conditions, Earthseed's Destiny (emigration to other planets) provides a consistent biosocial base. Earthseed offers a disciplinary apparatus that fuses structures of feeling, social organization, and labor organization. In the process of fulfilling this Destiny, Earthseed partially reconstitutes a secular public sphere over and against the social fragmentation of neoliberalism and the authoritarianism of religious fundamentalism.

Several scholars have usefully excavated Earthseed's origins in and challenges to other religious traditions, seeing especially its dialogic relationship with spiritualized Christianities and American fundamentalism.[5] The characters' sense of religious mission grows from a variety of commitments. Some, like Zahra Moss, eschew the Destiny and want "some kind of community where people look out for each other and don't have to take being pushed around" (*Sower* 223). As the leader of the movement, however, Olamina keeps the Destiny in the center and tries through evolving conditions to assemble a workable utopian program and a far future goal of total revolution. Earthseed's scripture, a collection of poetic aphorisms Olamina calls *The Books of the Living*, keeps the long-term goals and the short-term methods together by making the insight "God is change" into a flexible guide for organization and action. Olamina describes her books as both rupturing and organizing: "I'll use these verses to pry them loose from the rotting past, and maybe push them into saving themselves and building a future that makes sense" (79).

Earthseed theologizes a basic truth of biological evolution: all systems and species change. This truth recognizes human agency as a crucial power while simultaneously warning of the unintended effects of action. The resulting recognition of human limitation drives immediate social change and creates a more revolutionary hope for changes to human biology. Recognizing the relation between the social and the biological, however, Earthseed hopes for change that rejects a progressive idea of evolution: it eschews the eugenicist hope for "better" humans and instead changes the biological systems around humans (putting them on a different planet) in the hope for changes to both social and biological relations. Earthseed's hope does not lie in the idea that people can be improved or controlled or saved by God or anything else. Rather, Earthseed seeks biosocial adaptations that will help humans adapt to their own natures so as not to destroy their environments and themselves. This ambivalent religion combines optimism and pessimism; its element of constant contingency is intended to make effort continuous and thoughtful. Change may be inevitable, and difficult, and even disastrous. Human agency, however, can make it survivable, and for Earthseed, surviving is a religious duty.

Earthseed begins by elevating change to divinity. The epigraph of *Sower*'s first chapter reads: "All that you touch / You Change. / All that you Change / Changes you. / The only lasting truth / is Change. / God / is Change" (*Sower* 3). These lines frame the novels with a dialectical agency. Change happens both through agents and to agents, such that action and inaction have reciprocal, though perhaps not equal, consequences. The first third of *Sower* expresses this truth as ecological disaster, social fragmentation, and crime. Change may be the "only lasting truth," but these particular changes have traceable origins: unwise social policy and shortsighted exploitation of natural resources. The resulting poverty and drought have turned the Los Angeles area mostly dark. Olamina's stepmother reminisces about the lights of Los Angeles and wishes for them to return (5–6). Similar wishes for past abundance pervade the first novel. Olamina's father, Laurence, suggests that the family's only hope is to wait for the return of easier times: "Live. Hold out. Survive. I don't know whether good times are coming back again. But I know it won't matter if we don't survive these times" (76). Near the beginning of the second novel, Olamina's husband, Bankole, glosses the period of social and ecological disaster they're experiencing, which has come to be known as "the Pox": "I have also read that the Pox was caused by accidentally coinciding climatic, economic, and sociological crises. It would be more honest to say the Pox was caused by our own refusal to deal with obvious problems in those areas" (*Talents* 14). Olamina's father and husband, having both lived in the pre-pox United States, together present a knowledge about agency that is key to understanding Olamina's sense of truth: changes happen through human intention and accident, and inaction (Laurence's "holding out" or Bankole's recognition of people's "refusal to deal with obvious problems") represents a kind of intention, albeit a shortsighted one. Olamina rejects inaction, thinking as she overhears her father that it is not enough to survive, "limping along, playing business as usual while things get worse and worse. If that's the shape we give to God, then someday we become too weak—too poor, too hungry, too sick—to defend ourselves" (*Sower* 76).

Despite Olamina's contempt for inaction, however, accident and limitation are important throughout the novels: human action *and* inaction have led to the pox. Bankole says, "I have watched education become more of a privilege of the rich than the basic necessity it must be if civilized society is to survive. I have watched as convenience, profit, and inertia excused greater and more dangerous environmental degradation. I have watched poverty, hunger, and disease become inevitable for more and more people" (*Talents* 15). No single catastrophic event caused the pox; it has grown from a slow accretion of social and material factors. This presents an interesting problem for the characters: the largely accidental yet disastrous effects of human agency are clear, yet judging by her writing, Olamina clearly prefers action over inaction. What is to stop the actions from being as destructive as the policies that led to the pox? In part, Olamina addresses this by suggesting that change can be "shaped" through thoughtful action: "God is Power—Infinite, Irresistible, Inexorable, Indifferent. And yet, God is Pliable—Trickster, Teacher, Chaos, Clay. God exists to be shaped" (*Sower* 25). At first glance, this seems like therapeutic conventional wisdom: mindfulness makes a better life. But driven by this dialectic between accident and intention, Earthseed struggles to find a model of agency that rejects the mastery of Euro-American Enlightenment. Earthseed instead institutes a humble, partial commitment toward change that remains open to consistent revision.

Further, Earthseed's injunction to "shape change" celebrates agency with a contingency that theoretically prevents domination. Shaping change is less about domination and more about adaptation, with the goal not being control of nature and people, but people's survival within nature. Alain Badiou's discussion of St. Paul helps clarify how recognition of a truth can overturn domination. Badiou sees Paul as rejecting two equally powerful "subjective figures" of antiquity, whom Paul refers to in his letter to the Galatians as Greek and Jew: "There is no longer Greek or Jew, there is no longer slave or free, there is no longer male and female; for all of you are one in Christ Jesus" (Galatians 3:28). Badiou argues that Jew and Greek represent here two subjective figures of mastery. For the Greek figure, knowledge of the order of the cosmos allows a mastery of that cosmos, and one can achieve a specialness among people through that knowledge. For the Jewish figure, election—that is, being among the chosen people—creates a hierarchy of peoples, and recognizing the signs of this election is mastery. Paul suggests that Christ's resurrection undoes these figures of mastery.[6] Rejecting mastery in a public arena structured by official and unofficial hierarchies—in the Roman Empire or California in 2025—requires an act of faith but also requires a new way of structuring a social order.

Earthseed seems at first to echo the subjective mastery that Badiou describes as Greek: to shape change is to understand the forces of the universe and work with them. However, Earthseed's emphasis on continuous change makes clear that mastery can never be more than temporary since a form of adaptation suitable at one moment might not be suitable at the next. The rec-ognition that amoral, constant evolution invites yet confounds agency has im-mediate consequences for social relationships. These consequences come out as Olamina teaches converts while traveling in California, and later as Acorn, the Earthseed community, begins to grow. When others object that "your God doesn't care about you," Olamina responds, "all the more reason I should care about myself and others" (*Sower* 221). This idea is formulated in one of the more frequently recurring Earthseed aphorisms: "Kindness eases change" (*Sower* 167; *Talents* 47, 311). The promise of kindness alone suffices to win some converts; Olamina's friend Zahra, for example, is uninterested in anything but a supportive community (*Sower* 223). Olamina turns the absence of a justly or-dered cosmos into an injunction to care for one another.

This principle of kindness extends into communal democratic governance and ecological self-consciousness. The Acorn members make decisions com-munally, and they regularly hold meetings to consider the future of the com-munity (*Talents* 65). While the community has leaders, it also has informal rules that open leaders to challenges from members. When Olamina's brother, Marc, preaches a Christian sermon to the members of Earthseed, he is angry when they question him; like the characters of *Left Behind*, he expects that the unsaved will passively take in his preaching (136–40). With Olamina's leader-ship, the community manages its land sustainably, avoiding waste and poor land care. This thoughtful management is most dramatically illustrated when the fundamentalists who take over Acorn cut down all the trees, resulting in a landslide that destroys their own equipment (229). Ideally, the democratic and sustainable living at Acorn will make the Destiny possible. While these ar-rangements do suggest a utopian enclave of democracy, kindness, and ecolog-ical sustainability, these equitable social relations ultimately serve the more radical hope of planetary emigration and sociobiological change.

The connection between supportive communal relations and evolution comes through in Olamina's explanations to her closest confidants of the purpose of the Destiny: altering the species socially and biologically. Both el-ements of this intervention are interwoven throughout the novels, though two instances seem particularly illustrative. Olamina argues for social change based on a general view of history as driven by hierarchical tendencies. She explains: "When we have no difficult long-term purpose, we fight each other. We destroy ourselves" (*Talents* 163). Near the end of the second novel, Olamina gives more detail:

> I wanted us to understand what we could be, what we could do. I wanted to give
> us focus, a goal, something big enough to make us become more than we ever
> have been. We keep falling into the same ditches, you know? I mean, we learn
> more and more about the physical universe, more about our own bodies, more

technology, but somehow, we go on building empires . . . we go on having stupid wars that we justify and get passionate about, but in the end, all they do is kill huge numbers of people, maim others, impoverish still more, spread disease and hunger, and set the stage for the next war. (321)

The general idea that a united purpose prevents destructive tendencies can be found across the political spectrum. When Olamina pushes this further into biology, suggesting that "there seem to be solid biological reasons why we are the way we are. If there weren't, the cycles [of wasteful violence] wouldn't keep replaying" (*Talents* 321), she at first seems to be echoing an old canard: humans naturally, and therefore unpreventably, exploit each other. Olamina, however, clarifies that these violent tendencies, while rooted in biology, can be broken through a sociobiological agency: "We can choose . . . we can make something more of ourselves. We can grow up. We can leave the nest. We can fulfill the Destiny, make homes for ourselves among the stars, and become some combination of what we want to become and whatever our new environments challenge us to become. *Our worlds will remake us as we remake them*" (321–22, emphasis added).

This hope for social and biological change together marks the excess that pushes Earthseed out of the realm of secular movements and into the religious. The new worlds will remake the people: they will challenge people in social terms but also invite new sociobiological adaptations that will change the human species.[7] Olamina argues this explicitly: "we can be a long-term success and the parents, ourselves, of a vast array of new peoples, new species . . . or we can be just one more abortion" (*Talents* 48). This newly birthed species escapes an evolutionary cycle that holds most Earth-bound species: "We need to become the adult species that the Destiny can help us become! If we're to be anything other than smooth dinosaurs who evolve, specialize, and die, we need the stars" (163–64). Olamina reveals here the mission inherent in Earthseed: to change the human species, but not into particular images of super-people. Emigration invites challenges that will give rise to unforeseen sociobiological realities. In other words, Olamina's argument that the Destiny provides people with a unifying purpose contains a utopian impulse but not one with much potential beyond what has already been articulated in nationalisms and other collectivization efforts. It is the desire to abandon mastery, to allow the amoral forces of the universe to help change a group of thoughtful, purposeful humans (in ways unforeseen and invited) that makes Earthseed a radical project. Thus, the Destiny is necessary more than simply to provide what Butler in the novels and elsewhere refers to as a "positive obsession" (*Sower* 1; *Talents* 47, 157, 312; "Positive Obsession"). It instead opens a new possibility for humanity in a species-wide, transhistorical sense: a universalizing project that seeks evolution as salvation.

Adaptations of Faith

The Destiny holds the key to Earthseed's utopian vision: without sociobiological adaptations, there is no possibility of escaping the "same ditches," as Olamina puts it. The question for the novels, then, is how to meet the challenge of leaving Earth, given the landscape of "the Pox." How can a small group of poor, powerless people accomplish something so large? Just as Olamina adapts to her hyperemapthy within the challenging environment of the road and later Camp Christian, she learns to adapt Earthseed to aid first its survival as a movement and later its goal of interplanetary colonization. To make this happen, Earthseed must go through several changes: first as an intellectual exercise for a young Lauren Olamina in Robledo, then as a means of protection and recruitment on the road, and then as the foundation of an ecologically sustainable community. After Jarret's Crusaders enslave and ultimately destroy Acorn, Olamina decides that Earthseed must change again: a settled community opens itself to destruction amid the relatively lawless conditions of the pox, and constant self-protection will not allow Earthseed adherents to build toward the Destiny. For Olamina, a settled community is too unsafe and too slow to succeed. Instead, Olamina splits Earthseed apart and begins a program of targeted evangelization of people selected for their openness, their useful skills, and/or their relative wealth and influence. Once again, Olamina goes on the road, though with more specific goals than she and the others had in *Sower*.

This change has largely been framed in previous scholarship around the question of what makes a genuine utopian program. Tom Moylan, for example, sees the move as abrogating Earthseed's genuine revolutionary potential (238). Gerry Canavan goes further, suggesting that "we can see precisely why Earthseed ceases to be threatening to the powers that be on Earth; privately funded and enclavist in its methods . . . in its final formulation Earthseed is perfectly compatible with everything that had made life under neoliberal capitalism so utterly terrible" (*Masters* 138). Why wasn't Olamina's original communitarian vision adequate? That is, why did the utopian program need adjusting? And does its final form capitulate to neoliberal ideology? A universalizing project like Earthseed must be pursued within a particular context. Earthseed provides not merely a utopian vision that remedies the abuses of neoliberalism, it also provides the discursive material necessary to adjust the program to operate without a robust bourgeois public sphere. Olamina makes this adaptation by moving Earthseed to a parasitic organizational model. The novels thus provide an interesting challenge to the utopian imagination: to achieve a revolutionary end, revolutionary methods must be temporarily abandoned in favor of acquiring the capital and influence necessary to intervene in the largely inaccessible power structures of postdemocratic neoliberalism.

Butler's stories consistently show that human behavior grows out of genetics, such that historical conflicts, for example, are largely driven by the same human contradiction between intelligence and hierarchy. Her fiction explores how these two elements interact, suggesting that while humanity may be an inherently hierarchical species, human hierarchies are not inevitable. Jeffrey Allen Tucker argues in a reading of *Xenogenesis* that Butler reveals sexism and racism to be expressions of a human tendency toward hierarchy, but they are not in and of themselves natural, unavoidable social phenomena ("Human Contradiction"). Tucker provides a crucial insight: Butler's work argues for social contingency despite biological tendencies. In the *Parable* novels, Olamina pursues her universalist, sociobiological project within particular historical circumstances. Badiou provides a similar insight: in order to spread Christianity to gentiles, Paul recognizes that the Christian event occurs within a historical regime (the history of Israel and the Jewish faith). The Christian event can be extended while respecting its Jewish origins through an agreement to create partially distinct Christianities—one ministry to Jewish people, in which rules about circumcision, for example, remain intact, and one ministry to "the nations," in which the Mosaic law no longer applies (40–41). Recognizing the openness of the Christian truth event, Paul makes use of the networks of the Roman Empire, starting diverse churches around the Mediterranean and Asia Minor, but largely anchoring them with relatively wealthy people. Paul's truth may transcend the Roman Empire, but it must grow within it. As Badiou puts it, "every name from which a truth proceeds is a name from before the Tower of Babel. But it has to circulate in the tower" (110).

Butler wrote in an environment similar to the setting of the novels: an ecologically and socially chaotic California. The evolving project of Earthseed has to be understood, then, within 1990s Southern California. To help with this, I use Mike Davis's 1990 study of the city's social architecture, *City of Quartz*. Starting early in the U.S. settlement of California after the Mexican-American War, Davis describes a genealogy of social, political, and material circumstances that exacerbate a gap between rich and poor and remove the means to redress that gap: the concentration of political power in the hands of the wealthy; urban sprawl only opposed by parochial, often racist rhetorics; the conversion of the city into a "fortress" of privatized spaces; and the aggression of police forces that criminalize poverty (105, 206–10, 224–30, 280–91). *Sower* echoes Davis's diagnoses: there is a rigidly patrolled separation between rich and poor and an absence of space in which democratic resistance might be organized. In *Sower*, the walled community in which Olamina lives with her family maintains a boundary that separates the falling middle class from the homeless street poor. Abandoned by the police, the public sphere outside is nonexistent; to mount an organization without protection and without anyone watching would be impossible. The social architecture puts the truly rich and powerful entirely elsewhere, but the people outside the walls think of the residents of Olamina's community as wealthy. When the community is destroyed, it is by drug addicts who are part of a "burn the rich" movement (*Sower* 110, 215). Mounting a resistance using methods honed in the civil rights movement would be impossible in the absence of a public sphere wherein multiple social classes, races, and genders might occupy a similar space. There is nowhere to hold a sit-in, nowhere to march on, and no one to spread the news. Given this, the remnants of civil rights movement organizing—embodied in Laurence Olamina, a Baptist preacher who organizes via a combination of southern Black Christianity and West Coast, Black Panther–style self-defense—provide a leadership rendered irrelevant when the community is destroyed.

Lauren Olamina recognizes the impossibility of twentieth-century-style social movement organizing in the absence of a robust public sphere. Los Angeles is so fragmented that Olamina's entire neighborhood can be destroyed in one night—and its ashes picked over by scavengers over the next two days—without any official notice (*Sower* 153–64). What, then, does a twenty-first-century social movement do, given that it cannot rely on publicity and public spaces in which to mount protest? Jodi Dean writes two decades after *Sower* about the corporatization and individualization of the public sphere under what she calls "communicative capitalism": "the convergence of communication and capitalism in a formation that incites engagement and participation in order to capture them in the affective networks of mass personalized media" (*Communist Horizon* 215). As a result, Dean argues, leftist social organizations become less movements and more personal expressions of affective identification, and so they do more to feed global inequity and the extractive apparatuses of global capital than they do to organize any genuine alternative. The networks of communicative capitalism appropriate and foreclose alternatives: "These networks materialize a contradiction. They produce a common, a collective information and communication mesh of circulating affects and ideas. Yet these networks also presuppose and entrench individualism such that widely shared ideas and concerns are conceived less in terms of a self-conscious collective than they are as viruses . . . as if collectivity were nothing but an object of epidemiology" (Dean, *Communist Horizon* 215–16).

Awareness of the problems of communicative capitalism pervades Butler's work, particularly *Talents*. The destruction of the public sphere described by Mike Davis prevents the building of a revolutionary enclave; indeed, Jarret's Crusaders destroy Acorn without any interference from others. Enslaved, Olamina wonders in her diary, "We've been here for over a month and no one has noticed. Even our friends and customers don't seem to have noticed" (*Talents* 194). Meanwhile, the circulated "individuality" Dean describes has foreclosed the possibility of a mass social movement constructed through media apparatuses. Mere access to quality journalism is expensive and difficult to come by; most people who consume news do so through cheap, low-quality "news bullets." Olamina regrets the lack of free radio broadcasts in the area around Acorn (78). While Dean's solution lies in the revival of "the Party" (as in International Communist Party), Olamina seizes on a model that again is expressed through a biological metaphor. In response to change and a thoughtful recognition of the sociomaterial environment she's working in, Olamina re-creates Earthseed as a movement that draws from but does not visibly participate in the very capital networks that have made Earthseed necessary.

Whereas the enclave of Acorn had been based on production—Earthseed adherents bartered goods and services in the local economy near Eureka, California, as a way to learn the self-sufficiency and adaptation necessary to live on other planets—Olamina recognizes that such a model does not fit the current sociocultural circumstances. In biological terms, Earthseed needs to diversify; if it's located in one place, disaster can easily destroy it. Olamina shifts the program to a parasitic model, seeking out the beneficiaries of social disorder and adapting their privilege to serve the Destiny. I mean "parasitic" in the two senses Michel Serres uses the term in his 1980 work, *The Parasite*: in terms of a social parasite and in terms of "noise," or the background against and through which two beings communicate. Serres explains this with a fable of an uninvited guest coming to dinner and exchanging stories, conviviality, and novelty for energy and production—that is, for the energy provided by food and for the food provided by a process of production (15–16). The guest, at the same time, becomes a noise interrupting the meal, the original relationship between the diners, and the production of the food. The parasite has interrupted the exchange and thus changed it, drawing from it while also changing its character. Olamina literally becomes this guest many times, meeting people along the road, helping them with small chores, and at first seeming to add to the other's production: Olamina weeds gardens and helps with other odd jobs. The relationship shifts, however, as she begins to teach the hosts, winning them as converts to Earthseed and then putting them to work for the movement.

Olamina recognizes the potential of her own personality to form these parasitic relations through a semantic shift from "community" to "movement." Communities can be destroyed, but movements, spread out, diffuse, and working in assembly, can persevere:

> I must build . . . not a physical community this time. I guess I understand at last how easy it is to destroy such a community. . . . I must create not only a dedicated little group of followers, not only a collection of communities as I once imagined, but a movement. I must create a new fashion in faith—a fashion that can evolve into a new religion . . . that can help humanity to put its energy, competitiveness, and creativity to work doing the truly vast job of fulfilling the Destiny. (*Talents* 257)

Olamina describes here a "movement" but also a parasitic relation: the "energy, competitiveness, and creativity" are directed through the production and exchanges of the networks that exist in the pox. This means flows of production and consumption but also of resentment, fear, and loss. Olamina begins this work with her traveling companion, a formerly wealthy, skeptical young woman named Belen Ross. Belen objects that she wants no part of Olamina's work, but Olamina answers that her original Earthseed members "were willing to follow an 18-year-old girl because she seemed to be going somewhere, seemed to know where she was going" (326). Olamina confidently tells Belen that Belen will help Earthseed because, essentially, she has nothing better to do (327). Reorienting Belen's lack of purpose and fear—Belen has been abandoned by her wealthy family and has no other goal than trying to enter Canada, an almost certainly doomed venture—Olamina redirects Belen's energy and resentment.

Together, Olamina and Belen use this same parasitic function, becoming the noise that interrupts the relations between individuals and their social environments, drawing from the emotional and material exchanges between them and the political economy. Olamina begins by teaching Nia Cortez, a lonely widow who owns her own house and some farmland. Appealing to Nia's commitment to children (Nia is a former elementary school teacher in the now-defunct California school system), Olamina emphasizes Earthseed's concern with teaching. Olamina recognizes Nia's loneliness and hugs her as she cries.[8] Having won over Nia, Olamina asks her to take care of some of Earthseed's orphaned children (*Talents* 331–34), setting up both Nia and her house as a node in a loose, parasitic, largely invisible network. Olamina and Belen continue this approach with a childless, wealthy couple in Portland, the Elfords, who are "hungry for something to do" (344). The host-parasite relationship is explicit. After having worked for them, Olamina and Belen are invited "to eat with them at their table" (342). Teaching Irma Elford Earthseed verses, Olamina thinks, "we were an unexpected novelty, and the Elfords were curious about us" (343). The Elfords introduce Olamina to several of their well-connected and wealthy friends, and Olamina wins more converts who offer to help (347–48). Olamina and Belen get a more permanent shelter in the form of a house from one of the friends: "the people who own it have relatives in city and state government. They're the kind of people Jarret's Crusaders have learned to let alone" (349).

This new access to wealth and political influence draws from and re-forms the growing network of resentment over the fundamentalist fascism that now rules in the United States. Becoming "noise," Olamina constructs a largely invisible network, partially sheltered through its members' political influence and wealth and partially sheltered by its relative smallness. Olamina eventually becomes protected enough to sue the church of Christian America for the enslavement at Acorn, winning enough money for Earthseed to become a more public and nationally familiar movement (*Talents* 354–55). In abandoning the place-based community concept of Acorn and turning to this other method, Olamina gives up the enclave that lives alongside the ruins of neoliberal disaster. Instead, she interrupts the communication, this time between the individual people and the degraded environment they're living in. In effect, Olamina rebuilds the movement by forming nodes of parasitism and by interrupting and reorienting the communication so that in the conversations she and the other members are having with isolated, lonely, yet relatively secure people, the background destructiveness is the parasite. Linked together, they draw both from the material wealth that has survived and from the frustration and boredom of the people still in a position to do something. Rather than thinking of herself as a teacher approaching an individual student, she now intervenes in a relationship between the convert and the failed society—and the failed state. Olamina becomes the noise of interruption and reorients, regaling with stories and reorienting the relationship. The state is now the third aspect, the noise that lends affective weight to Olamina's message.

This parasitic model of movement building is an adaptation, but it's also clearly a means to an end. When Olamina and her friends are enslaved at Camp Christian, Olamina learns from Jarret's Crusaders even as she despises them: "any group wealthy enough to have seven maggots, to support at least several dozen men, and to have what seems to be an endless number of expensive collars must be able to spread any lies it chooses to spread. Perhaps our friends on the outside have been told believable lies. Or perhaps they've just been frightened into silence" (*Talents* 214). While Olamina has no particular interest in spreading lies, she does learn that wealth is just as important to a mission as devotion. During Olamina's second time on the road, Earthseed's rituals fade away as the localist community of Acorn no longer exists. The abandonment of this community allows her to build a movement through gaining the wealth and power necessary to launch people into space. There's a strange silence in the book for a number of years, and when readers meet Lauren Olamina again, it is through the narration of her long-lost daughter, Larkin, who has great skepticism about Olamina and Earthseed. Earthseed, now widespread, wealthy, and powerful, has a compound retreat headquarters a bit like a spa. Olamina spends much of her time traveling, speaking, and so on, but she returns often to this retreat, which is called Red Spruce.

In addition to showing Olamina and Larkin's alienation as a sign of what Olamina has had to sacrifice, Larkin's descriptions show a dramatic change in Olamina's style of leadership. Whereas Olamina previously led through close, intimate relations with others, she now has a kindly but distant relationship to others. When Larkin visits Red Spruce, all of the Earthseed members there refuse to let her see Olamina: "if I wanted to meet her, I should attend one of her

Gatherings or phone her headquarters in Eureka, Calif.... they protected her from me courteously, firmly" (*Talents* 397). While they feel love, Earthseed's younger members feel distant from Olamina. Edison Balter, a young acolyte working for Olamina, tells Larkin, "[Olamina] says I'm just about ready to go out on my own, and the idea scares the hell out of me." He follows this by telling Larkin, "You know you do look a lot like her. Like a softer version of her" (398). Olamina's comparative "hardness" and her seemingly unachievable abilities (Edison is afraid to act as an Earthseed evangelist without her) subtly display her distance from others. Moreover, Earthseed rituals and titles, absent since the destruction at Acorn, have returned: important people are called "Shaper," and Olamina and the Earthseed members exchange the ritual call-and-response greeting "God is Change—Shape God" (400). The meanings of these rituals, however, have changed. Rather than being connected to the embodied intersubjective relations of members of the community, they now signify something higher and more distant: a more permanent movement but also one with clear boundaries between insiders and outsiders. Larkin finds the ritual gestures and the general way people treat Olamina to be alienating and annoying (399–401).

Like Earthseed's adaptation from the settled community of Acorn to the decentralized movement, Olamina's change from interpersonal to distant leader appears at first to be a retreat from Earthseed's utopian goals. But this final change in *Talents* pays off a long-running commentary on evolution, adaptation, and diversification throughout the novels. Larkin's skepticism—her own distance from Olamina and the loving servant's distance—is a response to something that Bankole had warned of all along. *Parable of the Talents* opens with Larkin's overarching skepticism of Earthseed and her mother: "they'll make a God of her" (1). Bankole had raised a similar objection in *Parable of the Sower*. When Olamina tells him that the Destiny offers people "the hope of a heaven for themselves and their children. A real heaven ... that will be theirs to shape," Bankole quickly responds, "Or a hell.... Human beings are good at creating hells for themselves even out of richness" (*Sower* 261–62). He goes on to warn, "if you get people to accept it, they'll make it more complicated, more open to interpretation, more mystical, and more comforting." Olamina objects, "Not around me they won't!" Bankole offers something that will not be fully realized until the ships launch at the end of *Talents*: "You won't be able to stop them. All religions change.... if 'God is change,' surely Earthseed can change, and if it lasts, it will" (*Sower* 262). While Olamina concedes this point and has created a theology with an impersonal God and a resistance to deification, her own leadership has structured Earthseed and its changes all along. Olamina has made herself more distant in her national persona and her interpersonal interactions and by not accompanying the launched Earthseed spaceships. The Earthseed members may or may not make a god of her, but Olamina's immediate leadership, which centered Earthseed for decades and across several adaptations, has ended. God is change, and change can be shaped, but one person cannot control how other people will adapt.

While Earthseed seems not to have escaped neoliberal consumption models, it does remind that such things as leadership and religious practice will evolve. Just as Larkin narrates her mother differently than Olamina would like, all Earthseed adherents understand Olamina, Earthseed, and the Destiny differently in different conditions. Bankole's and Larkin's prophecies that Olamina will be deified despite her desire otherwise isn't surprising; if God is change, then Olamina cannot remain in control of the beliefs and relations of Earthseed's followers forever. The correspondence between deification and lack of control, however, is fascinating. Both novels are epistolary, mostly made up of Olamina's diary entries framed with the aphorisms she writes that become *Earthseed: The Books of the Living*. In *Parable of the Talents*, this scripture and diary are framed by narrators skeptical of Olamina: Larkin, Bankole, and Marc. The framing by narrators other than Olamina signals one of the most important ongoing themes of the *Parable* novels: while change can be shaped thoughtfully, change continues beyond any personal, individual efforts. Already, other voices are reinterpreting the sacred history and beliefs of Earthseed.

The Earthseed followers who travel to other stars will no longer have Olamina with them, and in light of their experiences on a new planet, they will most likely continue to change dramatically, perhaps for the worse.[9] While Olamina was a community leader at Acorn and on the road, she becomes a more aloof figure as she leads the parasitic movement to gain the money, power, and influence necessary to carry the Destiny forward. She is a more distant leader as the movement continues, and when the followers leave, she becomes a series of scriptures and legends of her words, deeds, and hyperempathy. In short, as conditions evolve, Earthseed will continue to as well. The most powerful character in the book experiences, at the end of the narrative, a simultaneous recognition of power and limitation. "I know what I've done," she says (*Talents* 408). But at the same time, we see the limits of her power and the limits of the shaping of change.

It's tempting to allow these limitations to be the final word of the books and to suggest that the novels' utopianism is permanently undercut. However, I argue that a more productive reading involves skeptical utopianism, a suggestion that the projects of adaptation and survival go on constantly as conditions change. Olamina hopes that emigrating to other planets will change people not in a simple reversal (for example, with the hierarchical tendencies of humans suddenly disappearing), but by requiring new biosocial adaptive responses to a new environment without support from Earth. Even near the end of *Talents*, however, the fruition of this hope is still up in the air. The starship that Earthseed sends to another solar system is named the *Christopher Columbus*, an irony Olamina notes: "This ship is not about a shortcut to riches and empire. It's not about snatching up slaves and gold and presenting them to some European monarch. But one can't win every battle. One must know which battles to fight. The name is nothing" (*Talents* 406). Canavan suggests contra Olamina that the name *is* something, that it suggests that "the Earthseeders aren't escaping the nightmare of history at all but are bringing it with them instead" (*Masters* 140). Canavan says that Earthseed attempts to suspend or escape history, but this name suggests that doing so is impossible.

Olamina's writings throughout the two novels suggest a slightly different reading to me: that the Earthseed project in all its phases—localist communities like Acorn, itinerant evangelization, settled wealth, and emigration to other planets—in no way implies an attempt to escape history any more than it suggests humans can fundamentally change. Like the novels' author, Olamina shares the sense that humans are essentially destructive. The question is one of adaptation and survival. Emigrating to a new planet isn't an attempt to escape history and to start over. Unlike the colonialist enterprise, Earthseed, ideally, is not searching for the fantasy of a virgin wilderness to exploit or resources to steal. It is instead a hope for thoughtfulness. The name *Christopher Columbus* does not undercut it so much as remind that the human contradiction remains, and it can't be undone by Olamina or by travel in space. Travel to another planet is an attempt to alter some of the environmental conditions through which these biological tendencies manifest.

Conclusion: Permanent [R]evolution

Parable of the Sower and *Parable of the Talents* throw a wrench into this volume about public religions. Both novels appear to present visions of ideal communities structured by religious commitments to ecology, justice, and community. Halfway through *Talents*, however, this public—characterized by expanded kinship among families, the environment, and local communities—collapses when far more monolithic religious zealotry wipes it out. It's tempting to read this as anti-utopian, as a cynical rejection of utopian projects altogether as hopeless. The Destiny, however, makes a different move involving public religion and utopia: by enshrining impermanence and suggesting that adaptation potentially contains the destructive human nature, the Earthseed novels present a skeptical, evolving utopia as a source of long-term hope. Ecologically sound, kind, and just relations are desirable, but by themselves they do not create a sustainable public. A deeper ecotheology, the novels argue, adapts to changing conditions and diversifies in the face of new circumstances.

Butler plays an interesting game in hailing multiple reading publics. She spoke frequently in interviews of her desire to open up new audiences for her work, noting, for example, that she wanted her book tours to include science-fiction, Black, and feminist bookstores. After receiving a MacArthur fellowship in 1995, she said that it introduced her work to new readers who might otherwise be inclined to dismiss science fiction. Butler wanted to write a bestseller, a "YES-BOOK," as she called it, that would make people feel good (Canavan, *Masters* 9). The *Parable* novels address many concerns of readers of the 1990s. On a sensational level, the novels present violence and crime in Southern California. Regarding social justice, they reject racism, sexism, and homophobia—contra white American Christian fundamentalism. On environmentalism, the books show a keen awareness of global warming as increasingly disastrous. Butler, however, flirts with rejection on all these fronts. Powerfully denying the narratives of U.S. conservatives like Ronald Reagan, she nonetheless draws on conservatives' alarm about urban violence and crime. Rejecting essentialist narratives of race, gender, and sexuality, she presents inequalities as manifestations of human tendencies toward domination. She is keenly aware of climate change, and there isn't even a hint in the novels that global warming might be reversed. The books dramatically diagnose the social and environmental troubles many readers recognize, but they take a biosocial turn that includes a strong doubt that human choice makes much of a difference.

Choices, social arrangements, and deliberate actions occupy important parts of Earthseed's philosophy. But at the same time, limitation, accident, and precarity provide a counterbalance. The *Parable* novels may not be the "YES-BOOK" Butler longed to write, but they do suggest that ongoing intentionality offers some hope for sustainability. In a cynical and somewhat pessimistic view of humanity, mere species survival may be the best thing to hope for. As Canavan writes, "Her cynicism led Butler to think humans, as a species, won't behave more decently toward each other and toward our environment until we literally have no other choice—and maybe not even then. But her optimism led her to believe that when push finally comes to shove we are actually capable of it, and might actually do it" (*Masters* 151–52). Whereas the *Xenogenesis* novels approach this same problem through alien intervention and eugenics (the removal of the human contradiction), Olamina's methods recognize adaptation as the key to long-term viability. Earthseed accepts the human contradiction but hopes for adaptation before that contradiction destroys everything. The key lies in difference, which, as Butler argues in her short essay "The Monophobic Response," humans seek out. In seeking difference, the novels reject neoliberal discourses of competition and fragmentation.

I turn next to Margaret Atwood's novels to consider some similar questions: What social arrangements lead to human survival? What are the costs of human survival? Is it even desirable?

CHAPTER 4

"Like Some Demented Theology Debate"

Postapocalyptic Junk Religions in Margaret Atwood's *MaddAddam* Trilogy

Margaret Atwood's *MaddAddam* series—*Oryx and Crake* (2003), *The Year of the Flood* (2009), and *MaddAddam* (2013)—defies easy fitting into the politics of the early twenty-first century. A terrifying "if this keeps up" story, the series exposes the abuses of biotechnology, privatization, and economization with special attention to global climate disaster. At the same time, the series satirizes may of the most common modes of response to environmentally destructive global capitalism. *MaddAddam* offers a strident critique of neoliberalism by showing the myriad, complicated ways characters fit into it. The series seems interested in two related sets of questions: first, how might people oppose the injustices (environmental, economic, sexual, and social) of global neoliberalism even while they are implicated in those injustices? And second, what kind of moral, metaphysical center can support social arrangements that value a sustainable community over individual pleasure and corporate profits? Overall, Atwood asks what kind of theological narratives structure a public that potentially offers justice and sustainability.

The books offer no certain answers to these questions. Whereas Butler's *Parable* novels respond to dystopia with a relatively unified vision of sociobiological evolution, the world of the *MaddAddam* series is awash in utopian ideas, and each has promises and problems. Extremely powerful biotechnological corporations use genetic engineering to create body-altering products; these corporations sell the whole system as a utopian society of individual fulfillment and economic opportunity. Organized resistance to this system almost always finds roots in religious thinking, whether in secularized but nonetheless metaphysical desires to "remake" humanity without environmental sin or in overtly religious organizations. Those combating this system include a post-Christian ecocult called the God's Gardeners; a group of secular bioscientist guerrillas called MaddAddam; and Crake, a brilliant young scientist who unleashes a plague meant to wipe out humanity and replace it with a new race of ecologically sound, culturally limited, childlike humans called

Crakers. The *MaddAddam* books satirize them all, showing their parallels and the ecological, cultural, and individual pain each visits on the world.

As the series continues, it becomes clear that no one of these programs contains the key to material sustainability and spiritual stability. Instead, the God's Gardeners, MaddAddam, and the Crakers (plus some genetically modified, transgenic animals) unite after the apocalyptic plague, and they reassemble remainders and refuse of these different utopian visions to create partial, evolving social and material structures. Through the survivors of the plague, the series posits partial, evolving religious commitments as key to reviving community. The result is an uncertain yet hopeful revolution: maybe, with different material, different narratives, and the junk of the past, humanity can start again and not destroy Earth this time. With some measure of cynicism, the characters in the *MaddAddam* series reject neoliberal values, but offer no monolithic alternative to them. Fighting the environmental degradation that results from privatization and economization, this junk utopia suggests, must happen through a variety of methods and ideas driven by commitments to Earth and each other.

In all three novels, characters narrate their lives leading up to an apocalyptic global plague. They describe a mid-twenty-first-century United States wherein privatization and responsibilization have created a highly stratified society. Inside secure corporate compounds, highly trained bioengineers design genetically engineered consumer goods. Outside the compounds lie the "pleeblands"—unsecured, decaying cities and suburbs containing customers, organized crime, and cheap, disposable labor for corporations. Even more disposable labor and resources come from outside the United States and particularly from the Global South. Nearly every element of the public sphere has privatized; corporate interests dominate widely available media, no one participates in local or national government, and a coalition of businesses runs the only police force, which protects corporate interests rather than the public good. These corporate police (the CorpSeCorps) hunt down corporate spies, run organized crime in the pleeblands, and generally operate as their own organized criminal business. Signs of environmental injustice lurk everywhere; Amanda, a refugee from catastrophic storms in Texas, for example, reports that relief efforts seem focused on keeping people in the disaster-ravaged southern states from moving northward as refugees (*Year* 85). Overpopulation and pollution suggest little hope for environmental justice or ecological recovery. The disaster that finally eradicates this order is designed by the young scientist Crake. Manipulating the resources of the biotech compounds, the CorpSeCorps, and organized environmentalist resistance, Crake designs a plague that kills most people on Earth; he distributes it in BlyssPluss, a drug promising greater sexual gratification. He also uses genetic technology to create a new human race, the Crakers, supposedly devoid of the fatal human flaws of hierarchy and imagination. All three novels give a different narrative perspective on this society.

While several religions appear in the novels, metaphysical questions that straddle the religious and the secular pervade these texts. Sorting out the competing religious ideas and utopian publics in the series requires a dive into interrelated questions that cross utopian studies, religion, and ecocriticism. As befits the wide-ranging quality of Atwood's work, scholars have approached this series from a variety of perspectives. Despite the novels' interest in metaphysics from secular, religious, and postsecular directions, examinations of religion in the *MaddAddam* novels have largely been limited to form.[1] Unsurprisingly, much of the work on these novels approaches them through ecocriticism. Curiously, much of this is an ongoing debate over whether the series sympathizes with Crake's apocalypse. All seem to agree that Crake's intervention allows Atwood to present some of the otherwise unimaginable implications of the deep ecological equivalence between *Homo sapiens* and other species.[2] Whether the novels do so to warn against deep ecology or to present it as the only ideology capable of redressing the Anthropocene depends more on the perspective of the scholar than on any permanent quality of the text, as all of them offer persuasive readings.[3]

Partially secularized religious ideas pervade the scholarly debates about Crake's deep ecology. They all treat the environmental degradation of the Anthropocene as a moral failure, the painful result of a secularized human sin—that is, a fundamental failure to protect the environment. Like Crake and the God's Gardeners, each of these critics indirectly asks and answers whether humanity can or even should be redeemed for the sin of environmental destruction. Some side with Crake, who believes *Homo sapiens* to be flawed by design and unchangeable; some side with the Gardeners, who see redemption as possible only after retributive elimination of the unredeemable; and some see the whole debate as monstrous and look for a different solution. I argue that the novels side with the third view. They present with some sympathy almost all the radical programs on offer but reject every one as a solitary correct solution. Instead, they take very seriously the diagnoses of the Anthropocene as irreversible; instead of undoing climate change, the novels imagine how to form a partial public devoted to solidarity within the damage already done.

I use two concepts to help illuminate this: partial faith and the junk city. The former comes from postsecular literary criticism, and the latter from science-fiction studies. By the end of the *MaddAddam* series, a junk religion featuring recombined partial beliefs and communal practices provides the basis of a new, interspecies communal solidarity. In *Partial Faiths*, John A. McClure examines a set of high postmodernist texts featuring what he calls "preterite spiritualities," or religious ideas inflected by self-doubt, incompleteness, mistrust of traditional religious hierarchies and institutions, and perhaps most important, engagement with progressive causes (3–4). Building on Gianni Vattimo's notions of "weak religion," McClure discusses characters in novels by Toni Morrison, Thomas Pynchon, Don DeLillo, and others who invest skeptically and partially in supernatural enchantment and religious ritual. Coming from a variety of positions and always believing only skeptically, the survivors of the plague in Atwood's series turn to their faith practices, although they are always unsure of whether they are genuinely helpful in the long term. McClure writes, "The partial conversions of postsecular fiction do not deliver those who experience them from worldliness into well-ordered systems of religious belief. Instead, they tend to strand those who experience them in the ideologically mixed and confusing middle zones" (12). *MaddAddam* presents these "ideologically mixed and confusing middle zones" as the spiritual basis of the new: the people left over from the plague can fit within the interspecies society forming in the not quite restored natural balance of the world.

The characters accomplish this through a junk community undergirded by junk religion. In an interview published in *Science Fiction Studies* in 1990, Samuel R. Delany suggests among other things that dystopia sometimes becomes utopia through what he calls "junk cities," where new social arrangements grow out of a decayed urban society and people reuse the left-behind garbage for new purposes. "Junk City has its positive side: it's the Lo Teks living in the geodesic superstructure above Nighttown in [William] Gibson's 'Johnny Mnemonic.' You can even see it presaged a bit among those who enjoy the urban chaos in my own *Dhalgren*—or the unlicensed sectors in the satellite cities of Triton" (Delany and R. M. P. 304). Delany's junk city suggests both material and social recombination. In *MaddAddam*, the partiality of the survivors' religious and ideological commitments creates a junk-city utopia.

These novels feature a wide range of utopian ideas that make use of religion in various ways. The series declines to champion any one of these utopian programs; instead, the survivors of the plague pick elements of each and recombine them to create a junk society capable of addressing their current circumstances. Each utopian program offers visions of an ecologically sound and just public; each fails or flips on its head. I begin by showing the utopian rhetoric of the neoliberal dystopia: the promise that technology and economization can provide endless enjoyment and pleasure. I then show how Crake's Paradice Project mimics the economized logic of the neoliberal system he seeks to destroy. Through a secularized concept of sin, Crake focuses excessively on material relations to the detriment of the spiritual. Next, I consider the God's Gardeners' model of community, which offers material support to the plague survivors but is limited in considering the place of humans in a restored ecology. I finish with a consideration of how the evolving myth structures of the Crakers extend the Gardeners' ecocommunal ideals to other species. The Crakers lead a new interspecies public that might rethink the relation between humanity and the global environment. By the end of the series, the characters have recaptured some partially transcendent meaning in the creation of a new public that may or may not be more environmentally friendly in the future. In the short term, the new public offers some hope of something different than the ruthless, destructive logics of neoliberalism.

Perpetual Youth: The Dystopian Promise

The three novels in the series take place across roughly the same period. During the months after the "waterless flood" plague, characters recall their lives in the two decades or so leading up to the event. Each novel focuses on different characters, thus lending different perspectives on their society and the events of the flood. In *Oryx and Crake*, Jimmy/Snowman cares for the left-behind genetically engineered Crakers and recalls his life. While Jimmy was among the privileged inside a corporate compound, his lack of talent in science relegated him to partial outsider status (alleviated slightly by his friendship with Crake). Jimmy's story shows his inability to sustain relationships with other people. While he dates women casually and without commitment, Jimmy's two closest friends—Crake and Oryx, a sex worker who works for Crake and teaches the Crakers—remain mysteries to him no matter how hard he tries to understand their lives. The second novel, *The Year of the Flood*, takes place concurrently with *Oryx and Crake*, but narrates the lives of Toby, a pleebland resident and reluctant member of the God's Gardeners, and Ren, a teenager who moves back and forth with her mother from the corporate compounds to the pleeblands with the God's Gardeners. Through Toby, whose family is torn apart by corporate machinations and who suffers sexual abuse at the hands of a fast-food boss, *The Year of the Flood* both highlights the exploitation suffered by unprotected people and the importance of solidarity. Ren's friendships with the other Gardener children similarly show the power of community as her friendships remain intact through hardships. The third novel, *MaddAddam*, extends *The Year of the Flood*'s focus on friendship and solidarity to other species, imagining an "eco-solidarity" that extends humanism. The novel provides more of Toby's perspective, but its flashbacks present the story of Zeb, a member of the God's Gardeners and MaddAddam. Through Zeb, a clever and often criminal environmental activist, *MaddAddam* satirizes environmental activism, showing Zeb as a highly effective, chameleon character driven only secondarily by activist motivations. Through Zeb's experiences—from abuse as a child by his Church of PetrOleum founder father to his infiltration of corporate compounds—the novels present environmental activism with sympathy and skepticism. Through the different narrative perspectives, the series builds a dystopian world and shows the materials, ideologies, and traumas the survivors will need to work with after the plague.

The pre-flood dystopia presented in *MaddAddam* features extreme but recognizable versions of neoliberalism. Wealthy corporations control all formerly public functions; as already mentioned, the private security force CorpSeCorps has taken the place of municipal and state police. Labor protections for safety and a minimum wage no longer exist, and neither do safety inspections of consumer products. Women especially suffer under this system; as in a wholly economized system, their sexual labor becomes exploitable. Sex trafficking abounds; Jimmy and Crake first encounter Oryx when they watch child pornography in which she is featured, and Jimmy later learns her story of being sold from her village somewhere in Asia (*Oryx* 121–43). Oryx, due in part to luck and in part to intelligence, manages to survive as a sex worker. Many other non-U.S. women, however, are treated as disposable, even at the high-end sex club Scales and Tails where Ren works and where "smuggled illegal-alien [temporaries] ... got ripped up all the time," subject to the violence of well-connected customers (*Year* 36). Protected male authorities commit sexual abuse with impunity, including Toby's boss, Blanco, who hates his job managing a fast-food SecretBurgers franchise but "figured the girls were his perks" (36). Even women with the kind of STEM-based skills valued by corporations still have to conform to sexual fantasies; Jimmy muses that his stepmother, Ramona, "was supposed to be a tech genius but she talked like a shower-gel babe in an ad" (*Oryx* 25).[4] The absence of environmental regulation leaves dangerous toxic waste everywhere, and, as in Butler's *Parable* series, global warming is practically a character. The experiences of all the main characters—from Jimmy's alienation to Toby's, Amanda's, and Oryx's exploitation—makes clear to readers that they live in a dystopian system built on neoliberal economization.

Nevertheless, this neoliberal system sells itself as utopian. Economic freedom in theory creates endless opportunity. Biotechnology promises to reverse the effects of aging, make all physical sensations possible, and produce endlessly entertaining products. Working at the AnooYoo spa, Toby sells a number of products that promise women youth and beauty but often disappoint them since the products of course cannot deliver on the promises: "They couldn't understand why even the most advanced AnooYoo treatments wouldn't make them twenty-one again. 'Our laboratories are well on the way to age reversal,' Toby would tell them in soothing tones, 'but they aren't quite there yet. In a few years ...'" (*Year* 264, ellipsis in original). The promise of these consumer products lies in the massive research and development projects undertaken by the corporations. These include creating transgenic animals that the characters encounter, like the pigoons, wolvogs, mo'Hairs (sheep that grow human hair), and liobams (lamb-lion crosses created by a religious group called the Lion Isaiahists). Less obvious are the beautiful transgenic plants that decorate the Watson and Crick Institute where Crake goes to college, though these are paired with horrifying and somewhat silly trans-genics like a spoat, a spider-goat cross that produces silk in milk that is useful in CorpSeCorps bulletproof vests, and a brainless hookworm-like animal that provides something like chicken meat (*Oryx* 199–201). Along with this techno-scientific promise comes the corporations' promise to establish social order. When the CorpSeCorps begins to consolidate its power, underfunded police departments and other public services have failed to maintain order, and peo-ple are initially glad to have the CorpSeCorps there to fulfill those functions (*Year* 25). At first, the CorpSeCorps maintains the appearance of serving the public, though it quickly turns to killing enemies and making money by work-ing with organized crime. Corporate interests and not the public good drive the force's actions.

The corporate system is the most rigorously secular of the utopian visions offered in the novels. There are two semiofficial religions with some power in the biotech corporations. The Petrobaptists, in an echo of the U.S. Christian theology called "dominionism," believe crude oil and other natural resources to be gifts from God to be exploited. For the Petrobaptists, environmental-ists are worshipers of Satan (*MaddAddam* 117). In an echo of the prosperity gospel, the Known Fruits recognize wealth as a sign of God's favor. The highly stratified society conforms to God's plan. Despite the presence of these reli-gions and their vaguely Christian orientations, the promises of the corporate compounds and their parallel crime organizations remain rigorously secu-lar. Nothing is required of people beyond enjoyment; they exist supposedly as consumers (though tacitly also as labor). While Crake designs his supervirus and the Craker people in secret, he hires Jimmy to write advertising copy for the RejoovenEssence compound where he works. Jimmy, whose talent with words goes underappreciated, writes ad copy that emphasizes the great plea-sures of the products offered. For the corporations, the commodification of the body and intellect opens a world of pleasure and fulfillment.

The corporate system features the absence of God, though this wouldn't in and of itself necessarily qualify it as wholly nonreligious. Instead, the novels suggest repeatedly that the consumer society has removed the intellect and the spirit from public and private life by rendering all words empty of tran-scendent meaning. This exclusive immanence, this total secularization, the novels suggest, empties meaning by transmuting all forms of culture to the material pleasure of the body. Atwood shows this in a variety of ways, begin-ning with the material differences between "numbers people and word peo-ple" (*Oryx* 25). The Martha Graham Academy, the humanities-centered college attended by Jimmy, Ren, Amanda, and Bernice, "was falling apart" (185), and its once proud motto, *Ars Longa Vita Brevis*, has been replaced with "Our Stu-dents Graduate with Employable Skills" (188). Jimmy's major, "Problematics," prepares students for work in advertising, a field in which he excels (288). The divorce from meaning becomes apparent as Jimmy keeps lists of fancy words to use in advertising and often makes up words: "It was his task to describe and extol, to present the vision of what—oh, so easily!—could come to be. Hope and fear, desire and revulsion, these were his stocks-in-trade.... Once in a while, he'd make up a word—*tensicity, fibracionous, pheromonimal*—but he never once got caught out" (248, emphasis in original). Later, alone on the beach after the plague, he often speaks words without any context in his head: "From nowhere, a word appears: *Mesozoic*. He can see the word, he can hear the word, but he can't reach the word. He can't attach anything to it" (39, emphasis in original). The God's Gardeners try to recapture some meaning with their hymns and rituals, but they also worry about the power of words, telling children that written words are impermanent, and writing is dangerous "because your enemies could trace you through it" (*Year* 6). Alone and thinking the plague has killed everyone, Ren thinks, "any writing I might do now is safe, because those who would have used it against me are most likely dead" (6). Similarly alone on a beach, Jimmy thinks about keeping a journal like a castaway on a desert island, but "even a castaway assumes a future reader, someone who'll come along later and find his bones and his ledger, and learn his fate.... Any reader he can possibly imagine is in the past" (*Oryx* 41). Under the corporate system, excessive immanence empties everything of meaning; before the surviving characters find each other after the plague, the absence of an audience similarly renders words meaningless. These characters crave something—if not God, then at least something transcendent.

The novels offer a metaphysical diagnosis of the corporate system: the absence of meaning beyond the embodied self has rendered life empty. As Stephen Dunning notes, the novels' consumer society and its ultimately disastrous plague suggest that great risk accompanies the abandonment of long-standing religious narratives (87). For the series, however, there's a broader problem that goes beyond the religious or the secular, and that's the divorce of body from mind and spirit. In the wholly material corporate system, human intellect and spirit exist only as means to create bodily experiences, and the spirit is used only to manipulate people into buying those bodily experiences. The clearest statement of this comes from Jimmy in *Oryx and Crake*, as alone on the beach after the flood, he recalls having encountered the words of *Macbeth* while watching Anna K, a woman who broadcasts her entire life in her apartment over the internet, reading Shakespeare as she washes her underwear or uses the bathroom (*Oryx* 84). Crake, watching with Jimmy, had rejected *Macbeth*, but Jimmy was enchanted. As he remembers, he muses:

> When did the body first set out on its own adventures? Snowman thinks; after having ditched its old travelling companions, the mind and the soul, for whom it had once been considered a mere corrupt vessel or else a puppet acting out their

dramas for them, or else bad company, leading the other two astray. It must have got tired of the soul's nagging and whining and the anxiety-driven intellectual web-spinning of the mind, distracting it whenever it was getting its teeth into something juicy or its fingers into something good. It had dumped the other two back there somewhere, leaving them stranded in some damp sanctuary or stuffy lecture hall while it made a beeline for the topless bars, and it had dumped culture along with them: music and painting and poetry and plays. Sublimation, all of it; nothing but sublimation, according to the body. Why not cut to the chase?

But the body had its own cultural forms. It had its own art. Executions were its tragedies, pornography was its romance. (*Oryx* 85)

Jimmy's diagnosis is striking given the material abuses suffered by people, animals, and the planet under the corporate system. Nonetheless, he sets up some important oppositions, describing the mind as "web-spinning" and the soul as "whining," opposite to and in the way of immediate bodily pleasure, "its fingers into something good." In the absence of the sublimation of bodily desire, muses Jimmy, the kind of art once studied at the Martha Graham Academy transmutes into different forms, forms of the body: "Executions were its tragedies, pornography was its romance."

The problems of the corporate society, Jimmy's pondering suggests, lie in the emphasis on the experience of the body. The corporations make their money off the health and pleasure of consumers and the exploitation of labor. The novels seem to hint at nostalgia here; a proper response to this system would return to a human wholeness (the kind once represented by the Martha Graham Academy). Through its exploration of solutions, however, the series suggests that integration—that is, a wholeness that notes the material security of body and planet, the intellectual possibilities of philosophy, and the spiritual fulfillment of religion and community—is hardly a matter of a simple return to the past. Through the alternative visions offered by characters in the books, it becomes clear that a merely material intervention fails to address human or environmental needs and that religious vision often neglects both the intellect and the baser material realities of the system they've been living in.

Designing Out Sin

Crake's plague and the transgenic Crakers offer the first utopian intervention, one based on a purely material calculation of what would make a sustainable human race. Crake designs the Crakers to be incapable of the two things that, according to Crake, guarantee the human race will destroy the environment: the need for animal protein and the need to create culture. Despite his atheism, Crake's intervention represents a highly secularized vision of the elimination of sin; the Crakers will live in a prelapsarian society only possible after

destroying the human race. Through the execution and rhetoric of Crake's project, the novels simultaneously establish the persistence of the power of symbolic thinking (even within the most materially minded) and the impossibility of a humanity without culture. Crake's attempt to design out the "cluster of
neurons" that creates God (*Oryx* 157; *Year* 258) fails because the Crakers crave
meaning and stories; eventually, they will invent their own. Crake's plague and
the new humans are religious on two levels. On the obvious level, Crake's project is awash with tongue-in-cheek biblical allusions. Selling it to his employers as experiments meant to create designer babies, Crake names his research
the Paradice Project. The first successfully created group of Crakers lives inside a dome with an Eden-like environment, protected entirely from any outside influence other than Oryx, who enters to teach them how to survive. The
Crakers are literally naked and unashamed, as Jimmy establishes: "They were
naked, but not like the Noodie News: there was no self-consciousness, none at
all" (*Oryx* 302). After the plague and the deaths of Oryx and Crake, Jimmy re-
moves the Crakers from the Paradice dome and introduces himself as "Snowman." He appears before the Crakers (who had been missing the presence of
Oryx) and leads them out of Eden like an angel guide, telling them in an echo
of some Christian rhetorics of salvation: "'I come from the place of Oryx and
Crake,' he said. 'Crake sent me. . . . And Oryx. . . . Oryx and Crake wish you to
have a better place than this'" (349). Later in the story (though earlier in the
book), as the Crakers demand more stories from Jimmy, he extends this biblical echo by telling them that the plague had been Crake "pouring away" the
chaos for them in "The Great Rearrangement" (103), an echo of Noah's flood.

Under these ironic biblical allusions lies an interesting secularization of sin
and death. Talal Asad gives a useful definition of secularization: despite overlap between secular and religious ideas, they are recognizably different. Secularization features a redefinition of religious ideas. His chief example is that of
pain: a religious definition of suffering might be that it's the result of sin (both
the original sin of mankind and individual transgressions of God's law). A secularized notion of suffering would be that it's caused by transgression against
the law of nature: for example, poor eating and lack of exercise cause health
problems (Asad 46–47). Crake explains his project and the plague in secularized terms of death and sin. He tells Jimmy that the Paradice Project is about
"immortality" (*Oryx* 292), but when Crake says that the Crakers possess a genetic feature that will make each die at age thirty without suffering, Jimmy objects that they aren't immortal. Crake explains: "Immortality . . . is a concept.
If you take 'mortality' as being, not death, but the foreknowledge of it and the
fear of it, then 'immortality' is the absence of such fear. Babies are immortal"
(303). Jimmy compares this to the spin of advertisers, rhetoric meant to ob-
scure truth, but like the promise of Christ's resurrection, Crake uses scientific
discourse and semantics to solve the problem of death. Crake further solves a

material problem by intervening in another frequent subject of religious concern, sexuality. For Crake, sexuality provides a major source of suffering (in his view, this is in the form of loneliness, rejection, and jealousy, rather than the violent abuse suffered by Oryx, Toby, and others). Crake solves this problem in the typically brilliant, horrifying, and silly manner the novels so often feature: the Crakers follow a heat cycle, wherein women ready to mate turn blue in the abdomen like baboons, men with giant blue penises perform a mating ritual, and then four men impregnate a woman. The Crakers do not feel sexual jealousy, and it's never clear which individual is the father of the baby. Jimmy thinks, "Maybe Crake was right . . . under the old dispensation, sexual competition had been relentless and cruel" (164–65). Crake's removal of the suffering in sex also echoes the corporate system's reorientation toward the body. Just as Jimmy observes that everything switched to the body when it "left behind" the mind and spirit, Crake hopes that biologizing sex in this way will remove it as a driving force of cultural production and therefore material destruction.

Crake's main concern lies in the destruction of the environment, which for him naturally grows from the human capacity to compete over sex and resources. According to Crake, human culture—the creation of narrative and symbolic meaning—is driven by this competition and, in turn, drives the destruction of the environment. He wants to design out these flaws. He tells Ren at one point that illness is a design flaw, and if he were designing the world, he would "do it better" (*Year* 147). His primary interest is sins against the environment. As Jimmy and Crake watch news coverage of conflicts between the CorpSeCorps and coffee-growing farmers in South America as well as the global movement to support these farmers (including protests and more violent actions—bombings, riots, and so on), Crake seems to Jimmy to side with the farmers: "'Those guys should be whacked,' Crake said. 'Which ones? The peasants? Or the guys killing them?' 'The latter. Not because of the dead peasants, there's always been dead peasants. But they're nuking the cloud forests to plant this stuff.' 'The peasants would do that too if they had half a chance,' said Jimmy. 'Sure, but they don't have half a chance.' 'You're taking sides?' 'There aren't any sides, as such'" (*Oryx* 178–79).

Crake's callousness toward the problems of the farmers pairs with his general callousness toward human suffering throughout. For Crake, peasants and corporations merely exhibit the same human tendency toward destroying the environment in order to pursue profit and dominance. Crake's idea here fits comfortably within the deep ecology formulation that lends human life no particular value compared with any other life. The propensity to "nuk[e] the cloud forests" exists in both the strong and the weak, as Jimmy points out. For Crake, "sides" are temporary, as is all human life. His lack of concern echoes in his and the corporations' willingness to experiment on people. For example, he tells Jimmy that BlyssPluss has used test subjects "from the poorer countries . . . and from the ranks of the desperate as usual" (*Oryx* 296). The human guinea pigs suffer terribly: "A couple of the test subjects literally fucked themselves to death, several had assaulted old ladies and household pets, and there had been unfortunate cases of priapism and split dicks. . . . One subject had grown a big genital wart all over her epidermis" (295). This awfulness has little effect on Crake, nor does the injustice visited when he has the CorpSeCorps kidnap, imprison, and even kill members of MaddAddam to help him design the Crakers (298–99). Jimmy finds this horrifying. Crake, accustomed to thinking on the mathematical level of design and the broader ecological balance, sees it as a necessary step to create the world better than God and/or evolution could.

While Crake intervenes in many aspects of humanity when he designs the Crakers, his chief concern lies in the human propensity for symbolic thinking, which leads to cultural and technological development and hence to hierarchy, domination, and destruction. Crake explains his design to Jimmy, making clear that a mix of bodily and cognitive transgenic alterations has allowed him to design out the need for adaptations that lead to cultural thinking:

> What had been altered was nothing less than the ancient primate brain. Gone were its destructive features, the features responsible for the world's current illnesses. For instance, racism—or, as they referred to it in Paradice, pseudospeciation—had been eliminated in the model group, merely by switching the bonding mechanism: the Paradice people simply did not register skin color. Hierarchy could not exist among them, because they lacked the neural complexes that would have created it. Since they were neither hunters nor agriculturalists hungry for land, there was no territoriality: the king-of-the-castle hard-wiring that had plagued humanity had, in them, been unwired. They ate nothing but leaves and grass and roots and a berry or two; thus their foods were plentiful and always available. (Oryx 305)

In this passage, Crake reduces all of human culture to neurons and need. The lack of a need to eat animal protein or even specific plants means that no agriculture—and therefore no land and no property—is necessary. Moreover, the Crakers lack the inherent cognitive abilities to see differences among themselves, which leads to racism and other "pseudospeciation." In a silly fashion, Crake and his scientists use a transgenic gene splice (presumably rabbits) to make it possible for the Crakers to consume their own excrement and thus redigest plant material (*Oryx* 305). Crake continues telling Jimmy about the Crakers: "they were perfectly adjusted to their habitat, so they would never have to create houses or tools or weapons or, for that matter, clothing. They would have no need to invent any harmful symbolisms, such as kingdoms, icons, gods, or money" (305). As far as Crake can tell, he has not only designed the Crakers for sustainability; he has designed them so that they will never need to change or develop any culture beyond eating and reproduction. Crake's utopia, while wholly secular and eschewing the idea of God and even the biological possibility of brains that could create religion, nonetheless represents an Edenic public. As Zeb later muses, Crake does not create a perfect world; it's "more like a reboot" (*MaddAddam* 334).

And in this reboot, the Crakers, just like Adam and Eve, discover good and evil. From an ecological perspective, Crake's design of the Crakers makes sense: he imagines a change to humanity so deep, so radical and bizarre, that readers can imagine a response to global warming comprehensive enough to change things. Given the politics of the Anthropocene, it's tempting to think of Crake as a possible hero, if not literally heroic. Problems within the narrative, however, call this into question: his callous treatment of human and animal life, for example, and most strikingly, his murder of Oryx for reasons that are at best unclear (and certainly, it's hard to imagine an adequate reason for doing so) (*Oryx* 329; *MaddAddam* 146). For me, it's pretty obvious that while the series has some sympathy for deep ecology, Crake's intervention is dramatically undermined by his colossal failures: the failure to destroy all of humanity, his failure to imagine possible dangers to the Crakers beyond their ecological footprint, and most of all his failure to prevent the Crakers from creating symbolic meaning. Even his best friend, Jimmy, curses him throughout the entire series and sometimes laughs with derision and wonder. Delirious from fever, Jimmy hears the Crakers singing and says to Ren and Toby, "You can't kill the music!" (*Year* 431).

While Crake expresses frustration at not being able to program out singing (Oryx 352), Jimmy, having lived among the Crakers for months, knows that the failure goes beyond music. The Crakers hunger for meaning, and they develop a rich symbolic culture. On the beach with Jimmy, they enact a ritual wherein they bring him a fish caught from the ocean and ask him to tell the story of how Crake created them and swept away the people who had been there before (101–2). Later, in *MaddAddam*, Jimmy, recovering from infection, passes this storytelling duty to Toby, and the Crakers ask for progressively more stories not only about Crake but about other mythical figures (most of whom they personally know) like Oryx and Zeb. This propensity for culture, however, had emerged even when they were still in the dome. After the plague has started to kill people, Crake has killed Oryx, and Jimmy has killed Crake, Jimmy listens to the Crakers speculate in somewhat mythical terms about the absence of Oryx from their dome: "'Where is Oryx? When is she coming back?' 'She always comes back.' 'She should be here, teaching us.' 'She is always teaching us. She is teaching us now.' 'Is she here?' 'Here and not here is the same thing, for Oryx. She said that.' 'Yes. She said it.' 'What does it mean?' It was like some demented theology debate in the windier corners of chat-room limbo. Jimmy couldn't stand listening to it for very long" (339–40). Jimmy may find it difficult to tolerate, but the Crakers engage in this "demented theology debate" not only with themselves, but with all the surviving human characters. Crake's failure to design out symbolic meaning is echoed by his failures to purify Earth from the sinful human race. Along with the humans who survive, the dangers of the biotech corporate system remains, including pigoons and wolvogs and, most dramatically, the Painballers, men reduced to violent sociopathy after having been sentenced repeatedly to gladiatorial combat (filmed for an internet audience) (*Year* 98).

Crake's primary failure, however, is conceptual. While he has rejected the destructiveness of the neoliberal economization of natural resources and people, he has created a race of humans economized through the back door. He has reduced them entirely to material reality, but it's a material reality he can't account for. Whether because of the dangerous garbage on the beach (*Oryx* 7) or the dangerous remaining humans, the Crakers are unprepared to survive by themselves. What allows them to do so, however, is precisely their symbolic communication, which lets them evolve, join with humans, and even communicate with pigoons and other transgenic species. Crake's plague has left junk: the actual objects of the consumer society, wasted or rendered useless because of their absence from circulation in the consumer economy. This junk, however, is available for repurposing by the survivors and Crakers. Similarly, the Paradice Project has left ideological refuse: Crake's not quite successful reboot. Out of this, the Crakers and the remaining humans need to create an interspecies public on the rubbish heap of the collapsed society.

Strong Ties from Weak Religion

The Crakers' emergent culture is just one position of three in the demented theology debate happening across the series. The first position consists of the secular promises of the corporations, and the second is offered by the God's Gardeners. A religious movement whose members live in the pleeblands in New New York and who have connections throughout the corporate compounds (including with Crake), the group is an "ecocult"—a vaguely Christian group that celebrates God's creation of various species. Deep ecologists, their rituals honor the relations among people and other species. They work to minimize their own ecological footprint, scavenging from the refuse of the corporate system, growing organic plants on their rooftops, and awaiting the waterless flood that they believe will remove most of humanity from Earth so that the remaining people can tend God's Garden. Through the God's Gardeners, the series imagines how a small community of deep ecologists can live within a destructive corporate system; however, the series also shows the limitations of this community, as the God's Gardeners are not prepared for evolving material conditions. While Gardener theology possesses specific positions about

God and demands particular practices from adherents, most of the individual Gardeners remain ambivalent toward Gardener religious belief, finding much of it silly. The perspectives of Toby, Ren, Zeb, and other Gardeners allow *The Year of the Flood* and *MaddAddam* to reject fundamentalist religion and absolutist deep ecology. Instead, the books develop a model of a public that similarly seeks sustainable survival but also pays attention to intellectual and material relations in a way that avoids some of the silliness and abuses present in the Gardeners. This partial commitment to Gardener religious practice allows the surviving humans to join the evolving, multispecies junk religion, which offers some hope at the end of the series.

The God's Gardeners practice a green theology that includes communal living, a canon of environmentalist saints (like Saint Rachel Carson), and the belief that humankind's divine purpose is to tend Earth as a garden. Before the plague, they stand in stark opposition to the corporate system and the CorpSeCorps, not only speaking against their environmental destruction, but increasingly aiding the escape of corporate researchers who want to fight corporate power, including Jimmy's mother, who escapes with information about the transgenic pigoons (*Year* 223). This opposition is written into the Gardeners' theology, which contrasts their own practices with the "exfernal world" of the compounds and pleeblands and looks forward to the waterless flood that will destroy everyone and leave only the Gardeners. To prepare, the Gardeners store food and supplies in "ararats" (named after the mountaintop landing site of Noah's ark) in various places. They also learn to scavenge from dumpsters and other refuse, which prepares them to make material use of the remainders after the flood. Eventually, the Gardeners are officially outlawed, and they must hide when the CorpSeCorps begins to hunt them (290). Fortunately, the God's Gardeners are more than a separatist ecocult: they're an oppositional movement with "truffle cells" hiding in various places throughout the system and the pleeblands (57). A push and pull between deep ecological commitment and religious skepticism characterizes the experience of all the Gardeners. The survivors draw on this partial commitment after the flood.

Gardener practice thus includes some partiality and skepticism. At an April Fish Day gathering, the God's Gardeners hear a sermon from Adam One titled "On the Foolishness within All Religions." In a message combining annual celebration, the moral equivalence of people and animals, and self-deprecating acknowledgment of personal imperfection, Adam One argues that playfulness is a quality of God the Creator that has been imbued in people and some animals (foxes, crows), all of which were created in God's image. Adam One concludes his sermon with a prayer to God, asking, "help us to accept in all humility our kinship with the Fishes, who appear to us as mute and foolish; for in Your sight, we are all mute and foolish" (*Year* 197). The group follows Adam One's sermon with a hymn, asking God's forgiveness for greed and vanity and celebrating April Fish Day's "[puncturing] of pomp and puffed-up pride" (198). Sermons and hymns begin chapters throughout *The Year of the Flood*, and each one grounds the theology of the God's Gardeners in the life of the community through a rhetorical ritual. Located near the middle of the novel, the April Fish Day message affirms the zealous commitment of the Gardeners to deep ecology's moral equivalence of people and animals while suggesting the need for religious humility in linking that principle with everyday actions.

Adam One's sermon calls for humility, but his sanctimony rankles Toby and Zeb. Despite all the Gardeners offer to utopian thinking, they offer insufficient practical, material means to adjust their ecological practices to new realities. They operate at levels of abstraction that undercut their practical efficaciousness. Toby, grateful to be rescued by the Gardeners from the abusive Blanco, nonetheless notes the "bossy sanctimoniousness" and "fuzzy theology" that pervade Gardener practice (*Year* 46–47). As she becomes a more permanent part of the Gardeners, Toby joins the Council of Adams and Eves, the leadership board of the Gardeners, and at one point witnesses a theological debate so abstract she has trouble holding her tongue. Why, if God created people to live in ecological harmony as equals with the rest of the life on Earth, do humans have teeth evolved for eating meat? Despite the Gardeners' acceptance of Darwinian evolutionary theory, this question is phrased in terms of the biblical Adam: why would the first man have carnivore's teeth? (240). When Toby asks Adam One whether such a question is necessary, the leader gives an answer that subordinates the group's theology to the group's deep ecological commitment:

> Most people don't care about other species, not when times get hard. All they care about is their next meal, naturally enough: we have to eat or die. But what if God's doing the caring? We've evolved to believe in gods, so this belief bias of ours must confer an evolutionary advantage. The strictly materialist view—that we're an experiment animal protein has been doing on itself—is far too harsh and lonely for most, and leads to nihilism. That being the case, we need to push popular sentiment in a biosphere-friendly direction by pointing out the hazards of annoying God by a violation of His trust in our stewardship. (241)[5]

Adam One's answer brings together theology, political pragmatism, and ecological commitment. Combining theology and modern science and featuring a pragmatic theology without denial of its truth, the answer is distinctly postsecular. The answer is also pedantic, and while Toby accepts it in the short term, she sees Adam One's explanation as at least somewhat deceptive.

While Adam One explains the debate over the biblical Adam's teeth as practical, in the series practicality often falls by the wayside with disastrous results. The Gardeners he's with nearly all die in the plague, and Adam One is eventually killed by the Painballers who escape the plague (*MaddAddam* 363). While the God's Gardeners seem to form a tight-knit community, they experience a variety of conflicts and hold their fair share of secrets. Zeb, who is the focus of much of *MaddAddam*, constantly goes on secret missions into the compounds and eventually helps lead the existing splinter group, MaddAddam (*Year* 268; *MaddAddam* 334). More strikingly, a Gardener named Burt is eventually exposed for using Gardener resources to grow marijuana; for having drugged his wife, Veena, for years; and for sexually abusing his stepdaughter, Bernice (*Year* 151, 289). This all happens in part due to the Gardeners' absence of formal structures and dogmatic trust of each other. As Toby muses, "Now they'd joined the long list of the religious faithful who'd woken one morning to find that the vicar had made off with the church building fund, leaving a trail of molested choirboys behind him" (166). The official absurdity of the God's Gardeners doesn't seem to lead to much self-consciousness to build on. For that, the series uses the experiences of Toby, Ren, and Amanda.

Ren and her childhood friends form ambivalent relations to Gardener practice at first due to their refusal to reject the "exfernal" corporate system. At the opening of *The Year of the Flood*, Ren is a young adult, stuck inside the quarantine chamber of the Scales and Tails animal-themed sex club where she works. In her flashbacks, however, she is a child in the God's Gardeners and then later lives inside the HelthWyzer corporate compound, where she dates Jimmy and befriends Crake. As children, Ren and her friends have mostly resistant relationships to Gardener practice, though they absorb much of Gardener education and belief in ways that help them shortly before and after the plague. The children go to classes about scavenging, growing and gathering food, and self-defense ("urban bloodshed limitation"), but like any other kids, they make fun of their teachers and find ways around the rules. They learn the Gardener chants but change the lyrics to be rhyming insults about their teachers (*Year* 62). These childish pranks form the basis of lasting friendships with other Gardener children, but most interestingly, their relations are cemented through the children's ambivalent fascination with the consumer products and pleebland cultures that the Gardeners so strongly reject. Ren remembers feeling fear of the Gardeners when, as a child, her mother took her from the relative safety of the HelthWyzer compound so they could live with her lover, Zeb: "They smiled a lot, but they scared me: they were so interested in doom, and enemies, and God. And they talked so much about Death.... And when they'd start talking about the Waterless Flood that was going to kill everybody on Earth, except maybe them—that gave me nightmares" (59).

Ren's comfort with the Gardeners grows, but her ambivalence takes real shape when she meets Amanda, an environmental refugee from Texas, whose toughness and possession of consumer goods enchant her: "Those girls were wearing the sort of clothes they usually wore: miniskirts and spangled tops, candyfloss boas around their necks, silver gloves, plasticized butterflies clipped into their hair. They had their Sea/H/Ear Candies and their burning-bright phones and their jellyfish bracelets, and they were showing off. . . . They looked as if they already owned everything from every single store and were bored with it. I envied that look so much. I just stood there, envying" (*Year* 72). Ren begins with fascination with Amanda's bracelet, which contains live jellyfish swirling inside. Ren brings Amanda home, and the Gardeners adopt her. She teaches Ren and the other kids about stealing, using consumer products, and the rules of street survival. At one point, after Burt is arrested by the CorpSeCorps for growing and selling marijuana, the kids steal some of his marijuana to smoke themselves (153–54). Amanda evinces the toughest elements of the corporate ideology: in streetwise terms, make everything economic, the subject of trade. Whenever Ren thanks Amanda, Amanda simply responds "you'll pay me back" (324). Ren finds her friendship consistently reliable, but Amanda seems to think of friendship almost entirely in terms of economic exchange.

While Ren rejects much of Gardener teaching, her memories of her Gardener friends keep her company when she's stuck, alone, in the "Sticky Zone" quarantine of Scales and Tails (*Year* 57–58). When she escapes—released by Amanda, who drives through chaos from Wisconsin to rescue her—she and Amanda find their young Gardener friends Shackie, Croze, and Oates, and their friendships provide companionship and allies in survival. Later, when they rejoin the Gardeners, they're prepared to scavenge, to tend herds of sheep, and to a limited extent, for combat against the dangerous Painballers. The children witness the waterless flood, and they draw on Gardener teaching without ever really committing to Gardener belief. Gardener practice is, however, the basis of their survival and solidarity among themselves. While they experience a long separation, the friends reunite as adults after the plague. Their suffering at the hands of the Painballers is intense, but their friendships persist.

While Ren and the other kids relate to the Gardeners in a childish, partial way, it turns out that most of the Gardeners have similar partial connections to Gardener theology and strong connections among themselves. Through *The Year of the Flood* and *MaddAddam*, Toby's feelings about the Gardeners evolve; though she never quite embraces the organization, her commitments to its practices grow stronger and help keep her connected to herself and others before and after the plague. Toby's childhood story is a capitalist nightmare. Her family's beautiful house is on desirable land, and corporations offer to buy it, but her father refuses. Mysteriously, not long after, her mother becomes ill, and the family goes into debt trying unsuccessfully to save her. They sell their home, and Toby's father commits suicide. Toby disappears into the pleeblands to avoid being arrested for her family's debt. She sells her eggs to make money, but an infected syringe sterilizes her for life. Eventually, she ends up at SecretBurgers, where she is relentlessly sexually abused by Blanco, the mob-connected supervisor of the franchise (*Year* 24–43). The God's Gardeners, having heard of Toby's abuse from Rebecca, a Gardener and former SecretBurgers employee, contrive to rescue and conceal her. They welcome her into their community without requiring much of her at first. Toby slowly becomes an important part of the community despite having doubts about their ecotheology and social organization, and despite remaining relatively uncommitted to their political agenda.

Toby's reaction to the God's Gardeners oscillates between gratitude and skepticism, forming an ambivalence that never leaves her even as she develops deeper commitments to Gardener practices, beliefs, and people. She finds immediate rescue from her abuse and marginal material security among the Gardeners, people who seem basically well intentioned. Upon arriving at the Gardeners' rooftop garden, Toby experiences gratitude and something like the presence of the divine:

> The garden wasn't at all what Toby had expected from hearsay. . . . She gazed around it in wonder: it was so beautiful, with plants and flowers of many kinds she'd never seen before. There were vivid butterflies; from nearby came the vibration of bees. Each petal and leaf was fully alive, shining with awareness of her. Even the air of the Garden was different.
>
> She found herself crying with relief and gratitude. It was as if a large, benevolent hand had reached down and picked her up, and was holding her safe. Later, she frequently heard Adam One speak of "being flooded with the Light of God's Creation," and without knowing it yet that was how she felt.
>
> "I'm so glad you have made this decision, my dear," said Adam One.
>
> But Toby didn't think she'd made any decision at all. Something else had made it for her. (*Year* 43)

Toby's sense of the quasi divine ("as if a large, benevolent hand had reached down and picked her up") suggests a sudden, partial openness to the possibility of something beyond the everyday market forces that have made her suffer. For the first time, the invisible forces that affect her life—that made her mother sick and allowed her abuse at Blanco's hands—have brought her somewhere that seems safe. Toby's direct thoughts aren't portrayed, and the text stops short of declaring an actual prayer of gratitude; it is only "*as if* a large, benevolent hand had reached down and picked her up." Toby's feeling of connection to the natural-like surroundings of the rooftop garden echoes the partiality of her feeling of gratitude to God. She feels the life of the garden as something benevolent and connected; nonetheless, this natural environment exists as a self-conscious creation of a group of people.

Later, when she survives alone after the plague at the ruins of the Anoo-Yoo spa, Toby maintains connections with the people she has lost through her performance of Gardener ritual and adherence to Gardener belief. Like Ren, she remembers advice on meditation and on basic physical survival, and she questions whether the Gardener teachings apply in her current context. Watching vultures and other carrion-eating birds fly around the spa in which she shelters from the plague, Toby remembers the Gardener teaching about vultures: "*Vultures are our friends.... They purify the earth. They are God's necessary dark Angels of bodily dissolution. Imagine how terrible it would be if there were no death!* Do I still believe this? Toby wonders. Everything is different up close" (*Year* 3–4, emphasis in original). The Gardener theologies around death seem comforting in the abstract; they focus on death as part of a necessarily natural and therefore morally good process of life. For Toby here, however, they remind of the plague and of her total, dangerous isolation, which opens her to attack from any other desperate survivor of the plague. Gardener teaching helps her prepare: "Even when she sleeps, she's listening, as animals do— for a break in the pattern, for an unknown sound, for a silence opening like a crack in the rock. When the small creatures hush their singing, said Adam One, it's because they're afraid. You must listen for the sound of their fear" (5). Faced with new circumstances, she must reevaluate some of the ethical stances she has developed through Gardener participation, but many of the same lessons and practices facilitate her physical and emotional survival.

Alone after the plague, Toby's recollections of Gardener teachings at first mostly remind her of loss and loneliness. Eschewing fanatical devotion, Toby adheres to Gardener practice in a way that recalls her past connections with people even as she tries to forget them. She tries to tell herself that the others must have died in the plague and that remembering them will only cause her pain that will interfere with her survival. As she walks through the hallways of the abandoned spa where she worked, she considers her survival as something apart from her life: "'Who lives here?' she says out loud. Not me, she thinks. This thing I'm doing can hardly be called living. Instead I'm lying dormant, like a bacterium in a glacier. Getting time over with. That's all" (*Year* 95). Her attempts to explain her survival according to Gardener narratives yield equally depressing results:

> She spends the rest of the morning sitting in a kind of stupor.... Paralyzing rage can still take hold of her.... It begins as disbelief and ends in sorrow, but in between those two phases her whole body shakes with anger. Anger at whom? Why has she been saved alive? Out of the countless millions.... She ought to trust that she's here for a reason—to bear witness, to transmit a message, to salvage at least something from the general wreck. She ought to trust, but she can't. (95)

Confronted with the realities of her current circumstances, Gardener ideology appears inadequate, esoteric, and inaccessible. Even as Toby tries to remind herself that "it's wrong to give so much time over to mourning," she cannot help but miss the others and even contemplates using her knowledge of herbal medicine to end her life (96).

Late in *The Year of the Flood* and throughout *MaddAddam*, when Toby is re-united with Ren, Zeb, and others, her partial commitment provides the basis for her to lead others in surviving. When Ren arrives at the AnooYoo spa, having been kidnapped and abused by Painballers, Toby immediately goes to work caring for her. Her initial ambivalence about their survival remains, however, as she thinks about poisoning sick Ren with mushrooms:

> Toby considers the Powdered Death Angels. Just a little, in Ren's weakened con-
> dition. Put her out of her misery. Help her fly away on white, white wings. Maybe
> it would be kinder. A blessing. I am an unworthy person, Toby thinks. Merely to
> have such an idea. You've known this girl since she was a child, she's come to you
> for help, she has every right to trust you. Adam One would say that Ren is a pre-
> cious gift that has been given to Toby so that Toby may demonstrate unselfish-
> ness and sharing and those higher qualities that Gardeners had been so eager
> to bring out in her. Toby can't quite see it that way, not at the moment. But she'll
> have to keep trying. (*Year* 357–58)

Toby's imagining of Ren dying as "fly[ing] away" recalls her own ambivalence at being alive, but more important, Toby vacillates between ethical models that demand different types of kind acts. Both are well intentioned, and Toby does not have a complete commitment to either one; she sees commitment as a goal reached through action. Toby later enacts one of the competing forms (mercy) in a somewhat less ambiguous manner. Having nursed Ren back to health, Toby goes with Ren in search of Amanda, Shackleton, Croze, and Oates, all of whom have been kidnapped by the escaped Painballers. Finding Blanco injured and ill beyond treatment, she gives him water laced with the same death angel mushrooms, finally eliminating him as a danger to her well-being (381–82). Toby's two different methods of treatment for Ren and Blanco do more than simply mark a difference between friend and enemy; they portray the flexible partiality of Toby's Gardener commitments. Poisoning Blanco is both selfish and kind; it ends both Toby's and Blanco's suffering at the same moment.

Despite the bossy sanctimoniousness and fuzzy theology of the God's Gardeners, they provide part of the model the series advances for community, political resistance, and sustainable living. The Gardeners develop much of the basis for living, including the gathering of food, the manufacture of medicines, and the general rejection of neoliberal fragmentation, outside the corporate system. While they maintain connections to the corporate compounds and the more violent forms of resistance of other groups—there's even some evidence that Adam One knew Crake was going to release the plague and provided some material support for doing so (*MaddAddam* 330)—they also provide the most organized questioning of neoliberal economization and of Crake's kind of overly material calculations. At one point, before the Feast of Serpent Wisdom, Adam One speaks about the importance of instinct and the limitations of human reason. Building on Matthew 10:16 ("be ye therefore wise as Serpents, and harmless as Doves"), Adam One argues that serpents provide a model for instinctive feeling, "as the Serpent feels the vibrations in the Earth. The Serpent is wise in that it lives in immediacy, without the need for the elaborate intellectual frameworks Humankind is endlessly constructing for itself. . . . The Human reason is a pin dancing on the head of an angel, so small is it in comparison to the Divine vastness that encircles us" (*Year* 233–34). The striking image of the inadequacy of reason flies in the face of Crake's intervention surely, but it also suggests some limitations in deep ecology generally, which would calculate human life as only a small part of an ecosystem without particular significance. The Gardeners suffer a similar limitation not merely through the fuzzy theology that dominates their lives but also in their faith that the waterless flood will have a result they want. Thanks, however, to the Gardeners, MaddAddam, Jimmy, the Painballers, the Crakers, and the pigoons and other transgenic animals, the post-flood world is hardly a restored Eden. For a way forward, Toby and the other characters need to reconsider human relations to other species materially, intellectually, and spiritually.

A Junk Theology

The Craker religion is the third position in *MaddAddam*'s demented theology debate, and despite the Crakers' childishness and misunderstanding of the human characters, their culture and biology provide the basis of the interspecies public present at the end of the series. Crake had tried to eliminate the "g-spot in the brain," the "cluster of neurons" that made the human brain capable of believing in God (*Oryx* 157), but through *Oryx and Crake* and at the end of *The Year of the Flood*, it becomes obvious that he has been unsuccessful. Craker theology develops in detail and sophistication, receiving the most elaboration in the third novel, *MaddAddam*.

At first, the evolving religion of the Crakers is limited mostly to a creation story and memories of being taught by Oryx. As time goes on, however, the Crakers develop their own stories, rituals, and social structures. These structures play a dual role in the series. First and most obviously, they prove Crake wrong: religious thinking may indeed be the result of a cluster of neurons, but it seems to be a fundamental part of human experience (even for transgenic humans). Second, the Craker religion shows that symbolic meaning is fundamental not only to humanity, but to survival. Symbolic thinking may indeed lead to dominance and environmental destruction, as Crake feared. However, the Crakers demonstrate that symbolic thinking similarly offers the imagination and devotion necessary to hold people together. The Crakers' genetic pre-disposition toward sustainable ecology leads them to create mythic structures that support sustainable living and interspecies community amid the refuse of the destroyed consumer society. While the God's Gardeners show the importance of solidarity within and outside religious practice, the Crakers extend this solidarity past humans and to all species. In doing so, they provide a model of deep ecology that unites the material, intellectual, and spiritual.

Craker mythology opens and closes the series, as the Crakers are introduced in *Oryx and Crake* in a section entitled "Flotsam" long before readers have a solid idea of what has happened in this world. In the Crakers' first appearance, the novel portrays them as hungry for an understanding of themselves in the world. The story begins with a ritual the Craker children have invented in which they bring garbage they don't recognize to Jimmy for identification: "Opening up their sack, the children chorus, 'Oh Snowman, what have we found?' They lift out objects, hold them up as if offering them for sale: a hubcap, a piano key, a chunk of pale-green pop bottle smoothed by the ocean. A plastic BlyssPluss container, empty; a ChickieNobs Bucket O'Nubbins, ditto. A computer mouse, or the busted remains of one, with a long wiry tail" (*Oryx* 7). These objects remind Jimmy of loss. He tells the Crakers that the objects won't hurt them, and "these are things from before" (7). For the Crakers, the "before" objects carry meaning only so far as they suggest a time before their creation, a mythical time separated from the present by Crake's flood. They ask Jimmy about his beard and if they can have "feathers" on their faces. After pretending to ask Crake by holding his watch up to his ear, Jimmy tells them to go away (8–9).

Through the presentation of the junk on the beach and the conversation about feathers, the Crakers indicate that they have separated both time and species: they understand they differ from Jimmy and the humans who came before them, and they divide time in two: before and after. The relative simplicity of Craker belief at this point is confirmed a little later when they ask Jimmy to tell their favorite story, the story of their creation and the plague. Jimmy says an internal, sarcastic prayer—"God of bullshit, fail me not" (*Oryx* 102)—and launches into a story about how Crake washed away the chaos from before, chaos that included "people . . . full of chaos themselves, and the chaos made them do bad things. They were killing other people all the time. They were eating up all the Children of Oryx [animals], against the wishes of Oryx and Crake. . . . they ate them even when they weren't hungry." Eventually, the Crakers start to join in: "'Crake made the Great Emptiness . . . ,' say the men. 'For us! For us!' say the women. It's becoming a liturgy" (103).

While the story features a familiar creation myth (chaos washed away, a new place made for the favored of God), the Crakers participate in it, gaining more agency over their beliefs as time goes on. The story was also preceded by the Crakers giving Jimmy a cooked fish, something he said Crake required (*Oryx* 101) and that becomes a ritual repeated in *MaddAddam* with Toby and later Blackbeard, a Craker who takes on storytelling duties. At first, Craker rituals happen through instincts programmed into their genetics by Crake. Using gene splices from crabs and birds with mating rituals, Crake produced a specific mating ritual for the Crakers involving penis waving, flowers, and group sex (165). In another example, possessing some genes from animals that mark territory with urine, the Craker men urinate around their encampments to ward away potentially dangerous animals (154–55). Eventually, however, the Crakers begin to ascribe symbolic meanings to their biological interactions. Remembering Oryx, the Craker women assert that "babies make Oryx happy," ascribing a mythical significance to their mating rituals and going off by themselves to "commune with Oryx" (157). While the Craker men continue their daily urination ritual, standing in a line, they invite Ren's friend Croze to join them—even though "his piss is weak"—as a way to acknowledge their friendship (*MaddAddam* 31, 44). The Crakers take this a step further when they begin to develop an animism. In *Oryx and Crake* when Jimmy goes back to the compounds to scavenge and does not return to the beach, the Crakers use trash and plants to construct an idol of him, chanting his name to summon him. When he returns at that moment, the Crakers tell him, "We made a picture of you, to help us send out our voices to you" (*Oryx* 360–61). Craker symbolic systems and practices become increasingly complex and involve more and more agency from the community and individual Crakers.

With the development of culture, the Crakers begin to recognize writing and increasingly assert agency over the construction of their own stories. Just as important, these stories begin to facilitate deeper, more equal relations with the surviving Gardeners and MaddAddam members. The Crakers' religion, in other words, facilitates greater, more self-conscious engagement with their environment. This begins with exerting control over how their stories are told to them. While Jimmy recovers from an infection in his foot, Toby assumes the responsibility of telling the Crakers' stories. Toby begins this practice over her own objections because the Crakers insist on it while they wait for Jimmy to wake up from his coma: "'Snowman-the-Jimmy is coming closer to us,' says the short woman. 'Then he will tell us the stories of Crake, as he always did when he was living in his tree. But today you will tell them to us.'" When Toby objects that she doesn't "know the stories of Crake," the Crakers have a solution: "You must put on this red thing ... it is called a hat" (*Madd-Addam* 38). The Crakers have invested ritual power in Jimmy's Red Sox hat, which they believe confers the power to tell the stories of Crake. Increasingly, they also demand stories of other heroes, including Zeb, who is still very much alive and laughs from a distance as Toby makes up semimythical stories about him (163–65). As Toby struggles through stories, the Crakers help and correct her when she says things they don't expect. Like Jimmy, she accidentally plants ideas in the Craker narratives and worries about their power: "Now what have I done? she thinks. What can of worms have I opened? ... What comes next? Rules, dogmas, laws? The Testament of Crake? How soon before there are ancient texts they feel they have to obey but have forgotten how to interpret? Have I ruined them?" (204).

Like Crake, Toby recognizes the danger of stories and worries that the Crakers will develop many of the same hierarchies and dogmas of human beings. The novel never assuages this fear, but it does take the question largely out of Toby's hands through the emerging priestly leadership of Blackbeard. Blackbeard's development begins with his interest in writing; lacking a concept of personal property, Blackbeard repeatedly takes Toby's diary to try to read it. He has difficulty understanding representation at first; when Toby writes his name and shows it to him, Blackbeard says "that is not me" (*MaddAddam* 203). Quickly, however, Blackbeard begins to absorb writing. This naturally leads him to the invention of his own stories and to intervention in the stories and rituals of the Gardeners. Not much later, when the survivors are scared about the pigoons and the Painballers, Toby performs a hallucinogenic ritual to commune with her old teacher, Pilar. As Toby feels the effects of the mushrooms she has ingested, a pigoon sow and two babies appear. While Zeb and Toby are afraid, Blackbeard sings and then tells them that Pilar appeared in the sow. Whatever the truth of Blackbeard's statements, his interpretation does help Toby and the others begin to trust the pigoons, a relationship that is crucial to the surviving humans and Crakers as the series continues (227–30).

Blackbeard's evolution takes him beyond helpful mystical sidekick and into multispecies leadership. The very end of the series features Blackbeard telling stories of the deaths of Zeb and Toby. Blackbeard wears Jimmy's Red Sox hat, and he relates the disappearance of two of their most important friends, who are made into mythical figures by the story. Very sick, Toby went away by herself into the forest to die. But the Crakers ascribe other significances to it:

> Where she went I cannot write in this Book, because I do not know. Some say that she died by herself, and was eaten by vultures. The Pig Ones [pigoons] say that. Others say she was taken away by Oryx, and is now flying in the forest, at night, in the form of an owl. ... Yet others say she went to find Zeb, and that he is in the form of a Bear, and that she too is in the form of a Bear, and is with him today. That is the best answer, because it is the happiest; and I have written it down. (*MaddAddam* 390)

Blackbeard—who recently has become acquainted with the fictional quality of these stories, having experienced a deep shaking of his faith when he encountered the corpses of Oryx and Crake at the Paradice Dome (356)—has recognized the importance of stories to the Crakers. He writes down the happiest ending, one that recognizes love for Toby and Zeb and connections among the Crakers, animals, and humans. He closes the story to the Crakers by saying "now we will sing," turning the story into part of a liturgy. Blackbeard creates an informal hierarchy and signals the development of a culture among the Crakers, one driven by spiritual meaning and material reality. This change appears to be in part hierarchical, and as Crake and later Toby feared, indicates that some of the attempts to design the Crakers to be immune to the dangers of human culture have failed. However, a difference hides within this that offers two bits of hope. First, Crake has failed, and through this failure, the series calls into heavy question the utility of an entirely material calculation about what makes people relate to their environment. Second and relatedly, the Crakers' myths invoke others: humans, pigoons, other species, and so on. There is danger in their developing agency, but their agency is different from that of the leftover humans, who may soon disappear, and offers the opportunity to rethink the relations among species in a more promising way than the Gardeners had.

Late in *MaddAddam*, all the remains of the pre-flood society start coming together: the material results of Crake's utopian, deep ecological intervention in the form of trash and loose transgenic animals; the material and spiritual practices of the Gardeners (several of whom survive); the genetic and scientific knowledge of the MaddAddam members; the pigoons and Painballers (representing possible or certain threats); and the developing Craker religion. The different groups seem necessarily in conflict due to their significantly differing practices and beliefs, but their differences complement each other. The Crakers seem helpless; lacking knowledge of good and evil (as it were), they cannot protect themselves against Painballers or anything else. The God's Gardeners are similarly nonviolent even when facing the Painballer threat. The plague still presents a danger. But in this environment, an unexpected alliance and community are made possible by an accident in the designs of the Crakers and pigoons: a linguistic and spiritual connection that excludes the humans. At this point, a new, junk assembly of ideas and materials comes together. The humans, so long the destructively dominant species on Earth, need the other species to face the threat of the violent Painballers. They must now step aside and no longer lead the new communal assemblage, but operate within it. They are capable of wielding weapons and knowledge but not of interspecies communication. As the post-flood society develops, humans are increasingly absorbed into the collective as equals and eventually become part of hybrid bioforms themselves.

Through most of the series, it seems that the different groups of people, animals, and Crakers share little frame of reference materially or culturally. The MaddAddam members debate epigenetics at breakfast one day, arguing over how much of Craker behavior is inherited and how much is cultural. To them, the Crakers seem interesting only as genetic experiments performed by Crake; they are obviously inferior to the humans, who can only present a colonialist-style danger to the Crakers. One MaddAddamite, Manatee, declares that the inferiority is obvious: "Well, we came up with Beethoven ... and, you know, the major world religions, and whatnot. Fat chance of anything like that with this bunch" (*MaddAddam* 140). Jimmy similarly worries that the Crakers would be "sitting ducks" without his protection, and indeed, their lack of understanding is a danger to them. Toby and Ren capture Painballers and tie them to a tree at the end of *The Year of the Flood*, but in the last book of the series the Crakers set them loose (5). Having no understanding of violence, the Crakers also do not fear the potentially dangerous transgenic species that have escaped from the compounds, including the bobkittens and wolvogs (*Oryx* 107–8). The greatest danger throughout the series comes from the pigoons, which are giant, dangerous pigs genetically engineered (largely by Jimmy's father) to grow human tissue (22–24). Possessing human brain tissue, the pigoons are capable of outsmarting humans and, it seems, eating them (55–56). They present problems in all three books, trapping and threatening Jimmy in the abandoned Paradice Dome, surrounding Toby's hiding place at the spa, and raiding the gardens at the AnooYoo spa and of the MaddAddamites (*Year* 18). The human survivors and Crakers are surrounded on all sides by danger, and their chances of lasting seem slim.

The God's Gardeners' prohibitions against harming animals (their spiritual equals), the MaddAddamites' tendency to intellectualize, and the Crakers' misunderstandings provide little chance against the dangers of the environment. However, in combination, the remainders of their practices—the junk—combine to open the possibility of interspecies solidarity. Previously unknown abilities of the Crakers open this possibility. When Toby performs the ritual to contact Pilar, Blackbeard seems to have the magical ability to understand, and while Toby and Zeb doubt that Blackbeard actually sees Pilar in the pigoon's body, they become a bit less afraid of the pigoons. Shortly after, Blackbeard announces that the pigoons are coming to talk to the humans: "They! Come! Come ... The Pig Ones. Very many!" (*MaddAddam* 266). The pigoons come to them because the Painballers have killed one of their young, and the pigoons rather than the humans have recognized the common threat of the Painballers. Through singing, the Crakers seem to be able to communicate with the pigoons, and Blackbeard provides the translation (266–68). Blackbeard facilitates an alliance, and together the pigoons and humans attack and capture the Painballers (losing Jimmy and Adam One in the process) (362–64). The Crakers, with a special, genetic connection to other species impossible even for the ecologically minded God's Gardeners, make possible the alliance between humans and pigoons, and so the leftovers dispose of the most pressing threat to their survival.

But what should be done with the Painballers? Through this question, the interspecies allies face a problem: would an act of collective violence (executing the Painballers) be acceptable in protecting themselves? The answer, as it turns out, is yes, and this decision is made through a vote with only Lotis Blue (a member of MaddAddam) voting to spare their lives. The novels have made clear that the experiences of the Painballers have so damaged them as to make them violent and threatening forever. Scholars have commented on this execution and whether or not it indicates that once again the survivors will develop hierarchical and violent cultures that will damage Earth (Heise). What's more interesting to me here is how they handle it and how the act of collective violence paves the way for the disappearance of the human law that requires such an execution. The pigoons get a vote in the process, but they make their decision quickly—the Painballers must die for the harm they did to the pigoons' young—and disappear. The humans debate and vote, using Jimmy's Red Sox hat (the series' chief ritual object) to collect the votes. After voting that they must execute the Painballers, Zeb, Toby, and others take them to the beach and kill and bury them. The Crakers and pigoons are kept out of the process, and it's tempting to read this as antidemocratic. It may be, but this act of collective violence does not serve to confirm human power nor that the pacifist tendencies of the God's Gardeners have fallen away. Toby remains uncomfortable with the execution, for example. Significantly, after the execution of the Painballers, the narrative shifts toward the disappearance of the current state of humanity. Ren, Amanda, and a MaddAddamite named Swift Fox are all pregnant but with half-Craker babies. It's not certain whether humans and Crakers can produce viable offspring (*MaddAddam* 206), but the narrative shifts, and Blackbeard takes over the telling, narrating the birth of human-Craker hybrids, the disappearance of Zeb, and the death and/or apotheosis of Toby. The final act of the humans has been to eliminate as best they can the threatening remainder of the society they had been part of. The horrifying entertainment and privatized justice system produced the Painballers, and after their elimination, humanity fades away.

Conclusion: An Uncertain Reboot

By the end of *MaddAddam*, the Crakers have taken over the narrative in a slowly recovering natural landscape. Deer and bears reappear; Ren, Amanda, and Swift Fox have babies (*MaddAddam* 379); and the Craker-human society makes peace with the pigoons. Some of the Crakers join some of the humans in a mediation group (377–78). Increasingly, the humans and Crakers blend biologically, socially, and culturally, but the Craker narratives increasingly dominate. In the end, while nothing is certainly settled—indeed, there are signs that other humans may be present, and they may be dangerous (388)—the

Crakers lead a new utopian public characterized by the accretion and recombination of things and ideas. In honor of their fallen heroes, they build statues out of junk (jar lids, mops, and so on) of Jimmy and Adam One (376) just as Ren names her child Jimadam after the same two, and Amanda names hers Pilaren, after Pilar and Ren (380–81). Jimmy's hat remains, as do all the stories Jimmy and Toby had told. At the end, Blackbeard urges the Crakers to learn to write, to make copies of his book, and to preserve the stories so they might circulate among the Crakers for years to come (387). Nothing is settled, but all absolutist ideas—whether capitalist, scientific, or Gardener—have been cut off. The loss is immense, and all the characters feel it. The pain of the corporate system continues. But the novels seem to suggest that meaningful recombinations can be created out of the system's leftovers. The rituals and stories of the Crakers extend humanist values in opposition to purely economic logics.

Like the other novels I examine in this book, the *MaddAddam* series features a radical intervention. Just as aliens intervene in Sagan, God in *Left Behind*, and planetary emigration in *Earthseed*, a plague puts an end to most of humanity, offering an opportunity for a reboot and a new humanity. The world, however, is not new; while nature seems in recovery, the signs of the old, destructive system stay. *MaddAddam* announces neither absolute despair nor Pollyannaish hope. Instead, it contrasts the limitations and damages of various fundamentalisms (capitalist, technoscientific, religious) with the possibilities of partiality and combination. Partial practice, the series seems to suggest, can enable the kind of healthy self-doubt that allows diverse people (even diverse species) to survive and thrive together. Totally fresh starts, the series seems to suggest, do not exist; trauma and trash haunt forever. But there is hope in a recovery of body, mind, and soul.

CHAPTER 5

"The World at an Angle"
Islam and the Hope of the Arab Spring in G. Willow Wilson's *Alif the Unseen*

The prologue ("Chapter Zero") of G. Willow Wilson's 2012 novel, *Alif the Unseen*, dramatizes the potentials and dangers of power. Reza, a medieval Persian scholar, has magically imprisoned a jinn and forced it to tell him the secret stories of the jinn so that he might gain power from them: "I will assign each element of each story a number . . . and in doing so create a code that determines their quantitative relationship to one another. I will gain power over them—" (*Alif* 7). The jinn mocks Reza, warning that any power contained within the stories is forbidden: "*Man was exiled from the Garden for eating a single fruit, and now you propose to uproot the whole tree without the angels noticing. You're an old fool, and the Deceiver whispers in your ear*" (6, emphasis in original). Written during the Arab Spring, *Alif the Unseen* offers hope: the power of the unseen can topple repressive regimes and elevate everyday, powerless people like Reza so high that they might have the whole world. At the same time, no one can truly control the power of the unseen. The novel also contains a warning to the Arab Spring: the possibility of equally repressive power accompanies the inherent good of toppling the corrupt, repressive regimes of the Middle East and North Africa.

Instead, through the conversion of the protagonist, a dissident hacker named Alif, the novel argues for an Islamic ethics of reverence; this reverence levels all social, political, economic, and religious distinctions in the oneness of God's creation. New technologies like social media and the internet may offer the power of anonymity, but the novel suggests that those technologies better serve to render all people "seen." For the novel, equality among all peoples is part of the oneness of God's creation, and reverence for that creation provides a necessary prerequisite to genuine democracy. By contrasting the "seen" and the "unseen," the novel hopes that counterpublics hidden by repression can move into and restructure the "seen" toward democracy.

It's become cliché to repeat that no governments, diplomats, or academics expected the Arab Spring. It was a series of protests, uprisings, and revolutions that began in Tunisia and Egypt in 2011 and led to the overthrow of several long-standing dictatorial regimes in the Middle East and North Africa. While disagreement abounds about the causes and progression of the protest movements (especially given some disappointing setbacks across the region), scholars and participants tend to agree on a few of the causes and hopes of the transnational movement. First, the region experienced a massive population bulge, wherein up to 30 percent of people in the region were under twenty-five. Second, due to rapid urbanization and uneven integration in a Western-dominated global economy, these youths experienced devastating unemployment. Third, thanks to the internet, smartphones, and other new media technologies, young people experienced a wider variety of social contact, which resulted in dramatic cultural differences with their parents: by and large, they were better educated, more inclined toward democratic models of authority, and much more likely to be secular. The rallying cry for these youths was *karama!*—dignity—and their demands centered around employment, basic freedoms, and protections from police.[1]

Alif the Unseen speaks both to the hopes of the Arab Spring and a global hope in the democratic potentials of digital communication technologies. The novel hardly offers a complete and accurate picture of the Arab Spring, but it does explore how Islam might be used to theorize the role of the internet in the uprisings. In response to the Arab Spring, *Alif the Unseen* imagines a new public that flattens distinctions of class, race, and religion through an Islamic version of secularism. Imagining Islamic versions of secularism is hardly unprecedented in literature by Muslim writers in the United States. In a 2014 article titled "The Postsecular Turn and Muslim American Literature," Danielle Haque reads Mohja Kahf's 2006 novel, *The Girl in the Tangerine Scarf*, as showing how Islamic practice potentially revives the promise of an inclusive secularism by providing a universalizing alternative to the default Protestantism of American secularism. Arguing against some literary scholarship that she says reduces postsecularism to weakened spiritual liberalism, Haque theorizes religion not as an identity category or regulatory regime, but as universalizing practice.[2] For Muslim writers in the United States, she argues, Islam provides the basis for a revived secularism that opens the dream of justice and representation for all. According to this theory, Muslim writers do not merely defend the legitimacy of American Muslims; they redefine what's possible and who's welcome in the public sphere.

Whereas *Contact* and *Left Behind* imagine intervention by God or gods, and *Earthseed* and *MaddAddam* imagine radical actions as the bases of radically new publics, *Alif the Unseen* imagines no particular divine or disastrous intervention. Instead, the novel suggests that new models of publics can be built on recognition of the equality of all beings written into creation. Despite the novel's fantasy elements, its Islamic secularism imagines a democracy based on a radical theology of equality. This democracy directly opposes the dictatorial governments of the Middle East and North Africa. Implicitly, the novel's democratic public also rejects the "freedom" of global neoliberalism, which ruthlessly economizes labor and fragments groups into narrow, competing interests.

In *Alif the Unseen*, Wilson, an American writer and adult convert to Islam, uses Islam to provide a theological basis for horizontal relations among all people before God.[3] In the context of the Arab Spring, the novel hopes for new models of horizontally organized publics open to equal participation by all within and across the nations of the Middle East and North Africa. The social dream of *Alif the Unseen* rests on two elements: first, conversion, where the characters reaffirm Islam and convert to a version of Islamic piety that acknowledges the equality of all people and jinn before God. This definition of conversion renders all earthly authority temporary and demands a horizontal, secular public based on inclusive cooperation. Second, the conversion from unjust to just and from amorality to piety comes through a religious recognition of infinite possibilities. The jinn, demons, and strange relations of space that Alif experiences throughout the novel require him to recognize that God's creation offers possibilities hitherto unimaginable. To explicate the role of Islam in the utopia that *Alif the Unseen* hopes for, I consider how the novel presents repressive structures and explores alternatives to them. While the novel presents no alternative as perfect, it ends with precarious hope for an Islamic ethics that will convert vertical, dictatorial power to horizontal democracy, encompassing the diverse people in the region.

I start by showing how the novel presents the problem of repression in the fictional emirate in which the main characters live. Using imprisonment, torture, and a well-funded surveillance apparatus, "State" maintains control over a city fragmented by racial and economic disparities. I then show how hackers like Alif thwart State's security apparatuses to create an online counterpublic that allows the crossing of geographic, racial, class, and political boundaries. This counterpublic, however, relies on anonymity, and while it welcomes diversity, it also relies on people like Alif, who have no stable moral or political commitments. The novel offers solutions: a new model of "public" resting on reverence for God, and a politics of seeing not merely unseen beings created by God, but all people normally hidden in the repressive society. Piety, it argues, rejects pedantry and absolutism, recognizing instead the equality of all. The novel hopes for a new public wherein the diverse people of the emirate and beyond "see" each other. I end this chapter with a consideration of the novel's hope that universalizing Islam can provide the basis for a revolution that—while dangerous—moves toward justice and equality among diverse peoples.

Seen and Unseen

Alif the Unseen takes place in a fictional city-state emirate on the Arabian Peninsula located between the Arabian Desert's Empty Quarter and the Persian Gulf. The royal family dominates a highly stratified society and polices it with a highly efficient security apparatus. The emirate is split between the rich made wealthy by oil and the diverse working class of laborers and servants (largely migrants from North Africa and South Asia). The geography of the city (shown in a map at the start of the book) embodies this split: there is the Old Quarter, the New Quarter, and the working-class slums between them. Alif, the son of a wealthy Arab man and his South Asian second wife, resides in a working-class neighborhood and makes his living as a highly effective hacker. An opportunist, Alif works for various dissidents across the Middle East and North Africa who seek anonymity from state surveillance; they range from Islamists to pornographers. Heartbroken when his wealthy Arab girlfriend and fellow hacker, Intisar, enters into an arranged marriage, Alif invents a program he calls Tin Sari to hide his online presence from Intisar. Tin Sari is so shockingly effective that it seems almost magical and dangles before Alif the possibility of an incredibly powerful new variety of computer programming that would render obsolete all state surveillance operations. This possibility becomes all the more tantalizing when Alif receives an ancient book from Intisar called the *Alf Yeom—Thousand and One Days*—which seems to contain the secrets of the jinn.

Before he can pursue these secrets, Alif has to run from state security with the help of his next-door neighbor, a devout, working-class woman named Dina; a terrifying, amoral jinn called Vikram the Vampire; a white American convert to Islam (referred to simply as "the convert"); and Sheikh Bilal of Al-Basheera, an ancient, celebrated mosque in the Old Quarter. Moving around the city between unseen jinn spaces, the university, and the mosque, Alif and the others research the *Alf Yeom*. Sheltering from State's lead hacker and Intisar's fiancé, Abbas the Hand, in the mosque, Alif attempts to use the *Alf Yeom* to create a new, metaphor-based computer programming structure, resulting in him melting Sheikh Bilal's computer and state security forces breaking into the mosque and taking him prisoner. For months, Alif endures torture in prison before a hacker and member of the royal family called NewQuarter01 frees him and Sheikh Bilal from prison. Escaping, they stumble upon the unseen jinn city of Irem, where Dina and the convert have been hiding with the *Alf Yeom*. Enlisting the help of jinn friends of Vikram, Alif, Dina, and NewQuarter return to the emirate, where a full-scale revolution has begun. After Alif and Dina defeat the Hand and his demonic allies, the novel ends with the revolution in progress and Alif returning home to marry Dina. Abandoning his quest for the powerful new jinn-driven computer programming language,

Alif steps back to allow the motley crowd of the revolution to work out their new public arrangements without the ultrapowerful tools of the unseen. This somewhat incomplete ending (the revolution in progress and Alif declining to lead it) warns against using social technologies to establish new hierarchies; instead, the end elevates the heteroglossic crowd of Arab Spring protestors.

A dual geography characterizes the unnamed emirate where Alif and his friends live. On the one hand, economic and national divisions structure the seen physical geography of the city, and state powers surveil the public through ideological, economic, and repressive means. On the other, unseen online citizens within and outside the emirate participate in a digital counterpublic; the hackers and dissidents online also experience state repression, but they have a fighting chance to thwart it through computer code. The physical public of the emirate maintains the hierarchies of power that allow the royal family and government to exploit the population. In the book's map of the emirate, to the east lies the Persian Gulf, to the north and south the Arabian Desert, and to the west the desert's famous Empty Quarter. The emirate (a small city) is similarly divided in four. On the north side lies the Old Quarter, where the rich live in ancient houses and the celebrated Al-Basheera mosque and Al-Basheera University are located. On the south side is the New Quarter, a place of Western businesses and skyscrapers. A large set of working-class neighborhoods, home to poor people and multinational migrants, sits between the two. Additionally, to the west lies the state prison on the edge of the Empty Quarter, and far to the north lies the "place of trash," the city's garbage dump. Alif's friend Abdullah jokes that the division of the city is economic: "old money, new money, and no money" (*Alif* 96). The city's geography allows State to keep the emirate's working-class population away from the centers of power.

The geographical division maintains racial and national hierarchies as well. Alif embodies this division. He lives in a diverse working-class neighborhood called Baqara District. Alif's father, a wealthy Arab businessman, took Alif's mother, an Indian woman who arrived at the emirate with other migrants looking for work, as an "adored, illicit second wife" (55). Alif has little relationship with his father, and his father's first wife and his own half siblings have little to do with him. As a man with an Arab and Indian background, Alif not only embarrasses his father's first family, but experiences limitations in his marriage and job prospects: "A problematic son with dark-skinned pagan blood in his lineage, the product of a union unsanctioned by his grandparents, impossible to wedge into good society. A daughter would have been preferable. If she was pretty and well-mannered, a daughter could marry up; a son could not" (55). Earlier, Alif muses that "Indian and Arab blood had merged pleasantly on his face . . . pleasant enough, but he would never pass for full-blooded Arab" (14). Dina, Alif's next-door neighbor, has Arab ancestry, but being from

Egypt she also experiences economic and racial discrimination. Alif's mother tells him to get a decent job and marry a nice Indian girl (12–14), but Alif has desires to move up within a system he knows to be repressive. He falls in love online with Intisar, a wealthy, well-educated Arab woman who lives in the Old Quarter. Even before he meets her, he can tell from their online interactions that "she obviously had a lineage" (26), and he admires her intellect and education (146–47). Intisar declares her love for Alif but refuses to marry him because of social pressure and her own refusal to live "in a two-room apartment in Baqara District, doing [her] own laundry" (214). Alif, Intisar, and most of the other characters—regardless of their political and social positions—have internalized the divided geography of the city.

State agents hunt Alif due to his relationship with Intisar and his possession of the *Alf Yeom* more than because of his hacking activities. When Alif must run, he experiences little solidarity from the citizens of the emirate. In a particularly telling passage, Alif runs from a State agent who shoots at him in the middle of a crowd. He ducks through a women's clothing store, a semiprivate space, where he is met with the violence of an invader (181). Shortly before, Alif had confronted "the rotund, officious belly of a doorman.... by way of a uniform, the man wore a pseudo-Ottoman robe and a feathered turban that gave him the air of a circus performer or a waiter at some touristy restaurant. The simulacrum was unbearable" (180). Frustrated at the doorman stopping him, Alif is angry at the fellow working-class resident of the emirate for acting on behalf of the wealthy. He shouts, "Is this your life, dressing up like a monkey for a bunch of rich fucks? . . . Do you think they're going to stop treating you like shit if you turn me in?" (180). Alif's shouting at the doorman highlights both the common interests of the working class in the hierarchical city and the distinct absence of solidarity. Alif's associates mostly exist online; stuck in the physical space of the city and cut off from his computer connection, Alif looks for and cannot find allies among the people he meets. For allies, he must turn to criminals, jinn, and finally to Al-Basheera. The mosque, once celebrated and powerful—the chief cleric, Sheikh Bilal, remembers a time before oil wealth when the mosque exercised influence over the royal family and the university—sits in the Old Quarter in disrepair (182–87). In a city characterized by geographic splits, the mosque's isolation most dramatically shows the structure of power: Islam practiced among rich and poor and across nations could provide a basis for interclass and international solidarity, but the mosque lies hidden away by the old rich.

The city physically reinforces the hierarchies of power that keep its citizens split and afraid. However, the unseen geography of the city holds hope: the city "sits at a crossroads between the earthly world and the Empty Quarter, the domain of ghouls and *effrit* [types of jinn] who can take the shape of beasts" (*Alif* 9). Due to his prowess with hacking and his new relationship with the jinn called Vikram the Vampire, Alif has access to two unseen worlds: the shadowy world of the jinn and the equally shadowy world of the internet. The digital counterpublics and undergrounds in which Alif has power and influence aren't free of state dominance or hierarchy, however; State has gotten steadily better at hacking and pursuing online dissidents (16). Like communicating with jinn, being unseen in the digital world carries power and danger. Through both unseen realms, Alif rethinks the geography of the city and sees possibilities for solidarity and the overthrow of state power. At the same time, Alif's nihilistic pragmatism threatens to contain any new possibility; without guiding principles, the power of computer code and of the jinn might be used to gain a similarly repressive power, thus leaving the hierarchical structure of the emirate fundamentally unchanged. Attempting to solve this problem, Alif finds inspiration from Dina, from Sheikh Bilal, and from the unseen world of the jinn.

Alif and his friends participate as citizens of an international counterpublic, but little of the novel features Alif's online interactions. Instead, *Alif the Unseen* explores the digital world so important to the Arab Spring through the metaphor of the unseen jinn. Having jinn characters and a visit to the jinn city of Irem in the Empty Quarter allows the novel to explore the pitfalls and potentials of digital counterpublics and multinational revolutions organized in part online. The unseen world of jinn reorients the geography of the emirate, making it possible (albeit confusing) to move in ways that thwart the strict class and racial separations that alienate the emirate's people from each other. Vikram explains to Alif, "My race is older than you—we think about the world differently, and *we inhabit it at an angle*" (*Alif* 107, emphasis added). Similarly, Vikram characterizes the Empty Quarter where many jinn live as a "world turned sideways" (106). Alif experiences this alternative orientation firsthand when they visit the Immovable Alley, a jinn location whose entrance moves: "the alley is stationary. That's the whole point. The world moves around it. So entrances and exits can pop up anywhere" (154). Alif and Vikram enter the Immovable Alley in one place in the city, but when they exit, Alif finds himself far to the north in the place of trash (177). Similarly, Alif; his royal hacker friend, NewQuarter01; and Sheikh Bilal enter the jinn world of the Empty Quarter when a mirage of a pond turns into an actual pond; diving in, they emerge in the jinn world (301–7). That world provides an alternative geography to that of the emirate; rather than move through the hierarchical spaces of the city, jinn geography suggests open possibility, wherein one can take a shortcut and emerge in new spaces. Bewildered, Alif moves through the hierarchical spaces of the city in less limiting ways, just as his online persona allows him to oppose the State regime, court the wealthy Intisar, work for people in other countries, and befriend NewQuarter01, a royal prince.

In the novel, digital counterpublics offer a model of democracy for those excluded from power by the governments of the Middle East and North Africa. Just as the jinn inhabit the world at an angle and experience different geographies than humans do, the citizens of the digital counterpublics defy hierarchical geography and government repression. However, the novel presents the power of the unseen (jinn and digital technologies) with ambivalence. The narrative repeatedly draws a distinction between amoral, self-centered resistance, on the one hand, and solidarity, on the other. By contrasting the characters of Abbas the Hand, Alif, and Vikram, the novel shows that knowledge of the unseen can potentially enable democracy or further exploitation. Digital counterpublics raise new problems: while they're certainly oppositional rhetorically, moving them to democratic revolution presents big challenges.

The novel makes the parallel between Alif's amorality and that of the jinn. A skilled hacker, Alif works without regard to the morality or positions of his clients. Similarly, when the Arab Spring begins in Egypt, many of Alif's clients experience arrest and harassment, and Alif cuts his ties to them to protect himself: "When the violence spilled off the Internet and into the streets, making the broad avenues of Tahrir Square a killing field, Alif dumped his Egyptian clientele without ceremony. . . . If the name Alif was leaked to an ambitious State security official, *a coterie of bloggers, pornographers, Islamists, and activists from Palestine to Pakistan would be put at risk*" (*Alif* 17, emphasis added). Without taking any particular position beyond his own immediate interests, Alif has sold his services to a spectrum of resistance clients across the Middle East and North Africa. Later, he tells Dina when she observes that he has worked for Islamists: "I've also helped the Communists. And the feminists. I'll help anybody with a computer and a grudge" (233). Vikram links Alif's amorality to a general statement about jinn: "there are many kinds of jinn . . . as there are many kinds of *banu adam* [children of mud, or humans]. Some good, like Sakina, some less good, like me. Most are scuttling moral cowards, like you" (170). Like the jinn, digital counterpublics are amoral. They do not lead necessarily to any one political structure.

The novel highlights the potential danger of computer code when Alif realizes he can make a new computer language out of metaphors found in the *Alf Yeom*. This language could potentially contain thousands of layers of meaning like, according to Sheikh Bilal, the Qur'an (*Alif* 192–93). The novel examines this problem through the power of metaphor, which the characters find simultaneously enticing and dangerous. Near the opening of the novel, together on the rooftop of their families' duplex in Baqara District, Alif and Dina discuss the 1996 fantasy novel *The Golden Compass* by Phillip Pullman. *The Golden Compass* narrates a parallel universe wherein human souls exist outside of bodies in the form of shape-shifting companions to their people (much like jinn). Returning the book to Alif, Dina asserts, "This book . . . is full of pagan images. It's dangerous" (11). When Alif answers that she is ignorant and does not understand that the images are metaphors, Dina responds, "Metaphors are dangerous. Calling something by a false name changes it, and metaphor is just a fancy way of calling something by a false name" (11). This is a bold statement in a novel structured by the metaphor of unseen jinn standing in for a motley, transnational, online counterpublic; the novel nonetheless takes Dina's statement seriously throughout by exploring the power of "false names" like the online handle Alif. Later in the novel, both Alif and the Hand try unsuccessfully to use metaphor to create a powerful new programming language.

False names, unseenness, and metaphor offer Alif and other dissidents across the Middle East and North Africa the ability to converse outside the control of the State censors. As Alif and Vikram try to figure out why Intisar sent the *Alf Yeom* to Alif, Vikram suggests that Intisar is protecting the book from destruction by the censors. Alif dismisses this idea: "The censors don't bother with fantasy books, especially old ones. They can't understand them. . . . They'd die if they knew what *The Chronicles of Narnia* were really about" (*Alif* 105). Just as fantasy literature allows for honest discussion under repressive regimes, so do the online handles or false names used by Alif and his friends. "Alif," the first letter of the Arabic alphabet, is written with a single stroke of the pen as a vertical line. Alif thinks of this as representing the secrecy that separates his physical existence from his online persona: "He had spent so much time cloaked behind his screen name, a mere letter of the alphabet, that he no longer thought of himself as anything but an alif—a straight line, a wall. His given name fell flat in his ears now. The act of concealment had become more powerful than what it concealed" (10). Alif and his friends see this concealment, this unseenness, as the prerequisite for genuine citizenship. As Abdullah tells Dina, "now that you pious brothers and sisters haven taken over half the planet, the Internet is the only place left to have a worthwhile conversation" (75). Prior to the protests and revolutions of the Arab Spring, online anonymity made possible free exchanges. Concealment online is a political act that lends power to individuals beyond their own physical existence or talents. It pokes religious and state authorities in the eye while the concealed sit invisibly among everyone else.

The unseenness allowed by internet handles provides the basis of a genuine public uncontrolled by censors. The novel warns, however, that the power of the unseen can serve selfish interests as much as it can serve genuine democratic solidarities. When Intisar breaks off her relationship with Alif and asks that he "make it so [she] never [sees his] name again" (*Alif* 23), he designs a computer program called Tin Sari that will prevent her from encountering him online again. Doing so requires the computer program to recognize Intisar no matter what email address or handle she uses—essentially, to recognize her "linguistic DNA" (44) and hide Alif from her in any form. Tin Sari succeeds in ways Alif never expected; the program grows and appears to develop intuitive abilities of its own. Abdullah observes, "If what you're saying is true, you have discovered an entirely new way of getting computers to think. . . . you have endowed your little desktop machine with intuition" (47). Tin Sari holds both a potential and an incredible danger. Its growing ability holds out the promise for computer programs to develop new kinds of intelligence, to mimic "intuition," and thus to hold great power. The ability to recognize a person online, however, no matter their handle or IP address, promises immense power to government censors and other surveillance operations. Alif and his friends are terrified when they realize that the as yet unidentified government operative known as the Hand digitally invades their systems, evidently looking to steal and use Tin Sari (57). Tin Sari reveals a central problem with digital code: it serves power, and just as it can help dissidents like Alif thwart state power, it can also be used by the strong to oppress the weak.

As a wall, a person hiding behind a false name, Alif has some of the power of being unseen. The book compares this invisibility to the unique powers that jinn have over time and space to redefine the relations among people and places. Ultimately, through anonymity and the rapid mobilization made possible by digital communication, regimes like that of the emir face popular uprisings. The book celebrates this possibility, but it also sees in these technologies an amorality that potentially undercuts the principles of democratization. As Vikram says, most jinn are moral cowards like Alif, operating on practical self-interest instead of principle (*Alif* 170). To some degree, the jinn tend to operate under economized neoliberal logics. The novel goes further, however, suggesting that Alif's pursuit of computing power instead of acting in a public sphere of real people results from his manipulation by demonic forces. After being caught by State and interrogated by Abbas the Hand, Alif sits in the dark of an empty cell. A demonic jinn taunts him, encouraging him to turn in all of his dissident friends to Abbas. When Alif refuses, the demon deploys a nihilistic rhetoric of self-protection: "You really think the One who is birthing stars and eating up the bowels of dysenteric infants cares whether you live as a traitor or die as a martyr? You think any of this matters?" (273). The demon (whom Alif refers to as Farakhuaz after the name of the main character in the *Alf Yeom*) portrays an indifferent God and a world devoid of permanent good and evil. The demon encourages Alif to retreat into self-interest as he always has: "I'm only here to keep you safe. You think we've just met, but I've been with you all your life. I have been the little whispers in your veins, numbing you, keeping you between the walls of your room when the world seemed too big. I have been the ringing in your ears, waking you in the small hours of the night to remind you of your wretchedness. You are alone, and I am the only real partisan you have" (273). In the tradition of torturous interrogation, the demon presents itself as an ally helping Alif protect himself not merely from an intimidatingly large world but from Alif's own limitations. The demon's argument appeals to nihilistic self-interest and encourages Alif to deploy his knowledges for the sake of his own power. To protect the dissidents on principle would be to sacrifice himself for a meaningless solidarity. Alif rejects the argument, and the jinn leaves, but Alif says aloud, "please don't let it be right" (274). Shortly afterward, Alif is rescued by NewQuarter.

Alif's struggle between amoral self-interest and solidarity develops further in the contrasting approaches he and Abbas the Hand take toward the computer language hiding in the *Alf Yeom*. Alif experiences tremendous excitement at the possibility of creating a whole new computer language, but he does not pause to consider its use or potential drawbacks. Alif first realizes the computing potential hiding in the ancient *Alf Yeom* while he shelters in Al-Basheera mosque from the State security forces and their demonic allies outside. Using Sheikh Bilal's out-of-date Toshiba laptop, Alif tries to design a new operating system based on the metaphors of the *Alf Yeom*; he bases the new computing language on the multiple interactions among literal and metaphorical meanings, which allow huge amounts of information to be embedded into relatively small amounts of code. He explains to Sheikh Bilal, "A quantum computer would theoretically perform data functions using ions—which are difficult to get, control, and manipulate . . . but you could do almost the same thing if you could get a normal silicon-based computer to think in metaphors. . . . Metaphors: knowledge existing in several states simultaneously and without contradiction" (*Alif* 228). Sheikh Bilal warns Alif that the dynamic nature of the *Alf Yeom* makes it impossible to use the book in such a way: "knowledge must be fixed in some way if it is to be preserved. . . . that's why the Quran isn't meant to be altered" (229). Alif believes he can "translate the strings of metaphor into strings of commands." For Alif, the possibilities are magical like alchemy: "the dervishes saw the Philosopher's Stone, but I see code" (229). Sheikh Bilal gives one final warning: "I would be very careful. . . . the greatest triumph of Shaytan is the illusion that you are in control. He lurks on the forking paths, lying in wait for those who become overconfident or lose their way" (230). Sheikh Bilal and Alif argue about metaphor and coding through metaphors. For Alif, the possibility of code is magical and divine yet amoral. Sheikh Bilal reframes the argument morally: to talk about computing knowledge is to talk about power beyond the everyday and human, and so it is a question of God and Shaytan, of good and evil.

As Alif works, he experiences a hallucination in which he builds a tower with Princess Farakhuaz, the protagonist of the *Alf Yeom*, urging him on. The hallucination reveals both the moral stakes and the foolishness of harnessing the power of the unseen, as the code structure he builds becomes unstable. Farakhuaz tells him: "*You're building a tower. . . . Up and up and up, and at the very top I am waiting. All things are possible at the top. All things take whatever form they like. They will call you a transgressor but I will call you free"* (*Alif* 236, emphasis in original). Farakhuaz promises that the program hiding in the *Alf Yeom* holds power, a great height from which all things are visible and possible. At her urging, Alif uses the program to hack the Hand's systems in the State security mainframe. Alif sees the incredible power of the Hand's hacking programs and begins using the *Alf Yeom* code to attack them. Alif's own system falls apart, and he cannot stabilize it. He then realizes that the tower structure cannot be stable, and he sees its collapse as a metaphor for his own moral cowardice: "he did not hide because he was better, he hid because he was afraid" (240). Despite Farakhuaz's later pronouncement to Alif in prison—"a few minutes more and you would have pierced the veil of heaven" (253)—Alif sees that a tower that elevates one person above others is inherently unstable and the product of the evil thinking of demons like Farakhuaz. He answers, "*The information had no integrity, no guiding principle.* The whole project was collapsing when the computer fused" (253, emphasis added). The code, Alif suggests, rests on shifting meanings and therefore cannot be stable. Metaphorically, however, Alif also suggests that amoral self-interest cannot build a stable structure; some principle must be in place. As if to emphasize the need for something permanent, Alif invokes God: "it occurred to him to recite the *shahada* ['there is no God but Allah, and Mohammad is his prophet']. The thing began to shriek. Encouraged, Alif bellowed every talismanic holy verse he knew, testifying to the oneness of God, the indivisibility of His nature, the perfidy of Satan" (254). In invoking the oneness of God, Alif begins to discover the guiding, foundational principle that will help him look away from tower building and toward pious solidarity.

While Alif begins to see the error of seeking power through the unseen (jinn or digital), Abbas the Hand argues that the inherent amorality of such power invites its use to exploit and repress others. Like Farakhuaz, Abbas wishes only to build a tower from which he can stand above others. Abbas argues against principles of equality and for self-rewarding dominance using some sexually violent metaphors:

> We all get off on the same thing, that's the problem. . . . You don't really care about revolution. I don't really care about the State. What gets us hard is the code itself. I created what I believed to be the most beautiful suite of security programs ever made, a continuation of my own flesh, in some way. I thought that was winning. It certainly helped me track down a lot of your friends. . . . And then you stole the greatest idea I'd ever had, and used it to destroy my life's work. (*Alif* 257)

Alif responds simply, "I'm better than you" (258).

For Abbas, mastery over computing serves no particular interest beyond his own desire to dominate others. Alif thinks at one point that Abbas has the "look of a rapist" (*Alif* 268). Abbas extends his will to dominate into an argument against the democratic politics he believes Alif hypocritically represents: "Tell me what you honestly envision for the City. A democracy? Plato's Republic? You've imbibed too much western propaganda. Give the citizens of our fair seaport a real vote and they'll do one of three things: vote for their own tribe, vote for the Islamists, or vote for whoever paid them the most money" (258). Abbas's cynicism about democracy grows out of his own desire to dominate, and for this reason he cannot believe that using the *Alf Yeom* isn't possible. When Alif argues for freedom of speech, Abbas responds dismissively: "what naïve garbage. People don't want freedom anymore—even those to whom freedom is a kind of religion are afraid of it. . . . They are so terrified by their own power they will vote to have it taken out of their hands. Look at America. Look at the sharia states. . . . the world is returning to its natural state, the rule of the weak by the strong" (268). For Abbas, dominance of the many by the few is the natural state of the world, and the split geography of the city and the digital towers merely embodies that natural state. To "pierce the veil of heaven" is a goal to be pursued by the strong, who naturally deserve to be closer to the power of the unseen and even to God.

Within Abbas's speech hides the absence of equality and, more significantly for the novel, the absence of piety. While Abbas has allies among the unseen— indeed, he manages to visit the Immovable Alley without any jinn guide (*Alif* 170)—he does not invoke God in his conversation with Alif. His arguments remain within the mundane, seen world, invoking everyday political interests and banal matters of state. Alif, on the other hand, invokes God, oneness, and principle as he fights the Farakhuaz demon, defends his relationship with Intisar to Abbas, and finally speaks of Abbas's tyranny and the hope for freedom. In this conversation (after a somewhat circuitous journey), the novel begins to arrive at its destination: the power of the unseen isn't the power to hide in a basement or dominate from a tower. Moral use of the power of the unseen requires a new geography, one that reconfigures social relations. National, class, and geographical separations do not apply online, and so online communication allows for expanded public interaction.

Prior to the revolution, Alif, like many of the jinn, suffers from the problem Vikram identifies: he is a coward who works merely in his own self-interest while announcing democratic commitments. This leaves an opening for someone like Abbas the Hand to use the power of digital technology to restore what he calls the world's "natural state, the rule of the weak by the strong." The book suggests that the new power of the digital can be used for good, but only through an Islamic reverence and recognition of all others as equal parts of God's creation. Whether digital or jinn-driven, new powers can eliminate geographic, class, and political divisions and enable people to see the world at a new angle. This is only possible, however, through a politics of seeing and through the recognition and respect for the unseen: the jinn, the politically repressed, and the multinational and multiracial working-class power that make the economy of the oil state run.

On Reverence and Being Seen

For most of the novel, Alif hides behind a fake name and, like Abbas the Hand, seeks the power of the unseen. Through Alif's relationship to Dina and references to the Qur'an throughout, Wilson suggests a different path: an Islamic secularism based on reverence for the unseen and participation in the seen. The novel roots this politics of the seen in the Qur'an. Along with representing a wall that Alif hides behind, alif, the first letter of the Arabic alphabet, is also recorded at the beginning of the second and longest surah of the Qur'an: Al-Baqara (The Cow). Alif defends his use of the letter as a handle to Dina based on its presence at the opening of surah 2: "'*Alif, lam, mim.*' He drew the letters in the air with his finger. 'One-digit symbol substitutions: God, Gabriel, the Prophet. I named myself after the first line of code ever written'" (*Alif* 77).[4] Dina and the novel generally do not put much stock in Alif's comparing himself with the code letter for God, but his alif functions as the first reference to surah 2. The more important reference comes from the name of the area in which Alif and Dina live, Baqara District. The narrator gives a short history of their neighborhood: "named for the cattle market to which it had once played host, Baqara District was all imported labor from India, Bangladesh, the Philippines, and the lesser Arab countries of North Africa" (32). Baqara District features a multinational, racially diverse group of workers who arrived in the emirate looking for work.

Beyond the Arabic word "baqara," the diversity of the district draws a strong link to surah 2. According to tradition, Mohammad delivered surah 2 to a growing Muslim community in Medina (in exile from Mecca). Whereas the early surahs revealed at Mecca are short and poetic, having largely to do with the relations among people, faith, and God, the later surahs revealed at Medina tend to be longer and contain more ideas and regulations to help govern the growing Muslim community. Al-Baqara is the longest of these and contains many rules to help the growing number of diverse adherents live together. Al-Baqara, in other words, provides some of the most important Islamic bases for a community. It attempts to govern and sanctify to God a growing community and to understand the appropriately godly relationships among diverse people. Instead of seeing the world at an angle, like the jinn, or from a tower, like God, surah 2 demands that the faithful see the world horizontally and understand relations among all as the interaction between the order of God and the everyday. By calling the diverse group of working-class people sandwiched between the wealthy New and Old Quarters "Baqara," the novel suggests that relations growing out of the reconfigured geographies of the unseen should be informed by the Qur'anic principles for interrelationship. Further, the diversity of Baqara District already makes it resemble a Qur'anic community.

The power of the unseen (jinn or digital) allows for the breaking of hierarchical power; as Abdullah argues, "the Internet is the only place left to have a worthwhile conversation" (*Alif* 75). However, while the unseen plays an important role in tearing down hierarchical power structures, the unseen must be accompanied by dedication to God. Alif undergoes a conversion from unseen amorality to seen piety largely through his experiences with Dina and Sheikh Bilal. Dina warns Alif against false names, but through veiling, she also provides a model for how to understand the relation of the self to the seen and unseen. Rather than an absolute division between public and private, Dina's wearing of the veil allows her to sanctify her actions while participating in both private and public relations. This is a new understanding of the seen and unseen that the novel slowly moves toward. Dina expresses discomfort with false names, particularly with Alif's use of a handle rather than his real name (77). Her decision to wear the veil is unusual among people in Baqara District, and she especially faces resistance from her parents, who believe it will be an obstacle to her employment and marriage. Alif recalls

> the day she announced, at the age of twelve, that she intended to veil her face. Her mother's tears and her father's angry retorts carried easily through the common wall of the duplex. For an upper-class Old Quarter girl like Intisar to veil was one thing; her silken, beaded cocoon was a mark of rank, not religion. But Dina was imported labor—a shabby Alexandrian, expected to become the barefaced, underpaid ornament to someone's office or nursery, perhaps even discreetly available to whomever was paying her salary. For her to declare herself sanctified, not by money but by God, looked like putting on airs . . . a saint was not profitable. (29–30)

Dina's declaration flies in the face of the expectations put upon her according to her national origin and class position. Veiling her face, Dina declares that her relationship to God and hence to everyone else is determined by faith rather than the hierarchies of the emirate.

Alif's conversion from amorality to piety begins with the recognition that Dina's "sanctification," her dedication to God, structures her relations with others. While Dina's veil appears at first to mark her unseenness, the novel draws an important distinction between sanctified veiling and amoral unseenness that will lead Alif and the others to reorient themselves toward others. The conversion begins slowly when, while hiding in Al-Basheera mosque, Alif cleans the floor and participates in daily prayers with Sheikh Bilal. At first, Alif does so mostly to thank Sheikh Bilal for sheltering him, but Alif's piety slowly builds. When the computer program he's building out of the *Alf*

Yeom collapses, Alif feels magically exhausted and overcome. He begs Dina for help: "It's so bright inside my head . . . help me, please. You're the only one who knows what to do." In response, Dina throws her veil over Alif's head so that he shares it with her and sees her face for the first time since they were children. He also sees the brightly colored silk fabric she has sewn inside her veil (*Alif* 244). This sharing of space inside the veil is both the beginning of their promise to marry each other and a moment in which Alif begins to understand sanctification: Dina is not unseen, but she has particular ideas about how to interact with others in a sanctified way. This includes holding back some private space but also participating in the world in a way that constantly declares an orientation toward God. Later, sitting in darkness in prison, Alif recalls Dina's veil as a place of shelter: "he wanted Dina, he wanted her consecrated darkness, so unlike this hostile absence of light" (250). Alone and terrified in the dark of his prison cell, Alif begins to draw a distinction between mere invisibility—the absence of light—and an invisibility in the service of God and others. After he is rescued from prison by NewQuarter, they crash in the desert while running away from prison guards. Alif, starving after days of not being fed, is about to eat food brought by NewQuarter, but he pauses first to pray, thanking God for deliverance. Sheikh Bilal recognizes the importance of this act, telling NewQuarter, "the boy has set down what is obviously the first plate of food he has seen in a long while in order to thank his Creator. There are few acts of piety more honest than that" (294). On a personal level, Alif's conversion into a pious Muslim is moving along.

This conversion transcends the personal and moves into the public when, after a visit to the jinn city of Irem in the Empty Quarter, Alif and NewQuarter return to the emirate to find a full-scale revolution in progress. While the characters comment on the importance of the online counterpublics to organizing this revolution, the narrator emphasizes two important things about the revolution: its dangerous lack of organization, on the one hand, and its diversity of language, nationality, and political positioning, on the other. NewQuarter and Alif both recognize their former hope for revolution and express fear over its course as they watch the riots unfold. Alif asks NewQuarter, "Is this it? Is this our revolution?" NewQuarter responds, "If it is, it's already scaring the shit out of me. . . . Where is everybody? Why are they stealing things? Is this really what happens when people can't get into their Facebook accounts? Where is our glorious coup?" (*Alif* 380). For Alif, NewQuarter, and the novel generally, revolution against the corrupt, authoritarian royal government terrifies while it tears apart all of the hierarchies that prop up the government: "A low roar issued from around the corner. Alif's eyes widened. A mass of protestors appeared, marching dozens deep across the breadth of the boulevard, holding signs and placards in Arabic, Urdu, English, Malay; there were women bareheaded and veiled, old men in the red armbands of the Communist Party, men with beards and robes" (380). Whereas the visible geography of the city had separated and kept hidden the power of the diverse people of the emirate, the revolution renders visible the formerly unseen people of Baqara District and the online counterpublics. "They're marching together . . . all the disaffected scum at once. I probably know a lot of these people," Alif observes. NewQuarter echoes, "We did this, *akh* [brother]. Computer geeks did this. We told these ruffians they could all have a voice, but they had to share the same virtual platform. And now that the virtual platform is gone—" (381). In real life, however, the revolution scares at the same time it offers hope; the three characters try to hide as they see security forces use tear gas and bullets to assault the crowd.

Like the unseen worlds of the jinn and the online counterpublics, the revolution proceeds amorally and with a lack of organized purpose. The novel argues that solidarity, not chaos or power, is the natural state of the world. NewQuarter worries over the crowd's lack of purpose: "It's like watching a half-melted ice cube—impossible to infer its original shape, or that of the puddle it will eventually become. . . . Revolutions only get names after it's clear who won" (*Alif* 397). When Abbas the Hand appears amid the chaos and confronts Alif, their conversation about power continues. Abbas argues that inequality and conflict are natural parts of human relations. He has no need to undermine the revolution: "I don't have to hurt them. I will set my little friends upon the crowd, and they will hurt themselves. Suspicions will grow, factions will arise, secularist and Islamist will discover they cannot cooperate, men will decide women are not their comrades. Someone will get bold and pull a knife. And that will be the end" (402). He declares his intention to continue using the *Alf Yeom* to increase his own power, arguing that dishonesty and power are natural things among computer programmers and his jinn allies: "what incentive does someone who is unseen have to keep his word? None. We are only honest because we must live in the light of day" (406). Alif, however, argues that dishonesty is a product of power rather than of nature: "it's because of people like you we have to go unseen to be honest. You've made truth impossible anywhere but in the dark, behind false names. . . . All the people you've chosen not to see out there are calling for your blood" (406).

Whereas Abbas the Hand argues that amorality and even evil are natural parts of power, Alif makes a countersuggestion: amoral counterpublics and the uncertain revolution are products of repressive power structures. That amorality provides an insufficient basis for stable power, let alone justice. This instability becomes a problem for Abbas when his demonic allies turn on him. Alif opens the *Alf Yeom* to show Abbas that two new stories have appeared at the end of the book: "The Fall of the Hand, or A Sad Case of Early Retirement" and "The Tale of Alif the Unseen." "I warned you . . . this book is tricky" Alif tells Abbas (*Alif* 411). The demons have turned on Abbas, and eventually he is exposed to the revolutionary crowd as the Hand, and they hang him in NewQuarter's apartment (426). In Abbas's attempts to wield the power of the unseen (both digital and jinn), he understood its potential but lacked understanding of its instability.

Near the end, the novel contrasts the unseen revolutionary counterpublic with the hope for a new public based on seenness, a horizontal power structure in which no one hides and revolution runs its course. Shortly before Abbas the Hand is abandoned to his treacherous demon allies, Abbas and Alif argue over Tin Sari, the software that had so accurately hidden Alif from Intisar by properly identifying her way of talking. Alif tells Abbas it worked because unlike the *Alf Yeom*, it did not rely on the power of the unseen. Abbas objects: "It shouldn't work. . . . No program can probe what is unseen in human hearts." Alif's answer is telling: "it works because it exposes the apparent. The words you use, how you use them, how you type them, when you send them. You can't hide those things behind a new name. The unseen is unseen. The apparent is inescapable" (*Alif* 418–19). Alif suggests that the "apparent"—that which is seen even in the digital realm of the mostly unseen—is key to recognizing people. The *Alf Yeom* continues to develop just as the counterpublic does. The hope of the revolution lies in abandoning attempts to harness the power of the unseen and instead to become seen, to join the motley crowd and recognize one's own equality within it.

At the very end of the book, Dina calls Alif by his real name, finally revealing it: Mohammad (*Alif* 428). It would be tempting to compare Alif to the prophet Mohammad; he does after all get to see some of the splendor of God in the form of the jinn city Irem, and he has (albeit not always deliberately) helped to reveal some of the unseen world. I argue, however, that Alif's name does less to elevate him to the status of prophet and more to establish him within the faceless crowd of the emerging revolutionary public. Mohammad is the name of Islam's holy Prophet; it is also among the most common names for men in the world, one that transcends class, race, nation, and even in some cases religion. Alif is not determined to reveal the designs of God; instead, he abandons that power, and in the last pages of the novel, he and Dina go home to talk to their parents about getting married (429–31). The revolution must be allowed to progress on its own. The diversity within the revolution is part of the grand diversity of God's creation of seen and unseen. Participation in an emergent secular public is based on recognition of the horizontal quality of that diversity. This is the moral center that the novel suggests: horizontal power, the visibility of all. Alif and Dina returning home doesn't qualify as a retreat, but as a reorientation: his mastery of the unseen is no longer needed by the revolution or himself.

Conclusion: Conversion and Transcendence

Alif has undergone a conversion that embodies the hope of the novel for the Arab Spring: from amorality to piety, from seeking power to participating in power, and from unseen to seen. *Alif the Unseen* places its hopes in the utopian possibility that faith in the oneness of God's creation can transform the power of the unseen into the seen. Whereas the digital counterpublic and the jinn have the power to reorient geographies, to destroy divisions, and to topple hierarchies, they also possess a counterrevolutionary amorality (seen post–Arab Spring in places like Egypt). The novel suggests that a properly understood Islamic faith renders all people equal and visible. When Alif, NewQuarter, and Sheikh Bilal meet an unnamed jinn in the Empty Quarter after escaping from a State prison, the jinn expresses contempt for the state of human religion, which he suggests is disappearing in a conversation with Alif: "Belief. . . . It doesn't mean the same thing it used to, not for you. You have unlearned the hidden half of the world." "But the world is crawling with religious fanatics. Surely belief is thriving." "Superstition is thriving. Pedantry is thriving. Sectarianism is thriving. Belief is dying out. . . . You are prepared to accept the irrational, but not the transcendent" (*Alif* 303). The jinn gives the novel's argument here: the hope for revolution cannot be based simply on religious rules or sectarian loyalties. The solution, in other words, is not Islam per se; the imposition of pedantic rules accomplishes little but simply reorienting a vertical power structure. A revolutionary public must believe in the unseen and make it visible in the same way that Alif is looking at the typically unseen jinn as they speak. Belief in possibility and in new geographies, the transcendence of all things that God has created—these are key. Contra Abbas's arguments, the hierarchical power structures of the Middle East and North Africa are not permanent. The possibility of speaking with jinn suggests otherwise: the unseen can be seen.

Alif the Unseen expresses hope for the Arab Spring, for newness, for transcendence, and for faith in the equal oneness of God's creation. It offers a new vision for a different orientation of the world. It's based in a version of Islamic secularism not characterized by pedantry or superstition, as the unnamed jinn says, but by reverence for the oneness of God, for the ability and willingness to see people and to interact, and for parts of the world not to be unseen. The Communists and the Islamists are on the same street in the hopeful and terrifying revolutionary marches. According to the novel's reading of the Qur'an, all must be seen and allowed to participate as equals. This religious belief offers the hope of an international, interreligious secularism. Through this postsecular public, the novel rejects the U.S. representation of global Islam as threatening to democracy. This move clearly criticizes the culture of the U.S. security state immediately after 9/11, which tended to depict a monolithic Islam hostile to Western democracy. Just as important, the novel rejects the naturalized logic of global neoliberalism. Like Butler's Earthseed novels, *Alif the Unseen* exposes the political structures of the emirate—and, by extension, all political arrangements—as impermanent and not necessarily natural. Combining Islamic oneness with secular ideas, the book hopes for an alternative globalization based on representation rather than capital.

CONCLUSION

Faith in the Future

All the public religions in the novels I have examined here contain religious fervor; all contain some counterbalancing doubt. In the previous chapter, I excavated the Islamic secularism undergirding *Alif the Unseen*'s technomagical hopes for the Arab Spring. Wilson's novel joins a wide literature imagining a revolutionary utopian future; the popularity of such utopias simultaneously obscures and testifies to the seizure of state power by right-wing movements in the United States, Great Britain, Poland, India, and elsewhere. Such seizures demand attention to the power of often ignored counterrevolutionary utopias like *Left Behind*. The slogan Make America Great Again, for example, hovers at the margins of secular and religious, oscillating between utopian and dystopian. Leading up to Donald Trump's election and during his presidency, the embrace of him by many prominent members of the New Christian Right caused more than a fair bit of consternation among liberal intellectuals from religious and secular perspectives.[1] How could a movement historically preoccupied with pietistic notions of sexual chastity, pious speech, and nuclear family stability embrace a thrice-married serial philanderer known for dishonest business behavior and unapologetic pridefulness? Asking and answering this question became somewhat of a hobby for a variety of cultural commentators, and a number of scholars have run their own investigations from various disciplinary perspectives. These scholarly studies share with nonscholarly commentaries a bewilderment and worry. They tend to situate the alliance between Trumpism and the NCR within particular political issues: official support for Israeli defense policy, selection of judges, and a general white populism that rejects progressive identity politics.[2] Whitehead and colleagues, for example, argue that Trump's rhetoric matches well with a version of Christian nationalism, which coincides with a variety of identity positions but operates independently and posits a uniquely Christian heritage and future for the United States.

While Christian nationalism certainly fits neatly within Trump's amorphous populism, the rhetorical appeal of Trump's utopianism hails a broader public that crosses the line between religious and secular. Whatever else one could say about Donald Trump's rhetoric (and I could say a great deal), the alliance between Trump and the NCR upends quite a bit of what many thought was understood of religion in the United States. However, recognizing Trumpism and the MAGA movement as a utopian public religion can bring new insight to the questions raised by the former president's political success. The Trump administration's policy and rhetoric rested on the kind of authority discussed in chapter 2 with a set of ritual practices (e.g., tweeted denunciations of professional football players, rallies with "lock her up" and "send them back" chants). These rituals express hope for the restoration of white men into their rightful places as the chosen (of God, of the United States, of history—it doesn't matter which). On an intellectual and material level, Trump's utopianism requires the active and passive oppression of whole categories of people, the closure of the protections and privileges of citizenship for millions, and endless lies.

Trumpism's aggressive authoritarianism thrives under specific cultural conditions, the same conditions that, on the one hand, allow reparative public religions to thrive and, on the other hand, threaten to crush and contain them. The uneasy alliance between Trumpism and the New Christian Right signals an important condition: the destabilization of political and religious distinctions. Such destabilization naturally grows out of the fragmentation and econ-omization that Wendy Brown identifies in *Undoing the Demos*; that is, absent a robust public sphere, political identifications harden and form into new kinds of alliances. Moreover, a consumer economy saturates media with targeted advertising and invitations to belong to particular groups of consumers. Po-litical and consumer marketing hails buyers into a public: you are one of the right people, the ones who know the truth, and you are right at home among the other true citizens. This hailing both divides citizens into target demographics and urges people to identify strongly with those target demographics, to be subjects that choose sides, as it were. In this environment, every single potential identification offers salvation and purpose (even if that purpose is contained within the networks of capital).[3] It does not matter that many of the most strident members of these divided groups have also been the most hurt by neoliberal fragmentation; there's simply no other obvious means to imagine something better. At the same time, a persistent, partially conscious knowledge calls for imagining utopian alternatives—namely, the knowledge that the global political economy is ecologically, politically, culturally, and eco-nomically unsustainable. This identification that "I belong among the pure" and the knowledge that this very division into oppositional political camps is destructive create an untenable aporia in which a public desperately desires reconciliation yet rejects nearly all means to reach it.

All the works examined in this book imagine solutions to this reconciliation-purity tension, and each has dramatic problems in doing so. Further, these works show that thinking through the religious utopian can help one see potential ways out of this bind, at least conceptually. The novels invite readers to think of the utopian as cutting across popular classifications of religion and politics, such that we can see how one's imagination of faith lends affective weight to political visions. Indeed, all these novels imagine a hopeful future that nonetheless carries some sort of immense—one might say dystopian—limitations. Within the bind I've identified—the search for purity and the knowledge that the very processes of purification create tension and violence—it seems that the novels still want to indulge a search for some complete utopian vision. Moreover, with the hope for alternatives to neoliberalism comes the persistence of neoliberal logics. Whether it was Slavoj Žižek or Fredric Jameson who said it, it's easier to imagine the end of the world than to imagine an alternative to capitalism (Fisher).

Each of the utopian visions I have examined in this book offers both hope and serious limitations. The *Left Behind* and *MaddAddam* series both imagine renewal only through an apocalypse that eliminates the vast majority of the world's population. For *Left Behind*, the utopia of Christ in fact requires the eternal, capital punishment of everyone who does not belong. In *MaddAddam*, hope for a future only happens after a much less precise die-off. The God's Gardeners in *MaddAddam* and Earthseed in Butler's *Parable* novels imagine a withdrawal, a disengagement with the world (whether it be through isolated communities or planetary emigration); in both cases, this withdrawal seems impossible in technological and ecological circumstances that connect everyone materially. Sagan's work, *Left Behind*, and to some extent Earthseed see evangelization as a possible solution; the protagonists seek to win over converts. Trouble lurks in this: the assumption that before a possible utopia can be achieved, a large number of people must first believe what the evangelist does. This assumption isn't so much aggressive as it is impractical: to wait until evangelization reaches a tipping point might require, like *Left Behind*'s Rapture or Earthseed's emigration, an intervention that culls.

Moreover, two affective problems—dominance and despair—arise with much more serious implications. I began this book with a short discussion of Perotta's *The Leftovers*, a novel that explicates the despair of the contemporary moment: the feeling that all meanings destabilize, and there's no stable position from which to construct a vision of any kind (let alone a utopian one). This despair shows up similarly in several of the novels in this study. *Contact* and *Left Behind* (despite the former's grand galactic optimism) both require outside intervention and, in the latter case, the universal elimination of everyone outside a narrowly defined set of ideologies and experiences. A different version of the same despair appears in the *Parable* and *MaddAddam* series. Earthseed requires a withdrawal and a surrender of Earth to those who show, in Butler's view, an unavoidable, genetic predisposition to destroy it. The radical remaking of Earth lies entirely outside of human possibility. Like *Left Behind*, *MaddAddam* also imagines a grand culling (though along much more arbitrary lines); recovery of the world and of humanity only becomes possible with drastically reduced and then dramatically changed populations of people.

Domination stands in dialectical relationship with despair. Unable to imagine a changeable humanity, the novels tend to imagine the solution in relatively repressive power. While this is obvious in *Left Behind*—Christ returns not so much as savior, but as big brother who punishes the Christians' unrepentant bullies—similar domination appears as a tool in the other novels as well. Butler expresses discomfort (in an interview accompanying *Parable of the Talents*) with Lauren Olamina's seeking of power, and whether heroic or villainous, Crake's technological manipulations have him employing the criminal apparatuses of the CorpSeCorps to kidnap, to assassinate, and finally to wipe out humanity. *Alif the Unseen* also identifies this problem of domination, embodying it in the character of Abbas the Hand. The novel warns against the seeking of vertical power structures, expressing support instead for the motley, self-arising, horizontal power of the diverse citizenry. It's telling, however, that the novel declines to imagine the move from revolutionary uprising to revolutionary governance; Alif and Dina simply return home, declining power for themselves and letting the mob sort it out.

These conceptual problems—domination, despair, withdrawal, destruction, evangelization—make these visions somewhat unsatisfying, but more important, also make them easy to appropriate and contain for counterrevolutionary interests. Despite these conceptual problems, however, the utopian, religious publics imagined in these novels offer several things to build on in the utopian imagination. Despite its problematic civilizational hierarchies and evolutionary cultural ideas, Carl Sagan's works demand an interest in truth in the sense of investigation and factual accuracy. For Sagan, science offers spiritual and cultural fulfillment, but underneath this lies something possibly even better: properly pursued and contextualized, the scientific method remains among the most useful tools to investigate and understand natural and social phenomena. *Cosmos, Contact,* and Sagan's other works contain a hope for truth that demands universal access to education and redefines citizenship as transcending identity. Sagan acknowledges the diversity of human experience but does so only aesthetically and with the thought that this diversity, while feeling good, is also a sign of immaturity. In other words, Sagan expresses wishes for universal citizenship that require adjustment, but nonetheless offers a much-needed focus on investigation and the seeking of truth. *Left Behind* has even more aggressive versions of the same problem with diversity. But while for Sagan diversity registers as an enjoyable element of childhood, for *Left Behind* it's an active threat. Nevertheless, *Left Behind* does offer some conceptual hope for utopian thinking: the series asks for Christians' commitment to something bigger than themselves, the belief that people can serve something beyond their immediate interests, experiences, pleasures, and therapeutic personal fulfillments. LaHaye and Jenkins imagine, though, that to do so is akin to joining a military in wartime: short-term action in an effort to restore an environment wherein the right people get to pursue their versions of personal fulfillment with the full blessing of God. The series offers no lasting vision for diverse democratic publics.

While Sagan's work and the *Left Behind* series ask readers to commit to visions bigger than themselves, to truths, the *Parable* and *MaddAddam* novels add productive complexity and partiality. Together, the latter two series imagine how commitment to a utopian vision requires evolution and reimagination. Butler's novels develop a model of commitment that transcends a particular historical context without dismissing that context. Her novels reimagine humans sociobiologically in models that humbly invite change and that alter relations to other species and environments. For the *Parable* series, positive change happens slowly and with setbacks, but remains possible with commitment from the "shapers" of change. This revolution has room for a diversity of experience and identity. Similarly, the *MaddAddam* novels offer peripherality, hesitance, and partiality as factors that strengthen, not weaken, utopian publics. Atwood's series further imagines how religions can function not as saving grace, but as actors, as cement for communities and interpersonal relations. *Alif the Unseen* adds enchantment to this partiality. Alif learns to turn his cynicism into healthy self-doubt, and then to turn his faith toward the power of God and away from the power of technologies. In Wilson's novel, God's power expresses itself specifically in the diversity of people in a newly imagined democratic public of seen and unseen together. Techno-enchantment offers power and the means to fight power, but ultimately cannot in and of itself provide the means for justice and equality. For that, the novel argues, reverential piety can inform a cultural and political shift.

These works together show that, unsurprisingly, one cannot imagine models of publics that are not in some way implicated in the things one wants to fight. These novels, however, offer some hope for crafting social dreams of better worlds beyond simplistic, destructive slogans like Make America Great Again. These novels hail readers into a broad public. They ask readers to reject despair, to recognize the need for constant evolution, to commit to truth, to imagine expanded kinship; they also ask readers to turn religion, technology, and political economy *against* power. These religious visions—their hopes for utopia—may just be a thin veneer over a nihilism that asks readers simply to allow unchecked power to dominate and destroy. For the visions in these novels to offer meaning for the future requires a revival and a reinvigoration of the long history of socially activist faith, a faith that imagines new forms of equality and reparation.

NOTES

INTRODUCTION. RELIGION IN THE SOCIAL DREAMS OF THE PRESENT

1. While many scholars have parsed, sharpened, and qualified this definition, few have challenged it and, indeed, many have defended it against the widespread popular misunderstanding of utopia as a "perfect society." The applications of the word "utopia" are so broad as to include literary depictions of "good places" (Eutopia), intentional communities, and simply any act of imagination that hopes for something better (or, in the case of dystopia, imagines something worse). One particularly interesting example of this last category is Richard Dyer's 1977 essay, "Entertainment and Utopia," in which Dyer argues that movie musicals provide imaginary opposites to the central affective problems caused by late capitalism.

2. For more on ancient utopian stories from the Old and New Worlds and on New World utopian communities, see Sargent, *Utopianism*.

3. Much of this work has focused on writing and other media from American Christian fundamentalist and evangelical perspectives. See Barkun; Boyer; McAlister, "Prophecy"; Stahlberg; Stillman; and Žižek.

4. "Weak religion" is a term from Gianni Vattimo's works *Belief* (1999) and *After Christianity* (2002). Weak religion locates religiosity, its secularized remnants, and beliefs and practices on the religious-secular line largely within the private, individual conscience; religious commitments remain fluid, and individuals dwell partly within and partly out of them as they construct their own partially religious maps of the world. Hungerford shows how the form but not the content of religious belief persists both in literary language and in how characters and writers relate to that language. McClure, by contrast, argues that postsecular literature presents a "mode of being and seeing that is at once critical of secular constructions of reality and of dogmatic religiosity" (ix). For McClure, postsecular literature highlights a deliberate uncertainty, a willingness of individuals to draw on religious and secular modes of knowledge without "choosing a side," as it were. McClure suggests that postsecular literature, like many traditions in Western religion, offers "open dwelling"—that is, the ability to live within a religious tradition without being confined to strict interpretations and rules (194–95).

5. In a review of the work of McClure, Hungerford, and others in postsecular scholarship, Tracy Fessenden expresses concern that their work, while opening up the definition of "secular" so as to make it a more permeable category, sidesteps the problems raised by the persistence of religion: "This liberating, pluralizing move implies redemption from a constraining past, in this case from the analytic and existential confines of secular categories that no longer serve as well as we would wish. But the postsecular turn I see in recent literary studies also promises release from the burdens of *religion*, that is, from the competencies, obligations, and complicities associated with a putative

past tense of shared religious belief and practice" ("Problem" 157, emphasis in original). Several scholars of literature have engaged the continued presence of these strong religious forms in American literature, looking at postsecularism as a new phase of public religious expression rather than as a "return" per se. Fessenden's work in *Culture and Redemption* similarly reveals the process by which recognizable ideas and practices of Protestant denominations became dominant though invisible through a process of secularization in American education and culture. For more on literature and strong religion, see Frykholm; Smith; McAlister, *Kingdom*; Haque; and Levitt.

6. In *The Structural Transformation of the Public Sphere* and several other works, Jürgen Habermas presents a definition of the "public sphere" based in spaces and texts. Coffee bars, public houses, and other public spaces, and newspapers and other widely circulated texts, create the real and virtual environment of the public sphere. This public sphere in theory flattens class distinctions and allows everyone to participate in the democratic discourses and organizations that constitute active citizenship in a modern democracy. Further, in theory but rarely in practice, the public sphere is secular in the sense of religiously neutral; to participate in it, citizens leave their religious affiliations at home, and everyone regardless of religion (or class, race, gender, sexuality, and so on) participates on an equal footing. From a variety of perspectives, thinkers have challenged and complicated Habermas's conceptions. Warner convincingly shows in several works that publics are multiple and overlapping and that dominant publics tend to exclude queer sexualities and genders. Warner reminds that publics are both intertextual, as groups of readers interact with texts depending on their interactions with other texts, and rhetorical, as they depend on the ways texts try to win audiences by hailing readers (in Althusser's sense) as members of multiple publics. For both Habermas and Warner, the public or publics overlap private and public (in the sense of state- and nonstate-owned and regulated) spaces and networks. Warner's theorization of publics presents their variation and their flexibility, though it also highlights the way the construction of publics relies on networks of circulation and consumption.

7. It would take quite a bit of text to define "neoliberalism" thoroughly (especially given the various ways people employ it in scholarly and popular discourse). For more on definitions and the historical and philosophical origins of neoliberalism, see Harvey; J. Wilson; and Hancock.

8. For more on the Reagan presidency politically, economically, and culturally, see Schaller; and Troy.

9. While Brown recognizes the difficulty in reconstituting a democratic system with people educated and prepared to participate, other thinkers warn against Brown's notion that a reconstituted democratic system that allows the full participation of multiple publics and citizens is possible or desirable. Dean adds to some of Brown's diagnoses of how neoliberalism works, including a particularly clever explanation of how the internet and social media technologies neutralize political action by turning all political actions and speech into "circulating" media objects. Whether they be passionate speeches, videos of direct action, videos of abusive action by authorities, their increased circulation (shares, views) are the most that can happen politically. Unlike Brown, Dean sees political organization—party, as in the Communist Party—and an elevation of incidents to conflicts between good and evil as the solution (see Dean, *Democracy* and *Communist Horizon*). For Dean, as long as class conflict is contained, economic inequality is inevitable. Only Communist revolution can remedy this. This puts her somewhat in line with Hardt and Negri in *Commonwealth*, who argue that the "public" is still a regime of ownership (by the state, rather than by citizens or cor-

porate entities). They argue instead for the "common," where life-sustaining resources like water are held in common by all. In *Public Things: Democracy in Disrepair* (2017), Honig joins these thinkers in their attempts to envision models of public engagement that combat the economization of neoliberalism. Implicitly, Honig builds on Habermas and Brown in that her work largely imagines the public or the "demos," which, for Honig, encompasses the multivariability and power differentials explicated by Warner. However, while Warner focuses on text and intertext, Honig centers on things: objects, infrastructures, and environments. Like Habermas, Honig sees spaces and places as important, but she also adds objects—public art, public parks, public places, and infrastructure (roads, pipelines, and so on)—into the mix. She uses public, then, in three senses: Habermas's "public," multiple textual and rhetorical publics, and state-owned public. Honig argues that public things constitute a "holding environment" that anchors people's investment in citizenship even as culture, economy, and politics change (12–17). These things, according to Honig, solve Rousseau's political paradox (which comes first—a good people or good laws?) by making an environment in which the conflict and consensuses of democratic society can play out (28–30). Honig's focus on things points out that not simply texts and rhetoric but also objects, constitute a public. For my purposes in examining utopian fiction, Honig usefully reminds to focus on how texts represent the networks of relations among human and nonhuman elements.

10. Casanova's *Public Religions in the Modern World* provides a foundational complication of secularization, showing how secularization is a multivalent process. While religion has not declined, he argues, throughout the world, public expressions of religiosity went through a variety of transformations over the nineteenth and twentieth centuries. For more on the philosophical bases of secularization and its possible postsecular transformations, see Asad; Taylor; Mahmood; and Connolly. Much of the work on postsecularism in literary studies has similarly been devoted to excavating either the persistence of religion, on the one hand, or the persistence of a false secularization thesis, on the other. In various forums, Vincent Pecora, Michael Kaufmann, Kevin Seidel, and Tracy Fessenden debate the influence of visible and invisible assumptions about religion and the secular in the profession of literary criticism.

11. One of Asad's chief examples is pain: under some religious models, pain exists in the world due to human sin, but similarly, a secular morality of pain could see pain as punishment for unhealthy behavior (46–47).

12. Jakobsen and Pellegrini's edited volume *Secularisms* contains several essays that, among other things, show the oppressive and liberatory potentials of various forms of secularism in different places and for different people. See also Warner and colleagues, *Varieties of Secularism in a Secular Age.*

13. For example, the theologian Vine Deloria Jr. reminds that, according to the U.S. Supreme Court decision in *Reynolds v. United States* 98 U.S. 145 (1879), Mormons were free to believe in polygamy but not to practice it (220–21).

CHAPTER 1. "THE WAY OF THE MACHINE"

1. The idea that modern technologies potentially bring people into closer contact with God, gods, or other deeper truths did not originate with Sagan; it was a popular theme throughout twentieth-century science fiction. See, for example, the work of Arthur C. Clarke, particularly *Childhood's End* (1953), "The Nine Billion Names of God" (1953), and *2001: A Space Odyssey* (1968).

2. Sagan biographer Keay Davidson argues that Sagan made conciliatory gestures

toward religion (including those in *Contact*) less because of any agnostic doubt and more as a matter of practical alliance with religious antinuclear and other social activists. Davidson provides several stories from Sagan friends that testify to his private contempt for religious faith. Reading Sagan's Gifford Lectures (published in 2006 as *Varieties of Scientific Experience*), it's hard to think of his atheism as particularly private. In the lectures, Sagan argues that the scientific method has a superior claim to truth in nearly all areas over any other knowledge regime. He specifies to a largely hostile audience that he has no objection to religious claims to ethical authority, but he rejects all claims to truth that cannot be investigated and recorded. In this sense, Sagan tends to view religions similarly (if less intensely) to atheists like Richard Dawkins: as discredited explanations for natural phenomena rather than as complex cultural systems. Sagan's other biographer, William Poundstone, argues that Sagan thought of the God of the Western monotheisms as a "myth" but "appreciated the diversity of spiritual experience. . . . he recognized spirituality as existing not only in conventional religion but also in the UFO myth, the marijuana experience, and the poet-scientist's contemplation of the universe" (342). Sagan's brief writings on marijuana appear pseudonymously in Lester Grinspoon's 1971 *Marihuana Reconsidered* and focus mostly on a vaguely defined "awareness," a spirituality born more of brain chemistry than anything divine. See Davidson; Sagan, *Varieties*; Dawkins; Geertz; Poundstone; and Grinspoon.

3. It's difficult to name a public intellectual more prominent than Sagan through the 1970s and 1980s. From the early 1970s until his death in 1996, he produced fifteen nonfiction books for popular audiences, one novel, and a PBS television series in addition to scores of scientific articles and more than twenty appearances on *The Tonight Show Starring Johnny Carson*. In 1980, Simon and Schuster granted Sagan a $2 million advance on a future novel, which became *Contact*, one of the largest publishing advances paid up to that point (McDowell). As his public profile grew in the early 1980s, Sagan crossed fields and advocated on many issues. Sagan appeared nearly everywhere as a symbol of liberal political causes, including nuclear disarmament and the environment. In December 1983, for example, the *New York Times* featured a short, somewhat condescending piece about longtime Equal Rights Amendment activist Sonia Johnson running for the Citizens Party's nomination for U.S. president. When asked about potential running mates, Johnson named Sagan alongside civil rights activist (and later U.S. representative) John Lewis and popular infant care writer Benjamin Spock. By 1983, Sagan's work on nuclear disarmament had secured him a temporary place as an icon of the American Left. He leveraged this to campaign for Democratic presidential candidate Gary Hart, appearing at university rallies across the northeastern United States (Barbanel). Sagan frequently met in the 1980s with Soviet scientists to urge cessation of Cold War hostilities (F. Lewis). When international dignitaries visited the United States officially, they sometimes met with Carl Sagan. He was visited by French culture minister Jack Lang in November 1984 (Freedman) and Indian prime minister Rajiv Gandhi in July 1985, who met with Sagan after addressing the U.S. Congress (Weinraub). Sagan continued to write against nuclear proliferation, to speak against the militarization of space in the Reagan administration's Strategic Defense Initiative, and to speak for other leftist causes, including appearances at Live Aid (Fein) and at nuclear test protests in Nevada, where he was arrested twice in 1986–1987 (Applebome; Lindsey). In 1986, *Foreign Affairs* advertised that Sagan would be writing regularly for the publication in much the same way *Scientific American* had fifteen years earlier ("World Doesn't Fit"). Sagan even became a reference in social debates, making appearances in

the laudatory quotes of self-help books ("What Will They Do") and getting a mention in a made-for-TV drama about a "family's crisis of faith" (O'Connor).

4. "Détente" describes U.S.-Soviet relations from the mid-1960s until the late 1970s. It was characterized by a relative thawing of the Cold War, featuring slowdowns in arms stockpiling, new treaties, and a general lack of direct hostility. It ended sometime in the late 1970s with the Soviet invasion of Afghanistan, confusion over the extent of possible cooperation between the United States and the USSR, and finally, the election in 1980 of Reagan, who advocated a generally more aggressive engagement with the Soviet Union. See Moss; and Villaume et al.

5. For more on this Reagan coalition, see Troy. For an especially clear and pointed explanation of the Reagan campaign's appeal to white working-class voters on the basis of racial resentment, see Schaller. For a general explanation of the rise of Sunbelt conservatism, see Schulman.

6. For histories of American Christian fundamentalism, see Harding; Marsden; Sandeen; and Shibley. For the relations between Christian Right thinkers and science, see Harding. On the rise of the antielitist Sunbelt conservatives, see Schulman; Schaller; and Flippen.

7. *Cosmos* was written by Druyan, Sagan, and astrophysicist Steven Soter. Druyan cowrote several books with Sagan, including *Comet* (1985), *Shadows of Forgotten Ancestors* (1992), and *Billions and Billions* (1997), as well as the screenplay for the film version of *Contact* (1997). Druyan was married to Sagan from 1981 until his death in 1996.

8. For an illuminating history of Mars and ecology, see Markley.

9. SETI is the name given to any project that involves searching for signs of intelligent life elsewhere in the universe. Most of this occurs through radio astronomy. The U.S. government helped fund official SETI projects in the 1980s, but most SETI work has been funded by other sources. See NASA History Program Office.

10. Regarding the relative advancement of extraterrestrial civilizations, see Sagan and Drake.

11. A transcendental number (something *Contact* discusses multiple times) is a number that neither repeats nor terminates but continues forever. The best-known example of this is pi, the ratio of the circumference to the diameter of a circle. Pi is 3.14159 . . . and on and on, neither repeating nor terminating at any point out to infinity.

12. Many readers will no doubt be familiar with the film adaptation of the novel, Robert Zemeckis's 1997 *Contact*. In the biggest senses, the events of the novel and the film are similar: Ellie Arroway (Jodie Foster) receives and helps decode a message from space; the U.S. government builds the machine described in the message; Ellie (by herself, without the international partners) travels to the center of the galaxy and talks with her deceased father; and she fights the defense establishment when she returns. The film focuses more on Ellie's spiritual development and downplays the global political elements and her relationships with everyone but Palmer Joss (Matthew McConaughey) and Michael Kitz (James Woods). While the film is interested in faith, it provides much less scientific detail than the novel does.

13. Reviewing the novel for the *Wall Street Journal* in December 1985, for example, Thomas J. Bray decries the generally liberal politics of *Comet* (Sagan and Druyan's 1985 nonfiction book) and *Contact*, contemptuously citing the latter's "woman president," "feminist scientist," "hackneyed, disjointed jabs at commercial civilization, nationalism, sexism, and other standard liberal bogeymen," and most of all, the novel's "paen to world government. The big powers get together to tax their citizens hundreds of bil-

lions of dollars to establish contact with the message-senders" (Bray 28). More politically sympathetic reviews stuck to *Contact*'s literary limitations. Peter Nicholls argues
that the book is "preachy," and "the tone is earnest, very much that of a youngish university lecturer who has had a few, but not too many, drinks" (BW6); science-fiction
writer Gregory Benford similarly says, "occasionally the narrative catches fire, then
sputters out under another lecture" (BR12).

14. Christopher Douglas critiques Sagan's representation of American fundamentalism, suggesting that it ranges from somewhat shallow to out-and-out inaccurate (citing, for example, the character Billy Jo Rankin's trafficking in false relics) (200–202).

15. Vaygay is clearly based on real-life Soviet astronomer I. S. Shklovskii. Unable to
leave the USSR, Shklovskii collaborated with Sagan by post to write *Intelligent Life in the
Universe* (1962 in Russia, 1966 in the United States), a book wherein the two speculated
about alien civilizations and possibilities of contact (Davidson 196–200).

16. Cygnus A is the brightest source of radio waves in Earth's sky. It is inside the constellation Cygnus (a northern sky constellation sometimes referred to as the Northern
Cross), and the "A" signifies that it is the brightest source of radio light in that constellation. A very bright source of light in any spectrum signifies a high amount of energy
being produced. See Astronomy Now.

17. The alien's explanation refers to cosmological theory. At the beginning of time, all
matter and energy exploded outward from a single point; this event is referred to as the
big bang. Observations of distant galaxies confirm that the universe is still expanding
from that initial explosion: almost all galaxies are moving away from ours, and the farther away they are, the faster they move away. Theoretically, if there were enough matter in the universe, gravitational attraction among matter would force the expansion to
halt, and eventually all the matter in the universe would come back together in the "big
crunch." Current theories suggest, though, that there is not enough matter in the universe to halt the expansion; theoretically, this means that concentrations of matter in
the universe (galaxies) will continue to move farther and farther from each other. As all
stars burn out over eons, galaxies become dark and lose all usable energy; this means no
new stars, no new planets, and no life of any kind—just cold and infinite disorder. What
the alien is telling Ellie about, then, is a gigantic engineering project to recover what
would normally be unusable matter and energy and to put it in the empty space created
by an expanding universe—to renew, in other words, the arrangements of matter and
energy that led to the formation of galaxies, suns, and planets billions of years ago.

18. Cygnus A is 350 million light years from Earth, so what is observed from Earth is
the state of Cygnus A 350 million years ago. The alien's reply suggests they have been
working on it for something more like a billion years

19. For an alternative reading of the convergence between Sagan's scientific religion
and American fundamentalist Christianity, see Douglas, who argues that *Contact* and
much of the NCR are engaged in forms of "postmodern religion," which privileges per-
suasion in the search for truths spiritual or scientific (203–20).

CHAPTER 2. "NOBODIES TRYING TO BE SOMEBODIES"

1. In *The Book of Jerry Falwell*, Susan Harding defines "born-again Christianity" as
"[referring] to Pentecostal and charismatic as well as fundamentalist and evangelical Protestants who mobilized politically and culturally in the 1980s" (xvi). I use the
terms "born-again," "fundamentalist," and "evangelical" throughout this chapter be-

cause, while *Left Behind*'s theology lies squarely within the late nineteenth- and early twentieth-century tradition of fundamentalism, I see the series' public engagement as part of the New Christian Right movement, which includes Christians from various born-again traditions. When addressing this cultural engagement, I use "born-again," and when describing *Left Behind*'s eschatology, I use "fundamentalist." A broader term than fundamentalist or born-again, "evangelical" denotes a Christian mission-focused orientation toward faith and the world.

Michael Barkun, Paul Boyer, and Linda Kintz all point out that premillennial dispensationalism includes utopian elements; it imagines an end to suffering and the beginning of a just government administered by Christ (Barkun 18–19; Boyer 318–23; Kintz 9).

2. For a short description of other prophecy popularizations, see Swirski. Boyer offers a book-length study of end-times culture. For a review of Rapture fiction (fiction written around the dispensationalist end-times narrative), see Frykholm. For a longer consideration of Rapture fiction, see Gribben.

3. Tim LaHaye, a coauthor of *Left Behind* and the author behind most of the books' theological explanations, wrote or coauthored eighty-five books, most of which have been distributed in Christian bookstores and among theologically friendly churches. Many of these are self-help books for Christian readers; others offer guidance for reading the Bible, and most of the latter focus in some way on end-times prophecy. LaHaye was an influential critic of secular humanism, and many of his works oppose a morally relativistic secular humanism to biblical truth. For more on LaHaye and his influence, see Shuck; and Frykholm.

4. For a reading of the series as political argument for pro-Israel foreign policy, see McAlister, "Prophecy." For more on *Left Behind* as commentary on proper Christian family life and gender roles, see Frykholm. For examinations of *Left Behind* within a globalized information economy, see Shuck; and Strombeck.

5. For more on the networks of readers who shaped the reception of *Left Behind*, see Frykholm. For more on fundamentalist and evangelical Christian reading practices, see Smith. For discussions of Christian political and cultural activism in the 1970s, 1980s, and 1990s, see Lienesch; and Shibley.

6. The New Christian Right is a name given to the loosely organized coalition of Bible-believing Christians pursuing conservative activism from the 1970s onward. This term signals a convergence among Christians of diverse denominations and theologies. As Lienesch puts it, "contemporary religious conservatives have converged in practice to the point that the old categories are effectively empty" (228). For more, see Lienesch; Harding; and Marsden.

7. To some extent, this impression of uniformity was calculated by activists like Jerry Falwell, who did the work of uniting various groups within fundamentalism around specific issues like abortion, school prayer, and tax-exempt status for Christian schools. However, from its inception in the late nineteenth century, fundamentalism has always been a contested movement. In his landmark study, *Fundamentalism and American Culture: The Shaping of Twentieth-Century Evangelicalism, 1870–1925*, George M. Marsden admits to difficulty defining fundamentalism because of its historical variations. He lands on "militant opposition to modernism" (in this case, historicist biblical criticism and rereadings of scripture based on modern science), but he admits that even that doesn't quite capture fundamentalism's complexity (4). Together with Joel A. Carpenter, who studied the movement in its 1930s and 1940s incarnations, Marsden shows how fundamentalism was formed in part by intramovement disagreements over the-

ology, biblical hermeneutics, politics, ideas about gender, and overall ideologies about relations between Christians and the rest of the world.

8. For descriptions of cultural, political, and theological conflicts among born-again Christians, see Gasaway; and Swartz.

9. For a thorough description of the myriad issues under debate at the Lausanne conference, see the fifth chapter of McAlister, *Kingdom*.

10. While dispensationalists are a small minority among Christians, they include particularly prominent American fundamentalist Christians, such as the late Jerry Falwell and Pat Robertson, who have access to mass media and people in state and federal power.

11. The term "millennial" comes from this prophecy of Christ's thousand-year rule and predates the development of premillennial dispensationalism. For the origins of dispensationalism and its prominence among American Christian fundamentalists, see Sandeen; and Marsden.

12. The idea that Orthodox Jews would be violently enraged by the conclusion that Jesus was the Jewish messiah—a nearly two-thousand-year-old idea—is symptomatic of the series' broader difficulty in imagining non-Christian thinking. For an illuminating reading of U.S. support for Israel and the absence of Palestinians in *Left Behind*, see McAlister, "Prophecy." For an insightful reading of *Left Behind*'s reinscription of anti-Semitic stereotypes, see Mleynek. For a reading of *Left Behind* as Holocaust denial rhetoric, see Lampert-Weissig.

13. Later in his book, Gribben argues pointedly that while the series has conservative politics, it would be a mistake to read it as merely reactionary in its views of race, gender, and sexuality. Gribben shows how the series gives voice to the variations within evangelical thought. As an example, the fact that *some* Catholics disappear in the Rapture shows, according to Gribben, some relatively progressive thinking for the genre. He further states that many evangelical and fundamentalist readers rejected—or were at least uncomfortable with—the theology and politics of the series (133–44).

14. "One world currency" is a staple of twentieth-century prophecy popularizers, who read several biblical passages to mean that when the end of the world approaches, the whole globe will trade in one currency. Institutions like the European Common Market and the European Union, together with the adoption of the euro by EU nations, are often seen as eschatological signs. See Lindsey; and Boyer.

15. For more on how the characters use digital technology, see Shuck.

CHAPTER 3. SMOOTH DINOSAURS VERSUS ADULT HUMANS

1. Just in the period 2016–2018, thirty articles and book chapters about Butler's work were listed in the MLA international biography. Scholars approach Butler's work from a variety of critical perspectives, including utopian studies, disability studies, Black feminism, and critical race theory.

2. Gerry Canavan returns many times to problematic elements of Butler's work, including the strange relations between her characters and neoliberal economics and her seeming flirtations with essentialism. He writes of her uncomfortable relationship with radical Black politics of the 1970s (Canavan, *Masters* 28–29) and with progressive politics more broadly. For discomfort especially around the *Xenogenesis* series, see Bonner; and Holden.

3. The uneasy relationship between Butler's fiction and essentialism drives much of the criticism of her work. See Tucker, "Human Contradiction." See also Thaler, who

reads *Parable of the Sower* as having a particularly troubling relation to African American agency that requires the subtle, constant presence of consumerism.

4. A belief that this contradiction drives all human tragedy and potential pervades Butler's fiction, nearly all of which features characters with some sort of changed biological circumstances: immortal super-telepaths (the *Patternist* series, 1976–1984), alien-human hybrids (*Xenogenesis*, 1987–1989), people who feel the pain of others and seek biological difference on other planets (the *Parable* novels, 1993–1998), and vampires living symbiotically with humans (*Fledgling*, 2005).

5. For a discussion of Christian fundamentalism in *Sower*, see Andréolle. Philip H. Jos argues that Earthseed fits within a spiritualized Christian tradition.

6. Badiou shows this as a consequence of Paul's subjective antiphilosophy, rather than an actual consequence in the history of Christendom (42–49).

7. Canavan reports on Butler's aborted drafts of *Parable of the Trickster*. They all describe the Earthseed adherents on an inhospitable planet. In many of these manuscripts, the characters experience new biological changes, such as telepathy, blindness, and other things experienced as the planet's antibody reactions to the human invasion (Canavan, "There's Nothing New" 143–51). Fore more detail on these unpublished drafts, see Canavan, *Masters*.

8. For more on kinship in the *Parable* novels, see Agusti; and Wegner.

9. For a lengthy discussion of Butler's drafts of *Parable of the Trickster*, see Canavan, *Masters*.

CHAPTER 4. "LIKE SOME DEMENTED THEOLOGY DEBATE"

1. See, for example, Bowen; and Northover. Dunning argues that the novels suggest that great dangers accompany the loss of all religious narrative. Hoogheem fuses religion and ecocriticism in a sustained "evolutionary criticism" reading that shows the power of symbolic narrative whether religious or secular.

2. For more on deep ecology, see Naess, who argues for a biocentric model of ecological action based on the idea that humans have no right to disturb ecology for any other reason than fulfilling the needs of survival.

3. A number of critics have noted the engagement of both the series and its author with deep ecology, but they disagree on whether the novels present deep ecology with sympathy or horror. Some critics, like Sharon Wilson, Karen Stein, and Shuli Barziali, place Crake within the long tradition of "mad scientists" who wreak havoc through their knowledge. Allison Carruth explicates the series' ambivalence toward deep ecology, noting that the series exposes deep ecology's tendency to set aside human rights in its equating of humans and other animals. On the other side, several critics, including J. Brooks Bouson, Greg Garrard, Hannes Bergthaller, Roman Bartosch, Allison Dunlap, and Gerry Canavan, see something positive about Crake's plague and the reboot of the human species.

4. I read the series in part as a companion to *The Handmaid's Tale* (1985), which warns that religious fundamentalism threatens the freedom of women and the advances of nineteenth- and twentieth-century feminism. The *MaddAddam* series suggests that neoliberalism offers an equal and opposite threat: the economization of women's sexuality has as much potential for domination and abuse as does fundamentalist repression and regulation.

5. For more on the *MaddAddam* series' treatment of religion as evolutionary adaptation, see Hoogheem.

CHAPTER 5. "THE WORLD AT AN ANGLE"

1. There's been extensive work on the Arab Spring, varying greatly depending on disciplinary approach and scholarly perspective. Certainly, optimism has fallen off since 2012 as so many of the movements were upended by counterrevolutionary pushes (Syria), civil war (Syria, Libya, Yemen), Islamic extremism (Syria, Yemen), coups (Egypt), and the imprisoning of activists (throughout the region). Only Tunisia seems to have transitioned to a stable democracy. For considerations of the evolution of the Arab Spring protest movements, as well as descriptions of the relative successes and failures of postrevolutionary transitions to democracy, see Asfandyar and Ullah; Conde; Aras and Falk; Rabbat; Halverson et al.; and Hodler. For more on the various roles Islam played in the protests, governmental reorganizations, and counterrevolutionary actions, see Bahlul; and Esposito et al. For studies of the role of social media and other media in the movements, see Al-Azdee and Metzgar; Watenpaugh; McDonald; and especially Tufekci. For discussions of the protests in specific national and historical contexts, see Gaffar. For historically, ethnically, and nationally specific close studies, see Halverson et al.; Saidin; Haas and Lesch; Yetiv; and Ryan. For ethnographic and journalistic engagements with organizers and protestors, see Cole; and Noueihed and Warren.

2. Haque argues against theories of postsecularism put forth especially by McClure and Hungerford. She joins Fessenden and Connolly in arguing that religion potentially revives the promises of secularism.

3. G. Willow Wilson is known among comic book fans as the writer of the new *Ms. Marvel* comic series. She's also the author of the graphic novel *Cairo* (2007, illustrated by M. K. Perker), the memoir *The Butterfly Mosque* (2011), and the novel *The Bird King* (2019). *Alif the Unseen* (2012) is her first nongraphic novel.

4. Twenty-nine of the 114 surahs (chapters) of the Qur'an begin with a short series of letters, referred to in Arabic as *muqatta'at* ("disjoined letters," "disconnected letters," or "mysterious letters"). Several theories have been proposed to explain the significance of the muqatta'at. Dina and Alif clearly subscribe to the theory that lends symbolic, divine meaning to the letters. For more on the muqatta'at, see Massey.

CONCLUSION. FAITH IN THE FUTURE

1. There are countless examples of news articles and commentary that oscillate between bewilderment and anger at the strange and seemingly hypocritical New Christian Right support for Trump. These responses range from a criticism of NCR values as decidedly un-Christian (a rhetorical move as old as the NCR itself) to amazement over the incompatibility of Christian beliefs with Trump's persona (e.g., crassness, dishonesty in business, treatment of women, multiple divorces). For just a couple of examples, see Berenson; and Morris.

2. As of the end of 2020, scholarly research on Trumpism was still limited and preliminary. For examinations of Trump rhetoric within conflicts over race and gender, see Hills; and Abraham. For examinations of Trump within evangelical views of the United States in relation to the rest of the world, see Martí; and Haynes.

3. For more on affect and identification as it circulates in social media, see Dean, *Communist Horizon* and *Democracy*.

WORKS CITED

Abraham, Susan. "Masculinist Populism and Toxic Christianity in the United States." *Concilium*, vol. 54, no. 2, 2019, pp. 61–72.

Agusti, Clara Escoda. "The Relationship between Community and Subjectivity in Octavia E. Butler's *Parable of the Sower.*" *Extrapolation*, vol. 46, no. 3, 2005, pp. 351–59.

Andréolle, Donna Spalding. "Utopias of Old, Solutions for the New Millennium: A Comparative Study of Christian Fundamentalism in M. K. Wren's *A Gift upon the Shore* and Octavia Butler's *Parable of the Sower.*" *Utopian Studies*, vol. 12, no. 2, 2001, pp. 114–23.

Applebome, Peter. "139 Arrested in Protest at Nevada Nuclear Site." *New York Times*, 1 Oct. 1986, p. A18.

Aras, Bülent, and Richard Falk. "Five Years after the Arab Spring: A Critical Evaluation." *Third World Quarterly*, vol. 37, no. 12, 2016, pp. 2252–58.

Asad, Talal. *Formations of the Secular*. Stanford University Press, 2003.

Asfandyar, Fakhr-Ul-Islam, and Muqaddas Ullah. "The Arab Spring Genesis: Implications for Global Politics." *Dialogue*, vol. 14, no. 1, 2019, pp. 1–16.

Astronomy Now. "Hotspots in Cygnus A: An Active Galactic Nucleus." *Astronomy Now*, 25 Oct. 2016, astronomynow.com/2016/10/25/hotspots-in-cygnus-a-an-active-galactic-nucleus. Accessed 8 Aug. 2018.

Atwood, Margaret. *The Handmaid's Tale*. McClelland and Stewart, 1985.

———. *MaddAddam*. Anchor, 2013.

———. *Oryx and Crake*. Anchor, 2003.

———. *The Year of the Flood*. Anchor, 2009.

Al-Azdee, Mohammed, and Emily T. Metzgar. "The Arab Spring: Beyond Media Effects." *Journal of Arab and Muslim Media Research*, vol. 11, no. 1, 2018, pp. 3–23.

Badiou, Alain. *Saint Paul: The Foundation of Universalism*. Translated by Ray Brassier, Stanford University Press, 2003.

Bahlul, Raja. "Religion, Democracy and the 'Dawla Madaniyya' of the Arab Spring." *Islam and Christian-Muslim Relations*, vol. 29, no. 3, 2018, pp. 331–47.

Barbanel, Josh. "Legislators Pass New State Budget: Spending Total Rises $2 Billion in $35.6 Billion Package." *New York Times*, 1 Apr. 1984, p. 1.

Barkun, Michael. *Disaster and the Millennium*. Syracuse University Press, 1986.

Bartosch, Roman. "Literary Quality and the Ethics of Reading: Some Thoughts on Literary Evolution and the Fiction of Margaret Atwood, Ilija Trojanow, and Ian McEwan." *Literature, Ecology, Ethics: Recent Trends in Ecocriticism*, edited by Timo Müller and Michael Sauter, Universitätsverlag Winter, 2012, pp. 113–28.

Barziali, Shuli. "From H. G. Wells's Island to Margaret Atwood's Paradice: Bio-Perversity and Its Ramifications." Bouson, *Critical Insights* 99–119.

Bellah, Robert, et al. *Habits of the Heart: Individualism and Commitment in American Life*. University of California Press, 1985.

Benford, Gregory. "Theology and the Interstellar Subway." *New York Times*, 3 Nov. 1985, p. BR12.

Berenson, Tessa. "Evangelical Leader Jerry Falwell Jr. Endorses Donald Trump." *Time*, 26 Jan. 2016, time.com/4194164/jerry-falwell-jr-donald-trump-evangelical. Accessed 6 Nov. 2020.

Bergthaller, Hannes. "Housebreaking the Human Animal: Humanism and the Problem of Sustainability in Margaret Atwood's *Oryx and Crake* and *The Year of the Flood*." *English Studies*, vol. 91, no. 7, 2010, pp. 728–43.

The Bible. The New Oxford Annotated Version, 3rd ed., Oxford University Press, 2001.

Bonner, Frances. "Difference and Desire, Slavery and Seduction: Octavia Butler's *Xenogenesis*." *Foundation*, Spring 1990, pp. 58–62.

Bouson, J. Brooks. *Critical Insights: Margaret Atwood*. Salem Press, 2013.

———, editor. "'A Joke-Filled Romp' through the End-Times: Radical Environmentalism, Deep Ecology, and Human Extinction in Margaret Atwood's Eco-Apocalyptic *MaddAddam* Trilogy." *Journal of Commonwealth Literature*, vol. 51, no. 3, 2015, pp. 341–57.

Bowen, Deborah C. "Ecological Endings and Eschatology: Margaret Atwood's Post-Apocalyptic Fiction." *Christianity and Literature*, vol. 66, no. 4, 2017, pp. 691–705.

Boyer, Paul. *When Time Shall Be No More: Prophecy Belief in Modern American Culture*. Belknap, 1992.

Bray, Thomas J. "Science Fact and Fiction: Sagan's Space Platform." *Wall Street Journal*, 5 Dec. 1985, p. 28.

Butler, Octavia. *Adulthood Rites*. Aspect, 1997.

———. *Clay's Ark*. 1984. Aspect, 1996.

———. *Dawn*. 1987. Aspect, 1997.

———. *Fledgling*. 2005. Seven Stories Press, 2011.

———. *Imago*. 1989. Aspect, 1997.

———. *Mind of My Mind*. 1977. Grand Central Publishing, 1994.

———. "The Monophobic Response." *Dark Matter: A Century of Speculative Fiction from the African Diaspora*, edited by Sheree R. Thomas, Warner, 2000, pp. 415–16.

———. *Parable of the Sower*. 1993. Grand Central Publishers, 2000.

———. *Parable of the Talents*. Seven Stories Press, 1998.

———. *Patternmaster*. 1976. Avon, 1979.

———. "Positive Obsession." *Bloodchild and Other Stories*. Seven Stories Press, 1995.

———. *Survivor*. Doubleday, 1978.

———. *Wild Seed*. 1980. Grand Central Publishing, 2001.

Brown, Wendy. *Undoing the Demos: Neoliberalism's Stealth Revolution*. Zone, 2015.

Canavan, Gerry. "Hope, but Not for Us: Ecological Science Fiction and the End of the World in Margaret Atwood's *Oryx and Crake* and *The Year of the Flood*." *LIT: Literature Interpretation Theory*, vol. 23, no. 2, 2012, pp. 138–59.

———. *Masters of Science Fiction: Octavia E. Butler*. University of Illinois Press, 2016.

———. "'There's Nothing New / Under the Sun, / But There Are New Suns': Recovering Octavia E. Butler's Lost Parables." *Los Angeles Review of Books*, 9 June 2014, lareviewofbooks.org/article/theres-nothing-new-sun-new-suns-recovering-octavia-e-butlers-lost-parables. Accessed 8 Nov. 2020.

Carpenter, Joel A. *Revive Us Again: The Reawakening of American Fundamentalism.* Oxford University Press, 1997.

Carruth, Allison. "Wily Ecologies: Comic Futures for American Environmentalism." *American Literary History*, vol. 30, no. 1, 2018, pp. 108–33.

Casanova, José. *Public Religions in the Modern World.* University of Chicago Press, 1994.

Clarke, Arthur C. *Childhood's End.* Ballantine, 1953.

———. "The Nine Billion Names of God." *Star Science Fiction Stories #1*, edited by Frederik Pohl, Ballantine, 1953.

———. *2001: A Space Odyssey.* New American Library, 1968.

Cole, Juan. *The New Arabs: How the Millennial Generation Is Changing the Middle East.* Simon and Schuster, 2014.

Conde, Gilberto. "On the Evolutions of the Arab Spring." *Regions and Cohesion*, vol. 7, no. 2, 2017, pp. 96–105.

Connolly, William. *Why I Am Not a Secularist.* University of Minnesota Press, 2000.

Contact. Directed by Robert Zemeckis, Warner Bros., 1997.

Curtis, Claire P. "Theorizing Fear: Octavia Butler and the Realist Utopia." *Utopian Studies*, vol. 19, no. 3, 2008, pp. 411–31.

Davidson, Keay. *Carl Sagan: A Life.* Wiley, 1999.

Davis, Mike. *City of Quartz.* Verso, 1990.

Dawkins, Richard. *The God Delusion.* Bantam, 2006.

Dean, Jodi. *The Communist Horizon.* Verso, 2012.

———. *Democracy and Other Neoliberal Fantasies.* Duke University Press, 2009.

Delany, Samuel R., and R. M. P. "On Triton and Other Matters: An Interview with Samuel R. Delany." *Science Fiction Studies*, vol. 17, no. 3, 1990, 295–324.

Deloria, Vine, Jr. *For This Land*, edited by James Treat, Routledge, 1999.

Douglas, Christopher. *If God Meant to Interfere: American Literature and the Rise of the Christian Right.* Cornell University Press, 2016.

Dunlap, Allison. "Eco-Dystopia: Reproduction and Destruction in Margaret Atwood's *Oryx and Crake.*" *Journal of Ecocriticism*, vol. 5, no. 1, 2013, pp. 1–15.

Dunning, Stephen. "*Oryx and Crake*: The Terror of the Therapeutic." *Canadian Literature*, no. 186, 2005, pp. 86–101.

Dyer, Richard. "Entertainment and Utopia." *Movie*, Spring 1977, pp. 2–13.

Esposito, John L., et al. *Islam and Democracy after the Arab Spring.* Oxford University Press, 2016.

Fabian, Johannes. *Time and the Other.* Columbia University Press, 1983.

Fein, Esther B. "'Live Aid' Concert Is Aiming for the Sky." *New York Times*, 12 July 1985, p. C5.

Fessenden, Tracy. *Culture and Redemption: Religion, the Secular, and American Literature.* Princeton University Press, 2007.

———. "The Problem of the Postsecular." *American Literary History*, vol. 26, no. 1, pp. 154–67.

Fisher, Mark. *Capitalist Realism: Is There No Alternative?* Zero, 2010.

Flippen, Brooks J. *Jimmy Carter, the Politics of Family, and the Rise of the Religious Right.* University of Georgia Press, 2011.

Freedman, Samuel G. "French Culture Minister Cites U.S. Influence." *New York Times*, 16 Nov. 1984, p. C1.

Frykholm, Amy Johnson. *Rapture Culture.* Oxford University Press, 2004.

Gaffar, Abdul. "Democratization and the Arab Spring: A Theoretical Perspective." *Mediterranean Quarterly*, vol. 28, no. 3, 2017, pp. 112–30.

Garrard, Greg. *Ecocriticism*. 2nd ed., Routledge, 2012.

Gasaway, Brantley W. *Progressive Evangelicals and the Pursuit of Social Justice*. University of North Carolina Press, 2014.

Geertz, Clifford. "Religion as a Cultural System." *The Interpretation of Cultures: Selected Essays*, Fontana Press, 1993, pp. 87–125.

Gribben, Crawford. *Writing the Rapture*. Oxford University Press, 2009.

Grinspoon, Lester. *Marihuana Reconsidered*. Harvard University Press, 1971.

Haas, Mark L., and David W. Lesch, editors. *The Arab Spring: The Hope and Reality of the Uprisings*. 2nd ed., Westview Press, 2017.

Habermas, Jürgen. *The Structural Transformation of the Public Sphere*. M.I.T. Press, 1989.

Halverson, Jeffry R., et al. "Mediated Martyrs of the Arab Spring: New Media, Civil Religion, and Narrative in Tunisia and Egypt." *Journal of Communication*, vol. 63, no. 2, 2013, pp. 312–32.

Hancock, David. *The Countercultural Logic of Neoliberalism*. Routledge, 2019.

Haque, Danielle. "The Postsecular Turn and Muslim American Literature." *American Literature*, vol. 86, no. 4, 2014, pp. 799–829.

Harding, Susan Friend. *The Book of Jerry Falwell*. Princeton University Press, 2000.

Hardt, Michael, and Antonio Negri. *Commonwealth*. Harvard University Press, 2009.

Harvey, David. *A Brief History of Neoliberalism*. Oxford University Press, 2007.

Haynes, Jeffrey. "Donald Trump, 'Judeo-Christian Values,' and the 'Clash of Civilizations.'" *Review of Faith and International Affairs*, vol. 15, no. 3, 2017, pp. 66–75.

Heise, Ursula K. "What's the Matter with Dystopia?" *Public Books*, 1 Feb. 2015, publicbooks.org/whats-the-matter-with-dystopia. Accessed 8 Nov. 2020.

Hills, Darrius. "Back to a White Future: White Religious Loss, Donald Trump, and the Problem of Belonging." *Black Theology: An International Journal*, vol. 16, no. 1, Apr. 2018, pp. 38–52.

Hodler, Roland. "The Political Economics of the Arab Spring." *Economic Inquiry*, vol. 56, no. 2, 2018, 821–36.

Holden, Rebecca J. "The High Costs of Cyborg Survival: Octavia Butler's *Xenogenesis* Trilogy." *Foundation*, Spring 1998, pp. 49–56.

Honig, Bonnie. *Public Things: Democracy in Disrepair*. Fordham University Press, 2017.

Hoogheem, Andrew. "Secular Apocalypses: Darwinian Criticisms and Atwoodian Floods." *Mosaic*, vol. 45, no. 2, 2012, pp. 55–71.

Hungerford, Amy. *Postmodern Belief: American Literature and Religion since 1960*. Princeton University Press, 2010.

Jakobsen, Janet R., and Ann Pellegrini, editors. *Secularisms*. Duke University Press, 2008.

Jos, Philip H. "Fear and the Spiritual Realism of Octavia Butler's Earthseed." *Utopian Studies*, vol. 23, no. 3, 2012, pp. 408–29.

Kahf, Mohja. *The Girl in the Tangerine Scarf*. Public Affairs, 2006.

Kaufmann, Michael W. "Locating the Postsecular." *Religion and Literature*, vol. 41, no. 3, 2009, pp. 68–73.

———. "The Religious, the Secular, and Literary Studies: Rethinking the Secularization Narrative in Histories of the Profession." *New Literary History*, vol. 38, no. 4, 2007, pp. 607–28.

Kintz, Linda. *Between Jesus and the Market: The Emotions That Matter in Right-Wing America*. Duke University Press, 1997.

LaHaye, Tim, and Jerry B. Jenkins. *Glorious Appearing*. Tyndale House Publishers, 2004.

———. *Kingdom Come*. Tyndale House Publishers, 2007.

———. *Left Behind*. Tyndale House Publishers, 1995.

———. *Nicolae*. Tyndale House Publishers, 1997.

———. *Tribulation Force*. Tyndale House Publishers, 1996.

Lampert-Weissig, Lisa. "*Left Behind*, the Holocaust, and That Old Time Anti-Semitism." *Journal of Popular Culture*, vol. 45, no. 3, 2016, pp. 497–515.

Lessl, Thomas M. "The Priestly Voice." *Quarterly Journal of Speech*, vol. 75, no. 2, 1989, pp. 183–97.

———. "Science and the Sacred Cosmos: The Ideological Rhetoric of Carl Sagan." *Quarterly Journal of Speech*, vol. 71, no. 2, 1985, pp. 175–87.

Levitt, Laura. "What Is Religion, Anyway? Rereading the Postsecular from an American Jewish Perspective." *Religion and Literature*, vol. 41, no. 3, 2009, pp. 107–18.

Lewis, C. S. *The Chronicles of Narnia*. Harper Trophy, 2002.

Lewis, Flora. "A Small U.S.-Soviet Step." *New York Times*, 1 July 1985, p. A15.

Lienesch, Michael. *Redeeming America: Piety and Politics in the New Christian Right*. University of North Carolina Press, 1993.

Lindsey, Robert. "438 Protestors Arrested at Nevada Nuclear Test Site." *New York Times*, 6 Feb. 1987, p. A8.

Ludwig, Kathryn. "Don DeLillo's *Underworld* and the Postsecular in Contemporary Fiction." *Religion and Literature*, vol. 41, no. 3, 2009, pp. 82–91.

Mahmood, Saba. *The Politics of Piety: The Islamic Revival and the Feminist Subject*. Princeton University Press, 2004.

Malone, Adrian, director. "The Backbone of Night." *Cosmos: A Personal Voyage*, PBS, KCET, Los Angeles, 9 Nov. 1980.

———. "Blues for a Red Planet." *Cosmos: A Personal Voyage*, PBS, KCET, Los Angeles, 26 Oct. 1980.

———. "The Harmony of the Worlds." *Cosmos: A Personal Voyage*, PBS, KCET, Los Angeles, 12 Oct. 1980.

———. "Heaven and Hell." *Cosmos: A Personal Voyage*, PBS, KCET, Los Angeles, 19 Oct. 1980.

———. "One Voice in the Cosmic Fugue." *Cosmos: A Personal Voyage*, PBS, KCET, Los Angeles, 5 Oct. 1980.

———. "The Persistence of Memory." *Cosmos: A Personal Voyage*, PBS, KCET, Los Angeles, 7 Dec. 1980.

———. "The Shores of the Cosmic Ocean." *Cosmos: A Personal Voyage*, PBS, KCET, Los Angeles, 28 Sept. 1980.

———. "Traveler's Tales." *Cosmos: A Personal Voyage*, PBS, KCET, Los Angeles, 2 Nov. 1980.

———. "Who Speaks for Earth?" *Cosmos: A Personal Voyage*, PBS, KCET, Los Angeles, 21 Dec. 1980.

Markley, Robert. *Dying Planet: Mars in Science and the Imagination*. Duke University Press, 2005.

Marsden, George M. *Fundamentalism and American Culture*. 2nd ed., Oxford University Press, 2006.

Martí, Gerardo. "The Unexpected Orthodoxy of Donald J. Trump: White Evangelical Support for the 45th President of the United States." *Sociology of Religion*, vol. 80, no. 1, Spring 2019, pp. 1–8.

Massey, Keith. "A New Investigation into the 'Mystery Letters' of the Qur'an." *Arabica*, vol. 43, no. 3, 1996, pp. 497–501.

Mayer, Sylvia. "Genre and Environmentalism: Octavia Butler's *Parable of the Sower*, Speculative Fiction, and the African American Slave Narrative." *Restoring the Connection to the Natural World: Essays on the African American Environmental Imagination*, edited by Sylvia Mayer, LIT Verlag, 2003, pp. 175–96.

McAlister, Melani. *The Kingdom of God Has No Borders*. Oxford University Press, 2018.

———. "Prophecy, Politics, and the Popular: The *Left Behind* Series and Christian Fundamentalism's New World Order." *South Atlantic Quarterly*, vol. 102, no. 4, 2003, pp. 773–98.

McClure, John A. *Partial Faiths: Postsecular Fiction in the Age of Pynchon and Morrison*. University of Georgia Press, 2007.

McDonald, David A. "Framing the 'Arab Spring': Hip Hop, Social Media, and the American News Media." *Journal of Folklore Research*, vol. 56, no. 1, 2019, 105–30.

McDowell, Edwin. "Sagan Sells First Novel to Simon and Schuster." *New York Times*, 13 Jan. 1981, p. C16.

Miller, Jim. "Post-Apocalyptic Hoping: Octavia Butler's Dystopian/Utopian Vision." *Science-Fiction Studies*, vol. 25, no. 2, 1998, pp. 336–60.

Miller, Steven P. *Billy Graham and the Rise of the Republican South*. University of Pennsylvania Press, 2009.

Mleynek, Sherryll. "The Rhetoric of the 'Jewish Problem' in the *Left Behind* Novels." *Literature and Theology*, vol. 19, no. 4, 2005, pp. 367–83.

More, Thomas. *Utopia*. 1516. Edited and translated by Robert M. Adams. 2nd ed., Norton, 1992.

Morris, Alex. "False Idol: Why the Christian Right Worships Donald Trump." *Rolling Stone*, Dec. 2019, pp. 66–97.

Moss, Richard A. *Nixon's Back Channel to Moscow: Confidential Diplomacy and Détente*. University of Kentucky Press, 2017.

Moylan, Tom. *Scraps of the Untainted Sky: Science Fiction, Utopia, Dystopia*. Westview Press, 2000.

Naess, Arne. *The Ecology of Wisdom: Writings by Arne Naess*. Counterpoint, 2008.

NASA History Program Office. "SETI: The Search for Extraterrestrial Intelligence." NASA, 29 Sept. 2014, history.nasa.gov/seti.html. Accessed 8 Aug. 2018.

Nicholls, Peter. "Carl Sagan's Messages from the Milky Way." *Washington Post*, 13 Oct. 1985, p. BW6.

Northover, Richard Alan. "Ecological Apocalypse in Margaret Atwood's *MaddAddam* Trilogy." *Studia Neophilologica*, vol. 88, no. 1, 2016, pp. 81–95.

Noueihed, Lin, and Alex Warren. *The Battle for the Arab Spring: Revolution, Counter-Revolution, and the Making of a New Era*. Yale University Press, 2012.

O'Connor, John J. "'Schoolbreak Special' Explores Crisis of Faith." *New York Times*, 1 Apr. 1986, p. C18.

"Octavia Butler: Science Future, Science Fiction." *YouTube*, uploaded by sonic1267, 10 Mar. 2008, https://www.youtube.com/watch?v=IgeyVE3NHJM.

Papke, Mary E. "Necessary Interventions in the Face of Very Curious Compulsions: Octavia Butler's Naturalist Science Fiction." *Studies in American Naturalism*, vol. 8, no. 1, 2013, pp. 79–92.

Pecora, Vincent. *Secularization and Cultural Criticism*. University of Chicago Press, 2016.

Perotta, Tom. *The Leftovers*. St. Martin's Griffin, 2011.

Pierce, Alexandra, and Mimi Mondal, editors. *Luminescent Threads: Connections to Octavia E. Butler*. Twelfth Planet Press, 2017.

Poundstone, William. *Carl Sagan: A Life in the Cosmos*. Henry Holt, 1999.

Pullman, Phillip. *The Golden Compass*. Alfred A. Knopf, 1996.

Rabbat, Nasser. "Heritage as a Right: Heritage and the Arab Spring." *International Journal of Islamic Architecture*, vol. 5, no. 2, 2016, pp. 267–78.

Reagan, Ronald. "Inaugural Address." 20 Jan. 1981. *Ronald Reagan Presidential Foundation and Institute*, www.reaganfoundation.org/media/128614/inaguration.pdf. Accessed 27 Feb. 2021.

Rensberger, Boyce. "Carl Sagan: Obliged to Explain." *New York Times*, 29 May 1977, pp. 181–82.

Rowell, Charles H. "An Interview with Octavia Butler." *Callaloo*, vol. 20, no. 1, 1997, pp. 47–66.

Ryan, Curtis R. "Jordan and the Arab Spring." Haas and Lesch, pp. 132–46.

Sagan, Carl. *Contact*. Simon and Schuster, 1985.

———. *The Demon-Haunted World*. Ballantine, 1995.

———. *The Dragons of Eden*. Ballantine, 1977.

———. *Varieties of Scientific Experience*. Penguin 2006.

Sagan, Carl, and Frank Drake. "The Search for Extra-Terrestrial Intelligence." *Scientific American*, vol. 232, no. 5, 1 May 1975, pp. 80–89.

Sagan, Carl, and Ann Druyan. *Billions and Billions*. Random House, 1997.

———. *Comet*. Random House, 1985.

———. *Shadows of Forgotten Ancestors*. Ballantine, 1992.

Sagan, Carl, and I. S. Shklovskii. *Intelligent Life in the Universe*. Translated by Paula Fern, Holden-Day, 1966.

Saidin, Mohd Irwan Syazli. "Rethinking the 'Arab Spring': The Root Causes of the Tunisian Jasmine Revolution and Egyptian January 25 Revolution." *International Journal of Islamic Thought*, vol. 13, no. 1, 2018, pp. 69–80.

Sandeen, Ernest R. *The Roots of Fundamentalism: British and American Millenarianism, 1800–1930*. University of Chicago Press, 1970.

Sargent, Lyman Tower. "The Three Faces of Utopianism Revisited." *Utopian Studies*, vol. 5, no. 1, 1994, pp. 1–37.

———. *Utopianism: A Very Short Introduction*. Oxford University Press, 2010.

Schalk, Sami. *Bodyminds Reimagined*. Duke University Press, 2018.

Schaller, Michael. *Right Turn: American Life in the Reagan-Bush Era, 1980–1992*. Oxford University Press, 2007.

Schulman, Bruce J. *The Seventies: The Great Shift in American Culture, Society, and Politics*. Free Press, 2001.

Schute, Nevil. *On the Beach*. Heinemann, 1957.

Seidel, Kevin. "Beyond the Religious and the Secular in the History of the Novel." *New Literary History*, vol. 38, no. 4, 2007, pp. 637–47.

Serres, Michel. *The Parasite*. 1980. Translated by Lawrence R. Schehr, University of Minnesota Press, 2007.

Shibley, Mark A. *Resurgent Evangelicalism in the United States: Mapping Cultural Change since 1970*. University of South Carolina Press, 1996.

Shuck, Glenn W. *Marks of the Beast: The "Left Behind" Novels and the Struggle for Evangelical Identity*. New York University Press, 2005.

Smith, Erin A. *What Would Jesus Read: Popular Religious Books and Everyday Life in Twentieth-Century America*. University of North Carolina Press, 2016.

Sorensen, Karen Schroeder. *Cosmos and the Rhetoric of Popular Science*. Lexington, 2017.

Stahlberg, Ben. "Theocratic America? Christianity and the Structure of Political Discourse." *The Sleeping Giant Has Awoken: The New Politics of Religion in the United States*, edited by Jeffrey W. Robbins and Nal Magee, Continuum, 2008, pp. 97–116.

Stein, Karen. "Problematic Paradice in *Oryx and Crake*." *Margaret Atwood: The Robber Bride, The Blind Assassin, Oryx and Crake*, edited by J. Brooks Bouson, Continuum Press, 2010, pp. 141–55.

Stillman, Peter G. "Dystopian Critiques, Utopian Possibilities, and Human Purposes in Octavia Butler's Parables." *Utopian Studies*, vol. 14, no. 1, 2003, pp. 15–35.

Strombeck, Andrew. "Invest in Jesus: Neoliberalism and the *Left Behind* Novels." *Cultural Critique*, vol. 64, 2006, pp. 161–95.

Suvin, Darko. *Metamorphoses of Science Fiction*. Yale University Press, 1979.

Swartz, David R. *Moral Minority: The Evangelical Left in the Age of Conservatism*. University of Pennsylvania Press, 2012.

Swirski, Peter. "'To Sacrifice One's Intellect Is More Demonic than Divine': American Literature and Politics in *Left Behind: A Novel of the Earth's Last Days*." *European Journal of American Studies*, vol. 9, no. 2, 2014, pp. 1–18.

Taylor, Charles. *A Secular Age*. Belknap, 2007.

Thaler, Ingrid. *Black Atlantic Speculative Fictions*. Routledge, 2010.

Troy, Gil. *The Reagan Revolution: A Very Short Introduction*. Oxford University Press, 2009.

Tucker, Jeffrey Allen. "Dear Octavia Butler." Pierce and Mondal, p. 172.

———. "'The Human Contradiction': Identity and/as Essence in Octavia E. Butler's *Xenogenesis* Trilogy." *Yearbook of English Studies*, vol. 37, no. 2, 2007, pp. 164–81.

Tufekci, Zeynep. *Twitter and Tear Gas: The Power and Fragility of Networked Protest*. Yale University Press, 2017.

Twain, Mark. *A Connecticut Yankee in King Arthur's Court*. 1889. Dover, 2001.

Vattimo, Gianni. *After Christianity*. Translated by Luca D'Isanto, Columbia University Press, 2002.

———. *Belief*. Translated by Luca D'Isanto, Stanford University Press, 1999.

Villaume, Poul, et al., editors. *The "Long 1970s": Human Rights, East-West Détente and Transnational Relations*. Routledge, 2016.

Warner, Michael. *Publics and Counterpublics*. Duke University Press, 2002.

Warner, Michael, et al., editors. *Varieties of Secularism in a Secular Age*. Harvard University Press, 2010.

Watenpaugh, Heghnar Z. "Cultural Heritage and the Arab Spring: War over Culture, Culture of War and Culture War." *International Journal of Islamic Architecture*, vol. 5, no. 2, 2016, pp. 245–63.

Wegner, Phillip E. *Life between Two Deaths, 1989–2001: U.S. Culture in the Long Nineties*. Duke University Press, 2009.

Weinraub, Bernard. "Gandhi, in a Speech to Congress, Calls for a Nonaligned Afghanistan." *New York Times*, 14 June 1985, p. A1.

"What Were We Reading 30 Years Ago? 1985's 10 Bestselling Books." *Aerogramme Writers' Studio*, 6 Oct. 2015, aerogrammestudio.com/2015/10/06/what-were-we-reading-30-years-ago-1985s-10-bestselling-books. Accessed 8 Nov. 2020.

"What Will They Do when They Find Out I'm Me?" [advertisement for Random House]. *New York Times*, 29 June 1986, p. BR5.

Whitehead, Andrew L., et al. "Make America Christian Again: Christian Nationalism and Voting for Donald Trump in the 2016 Presidential Election." *Sociology of Religion*, vol. 79, no. 2, Summer 2018, pp. 147–71.

Wilson, G. Willow. *Alif the Unseen*. Grove Press, 2012.

——. *The Bird King*. Grove Press, 2019.

——. *The Butterfly Mosque*. Grove Press, 2011.

Wilson, G. Willow, and M. K. Perker. *Cairo*. DC Comics, 2007.

Wilson, Julie A. *Neoliberalism*. Routledge, 2018.

Wilson, Sharon. "Postapocalyptic Vision: Flood Myths and Other Folklore in Atwood's *Oryx and Crake* and *The Year of the Flood*." Bouson, *Critical Insights* 334–52.

"The World Doesn't Fit on a 12 Inch Screen" [advertisement for *Foreign Affairs*]. *New York Times*, 13 Apr. 1986, p. BR25.

Yetiv, Steve A. "How Saudi Arabia Has Dodged the Arab Spring." Haas and Lesch, pp. 113–31.

Žižek, Slavoj. *On Belief*. Verso, 2006.

INDEX

affect, 3, 151–52: in *Contact* (Sagan), 33, 34–35, 47; in *Left Behind* series, 66–67, 70–71, 75; in *Parable* novels, 92, 95

agency: in *Left Behind* series, 57; in *MaddAddam* series, 122–23, 125; in *Parable* novels, 85–89, 162–63n3

Alif the Unseen (Wilson), 12, 129–48, 149, 152, 153; digital counterpublics, 133, 135–42, 144–45, 147; neoliberalism, 131, 138–39, 148; secularism (Islamic), 129, 130–31, 142–46, 147

anonymity, 129, 131, 132, 137, 138. See also *Alif the Unseen*; counterpublics: digital

Anthropocene, 102, 112. *See also* deep ecology

antifeminism, 49, 71, 75

apocalypse: in *Left Behind* series, 48–49, 59, 60, 65–66, 75, 151; in *MaddAddam* series, 101–2, 151; in Sagan's works, 24, 26

Arab Spring, 129–30, 164n1 (chap. 5). See also *Alif the Unseen*

Asad, Talal, 8, 28, 109, 157n10

astrology, 15, 16, 20–22

astronomy, 16, 18–19, 20–22, 47, 159n9

Atwood, Margaret: *The Handmaid's Tale*, 163n4; *MaddAddam* novel, 104, 114–15, 117, 120–21, 125; *Oryx and Crake*, 104, 107, 121, 122, 123; *The Year of the Flood*, 104, 114–15, 117, 120–21. See also *MaddAddam* series

Badiou, Alain, 36, 87, 91, 163n6

Bible. *See* dispensationalism, premillennial

big bang, 23–24, 160n7

biosocial, 77–78, 85–89, 97, 99. *See also* sociobiology

biotechnology, 100, 105–6, 113. *See also* genetic engineering

Blackness, 92, 162n1, 162n2

born-again Christianity, 7, 160–61n1. See also *Left Behind* series; New Christian Right

Brown, Wendy, 6, 59, 150, 156–57n9

Butler, Octavia, 90–91, 98–99, 163n4; *Parable of the Sower*, 80–81, 86; *Parable of the Talents*, 81–82, 86, 96, 97, 152; *Xenogenesis*, 91, 99, 162n2. See also *Parable* novels

Canavan, Gerry, 90, 98, 162n2, 163n7

capitalism, communicative, 92–95

Casanova, José, 4–5, 157n10

Christianity, 160–61n1, 161n7. See also *Left Behind* series; New Christian Right

climate change, 86, 99, 100, 102. *See also* ecology; ecology, deep; environmental destruction; global warming

Cold War, 35, 58, 158–59nn3–4

colonialism, 24, 25, 98

conservatism, 5, 16, 50–51, 75–76; in *Left Behind* series, 10, 49, 52, 60, 64–65, 70–71, 75; New Christian Right, 18, 161n6

consumerism, 72, 150–51; in *MaddAddam* series, 101, 105–8, 113, 116–17

Contact (film), 159n7, 159n12

Contact (Sagan), 10, 14, 26–47, 151–52, 159–60n13; Christian fundamentalism, 28, 29–30, 31–32, 45

conversion: in *Alif the Unseen*, 129, 131, 143–44, 147; in *Left Behind* series, 55–56, 65–66, 67, 71–72, 73. *See also* evangelization; proselytization

corporate systems, 71, 92; in *MaddAddam* series, 101, 104, 106–8, 110, 113–14, 116–17, 120

cosmic citizenship, 18, 22, 27, 41–43, 152–53

cosmological theory, 160n17

Cosmos (television series), 10, 18–26, 153, 159n7

counterpublics, 129, 131; digital, 133, 135–42, 144–45, 147

creation science, 18, 28, 53–54

Cygnus A, 42, 43, 45, 160n16, 160n18

kinship, 2, 12, 98, 153
Kintz, Linda, 70–71, 72

LaHaye, Tim, 161n3; *Glorious Appearing* (with Jenkins), 60, 63, 74; *Kingdom Come* (with Jenkins), 60; *Left Behind* novel (with Jenkins), 53, 73, 151; *Nicolae* (with Jenkins), 53, 63–64, 68, 72–73; *Tribulation Force* (with Jenkins), 53, 55, 56–57, 67, 68. See also *Left Behind* series
leadership, 57, 92, 95–97, 124
Left Behind novel (LaHaye and Jenkins), 53, 73, 151. See also *Left Behind* series
Left Behind series (LaHaye and Jenkins), 10, 48–50, 51–53, 54, 55–75, 149, 151–52, 153, 160–61n1; masculinity, 49, 54, 55, 58, 64, 68, 70–71, 71–73; neoliberalism, 10, 49, 58–59, 69, 72–75, 78
Leftovers, The (Perotta), 1–2, 5, 151
Lessl, Thomas, 19, 46
Liberty University, 54
lifestyle enclaves, 71
Lowell, Percival, 18, 22
Ludwig, Kathryn, 9

MaddAddam novel (Atwood), 104, 114–15, 117, 120–21, 125. See also *MaddAddam* series (Atwood)
MaddAddam series (Atwood), 11–12, 100–128, 151, 152, 163n1, 163nn3–4; neoliberalism, 12, 100–101, 103–4, 105, 113, 120–21, 163n4; religions (partial and strong), 100–101, 106, 113–21, 121–28
"Make America Great Again," 149, 150, 153; Trumpism, 12, 149–51, 164nn1–2
Marsden, George, 53, 55, 161n7
masculinity, 49, 54, 55, 58, 64, 68, 70–71, 71–73
McAlister, Melani, 49, 50
McClure, John A., 3, 4, 7, 102–3, 155n4
metaphor: in *Alif the Unseen*, 135, 136–37, 139–40; in *Contact* (Sagan), 38, 39–40, 43; in *Parable* novels, 82, 84, 93
metaphysics, 100, 102, 107
Middle East, 12, 129, 130, 131, 132, 136, 147
militarism: in *Left Behind* series, 59, 63, 68–69, 72–73; in Sagan's works, 10, 15, 16–17, 28–29, 31, 47
Miller, Steven P., 7, 64–65, 67, 68
mission: in *Left Behind* series, 49, 50–51, 52, 64, 161n1; in *Parable* novels, 85, 89, 95

Mormons, 157n13
multiculturalism: in *Contact* (Sagan), 10, 27, 35–36, 40–41; in *Cosmos*, 10, 20, 23; in *Left Behind* series, 48, 62

Negri, Antonio, 6, 156–57n9
neoliberalism, 5–9, 150, 151, 156–57n9
New Christian Right (NCR), 4, 7–8, 17–18, 47, 50–51, 52, 54, 161nn6–7; *Left Behind* series and, 49, 69, 160–61n1; Sagan and, 15, 17, 47, 160n19; Trumpism and, 149–50, 164n1
Nicolae (LaHaye and Jenkins), 53, 63–64, 68, 72–73. See also *Left Behind* series
9/11, 58, 147–48
North Africa, 129, 130, 131, 132, 136, 147
nuclear disarmament, 17, 24, 25–26, 158nn2–3

Oklahoma City bombing, 68
Operation Desert Storm, 72
Oryx and Crake (Atwood), 104, 107, 121, 122, 123. See also *MaddAddam* series

Parable novels (Butler), 11, 77–99, 100, 151, 152, 153, 162nn1–3, 163n7; adaptation, 77–78, 84, 87, 96–97, 98–99; neoliberalism, 11, 78–79, 81, 84, 86, 90, 99, 100, 101, 105, 162n2
Parable of the Sower (Butler), 80–81, 86. See also *Parable* novels
Parable of the Talents (Butler), 81–82, 86, 96, 97, 152. See also *Parable* novels
parasitic organizational model, 90, 93–95
partial religious forms, 3–4, 7, 155n4; in *MaddAddam* series, 101, 102–3, 114, 117, 120, 128, 153; in *Parable* novels, 87
Paul (biblical figure), 36, 87, 91, 163n6
Perotta, Tom, 1–2, 151; *The Leftovers*, 5
pi (transcendental number), 159n11; in *Contact* (Sagan), 14, 28, 44–45, 46
pleasure, 33, 103, 106. See also affect; embodiment
populism, 48, 53–54, 149–50
postsecularism, 3–9, 12, 102–3, 155–56nn4–5, 157n10; Islamic secularism, 129, 130–31, 142–46, 147
Poundstone, William, 158n2
premillennial dispensationalism. See dispensationalism, premillennial
priestliness, 15–16, 19, 46, 124
privatization, 4–6, 8; in *MaddAddam* series, 100, 101, 105, 127; in *Parable* novels, 81, 91; in Sagan's works, 18, 20, 47

proselytization, 66–67. *See also* conversion; evangelization

pseudosciences, 15, 16, 22

public religion, 4–5

publics, 5–7, 156n6, 156–57n9

Qur'an, 142–43, 147, 164n4

rapture fiction, 60–61, 162n13. See also *Left Behind* series

Reagan administration, 5, 16–17, 47, 158–59nn3–4

religion, 3–9; weak, 103, 155n4. *See also* partial religious forms

responsibilization, 6; in *Left Behind* series, 48, 51, 59–60, 69; in *MaddAddam* series, 101; in *Parable* novels, 79

revelation, 15–16, 18; in *Contact* (Sagan) 14, 26–27, 28–29, 30–31, 31–32, 36, 37, 45–46; in *Cosmos*, 19, 24

Revelation, book of, 53, 61, 68, 74

Reynolds v. United States (1879), 157n13

Sagan, Carl, 9–10, 14–16, 47, 157–58nn1–3, 160n15; cosmic citizenship, 18, 22, 27, 41–43, 152–53; *Contact* (film), 159n7, 159n12; neoliberalism, 10, 15–16. See also *Contact* (Sagan); *Cosmos*

Sargent, Lyman Tower, 3, 6

Schalk, Sami, 82–83

Schulman, Bruce, J., 5, 7, 17

science, secular, 11, 19, 46, 52, 53, 55

scientific investigation, 10, 29, 31, 32, 33, 38, 45–46

scientific method, 15–16, 22, 30, 35, 152, 158n2

Scottish common sense realism, 55

Search for Extraterrestrial Intelligence (SETI), 27, 159n9

secularism, Islamic, 129, 130–31, 142–46, 147

secularization, 8–9, 109, 157n10

secular science, 11, 19, 46, 52, 53, 55

self-help, 17, 158n3, 161n3

Serres, Michael, 93

sexuality, 110, 163n4

Shklovskii, I. S., 160n15

Shuck, Glenn, 53

slavery, 81–82, 84, 90

social dreaming, 3, 6

social media, 129, 133, 156n9. *See also* counterpublics: digital

sociobiology, 79, 83–85, 89–90, 91. *See also* biosocial

solidarity: in *Alif the Unseen*, 134–35, 136, 137, 138, 140, 145; in *MaddAddam* series, 102, 104, 117, 122, 126

Soter, Steven, 159n7. See also *Cosmos*

Soviet Union, 16–17, 158–59nn3–4

spirituality, 16, 17, 34, 85, 102, 158n2, 163n5

storytelling, 112–13, 122–25, 128

suffering, 79, 81, 82–83, 109–10

surveillance, 131, 132, 138. *See also* counterpublics: digital

symbolic meaning, 110, 111, 112–13, 121, 123

Taylor, Charles, 9

transcendental numbers, 27, 159n11. *See also* pi

Tribulation Force (LaHaye and Jenkins), 53, 55, 56–57, 67, 68. See also *Left Behind* series

Trumpism, 12, 149–51, 164nn1–2

truth event. *See* Badiou, Alain

Tucker, Jeffery Allen, 80, 91

utopia, 2–3, 5, 7–8, 151, 155n1

Vattimo, Gianni, 155n4

violence: in *Left Behind* series, 54, 68–69, 74; in *MaddAddam* series, 126, 127; in *Parable* novels, 80, 82, 89

Warner, Michael, 5, 156n6, 157n9

wealth: in *Alif the Unseen*, 132, 134; in *Left Behind* series, 69–70, 71–73; in *MaddAddam* series, 106; in *Parable* novels, 90, 94–95, 98

whiteness, 150; in *Left Behind* series, 50, 51, 58, 71, 75

Wilson, G. Willow, 131, 164n3. See also *Alif the Unseen*

women, exploitation of, 105, 163n4

Xenogenesis (Butler), 91, 99, 162n2

Year of the Flood, The, (Atwood), 104, 114–15, 117, 120–21. See also *MaddAddam* series

Since 1970: Histories of Contemporary America

Jimmy Carter, the Politics of Family, and
the Rise of the Religious Right
    by J. Brooks Flippen

Rumor, Repression, and Racial Politics: How the Harassment
of Black Elected Officials Shaped Post–Civil Rights America
    by George Derek Musgrove

Doing Recent History: On Privacy, Copyright,
Video Games, Institutional Review Boards, Activist
Scholarship, and History That Talks Back
    edited by Claire Bond Potter and Renee C. Romano

The Dinner Party: Judy Chicago and the Power
of Popular Feminism, 1970–2007
    by Jane F. Gerhard

Reconsidering Roots: Race, Politics, and Memory
    edited by Erica L. Ball and Kellie Carter Jackson

Liberation in Print: Feminist Periodicals
and Social Movement Identity
    by Agatha Beins

Pushing Back: Women of Color–Led Grassroots
Activism in New York City
    by Ariella Rotramel

Remaking Radicalism: A Grassroots Documentary
Reader of the United States, 1973–2001
    edited by Dan Berger and Emily K. Hobson

Deep Cut: Science, Power, and the Unbuilt Interoceanic Canal
    by Christine Keiner

America's Other Automakers: A History of the Foreign-
Owned Automotive Sector in the United States
    by Timothy J. Minchin

Public Religions in the Future World: Postsecularism and Utopia
    by David Morris